ROUTLEDGE LIBRARY EDITIONS: EMPLOYEE OWNERSHIP AND ECONOMIC DEMOCRACY

Volume 14

MONDRAGON

MONDRAGON

An Economic Analysis

HENK THOMAS AND CHRIS LOGAN

Routledge
Taylor & Francis Group

LONDON AND NEW YORK

First published in 1982 by George Allen & Unwin

This edition first published in 2018
by Routledge
2 Park Square, Milton Park, Abingdon, Oxon OX14 4RN

and by Routledge
711 Third Avenue, New York, NY 10017

Routledge is an imprint of the Taylor & Francis Group, an informa business

© 1982 Institute of Social Studies at The Hague

British Library Cataloguing in Publication Data
A catalogue record for this book is available from the British Library

ISBN: 978-1-138-29962-7 (Set)
ISBN: 978-1-315-12163-5 (Set) (ebk)
ISBN: 978-1-138-56122-9 (Volume 14) (hbk)
ISBN: 978-1-138-56137-3 (Volume 14) (pbk)
ISBN: 978-0-203-71082-1 (Volume 14) (ebk)

Publisher's Note
The publisher has gone to great lengths to ensure the quality of this reprint but points out that some imperfections in the original copies may be apparent.

Disclaimer
The publisher has made every effort to trace copyright holders and would welcome correspondence from those they have been unable to trace.

MONDRAGON:
An Economic Analysis

HENK THOMAS
and
CHRIS LOGAN

Published in co-operation with
The Institute of Social Studies at The Hague

London
GEORGE ALLEN & UNWIN
Boston   Sydney

George Allen & Unwin (Publishers) Ltd,
40 Museum Street, London WC1A 1LU, UK

George Allen & Unwin (Publishers) Ltd,
Park Lane, Hemel Hempstead, Herts HP2 4TE, UK

Allen & Unwin Inc.,
9 Winchester Terrace, Winchester, Mass 01890, USA

George Allen & Unwin Australia Pty Ltd,
8 Napier Street, North Sydney, NSW 2060, Australia

First published in 1982
Reprinted in 1983

British Library Cataloguing in Publication Data

Thomas, Henk
   Mondragon.
1. Cooperation – Basque Region – Mondragon
I. Title   II. Logan, Chris
334'.6'09466   HD2884.Z8
ISBN 0–04–334006–7

Printed in Great Britain

CONTENTS

FOREWORD

This study forms part of the Labour and Development programme of the Institute of Social Studies, The Hague. Self-management is a research priority of that programme, and it had long been felt that an economic analysis of 'Mondragon' would help to clarify a number of fundamental issues. Our initiative fortunately met with a positive response in Mondragon, where leading officials not only gave us the green light but also a special assignment:

> There have been many visitors to Mondragon and much has been written about us, but the time has now come for a thorough analysis of our experiences and that is what we expect from you. We have no time to do it ourselves, and in any case, it is better to be evaluated by outsiders.

While tremendous support has been received from all sides, special thanks are due to Iñaki Gorroño, Antonio Perez de Calleja Basterrechea. Iñaki Aguirrez Zabale and Juan Larrañaga who, at each stage of our field work, generously shared their time and were outstanding resource persons; and also to Josefina Claramunt de Irialba who conducted a number of in-depth interviews.

Above all, I must thank Chris Logan, my colleague during the Mondragon fieldwork. The time which we spent together in the Basque Provinces in 1977 and again briefly in 1979, constituted a joint venture in which his peculiar knowledge of the Basque situation and language was invaluable. Furthermore, much credit is owed to him for dealing with the historical background and the organisational dimensions of the Mondragon group.

I am very grateful to Derek Jones and Hank Levin as well as to anonymous readers who examined an earlier draft and made many suggestions for its improvement. Colin Lacey's comments on the educational sections and Frits Wils's ideas about the structure of the introductory chapter were most welcome.

Jeff Harrod, Gerard Kester and Geertje Thomas challenged the work from the viewpoint of other disciplines and the tremendous support that they gave will never be forgotten.

Louis Emmerij, Rector of the ISS, took a personal interest from the start of the project, stimulating the work whenever possible. My thanks also go to him.

Jean Sanders has been an untiring and highly competent editor, who also efficiently handled the complicated logistics. I deeply appreciate the work she has done; without it, the manuscript would never have attained its present form.

Through the years Trudy Creutzburg, Pien Moonen, Shirley Myers and Rose-marie Plug have typed and re-typed the various drafts, each of which marked a new stage of progress. I also owe thanks to Netty Born who did a fine job in preparing the camera-ready copy and to Koos van Wieringen who prepared the graphs and diagrams.

Institute of Social Studies   Henk Thomas
The Hague

I

WHY 'MONDRAGON'?

The Mondragon group actually started in 1943 with a few classes at the lowest level of technical education for the training of unemployed young people; in 1956 a small workshop was opened for the manufacture of cookers and stoves; and in 1959 a credit cooperative opened its first branch office. All this happened in Mondragon, a small town in the province of Guipúzcoa — one of the Basque provinces in the north of Spain. According to the Guipúzcoa census for 1970, Mondragon then had 22,421 inhabitants and the province as a whole approximately 631 thousand.

Since those beginnings in the 1950s, huge expansion has occurred in three directions: education, industry, and banking. By the end of the 1970s there existed in the province a modern cooperative system of technical education, 70 cooperative factories with a work force of more than 15,000 cooperators, and a credit cooperative bank with 93 branches and 300,000 deposit accounts.

This spectacular development in cooperative history has attracted considerable attention. Many people have written about 'Mondragon',[1] and their opinions can best be summarised as 'This is a success story in a field where failure has been the general rule...' (Gutierrez Johnson & Foote Whyte 1977: 18). Observers have been impressed by its expansion and by its complexity: two unusual features for cooperatives. Producer cooperatives, in fact, usually face countless bottlenecks which prevent rapid expansion; furthermore, they function in isolation rather than as a group as is the case in Mondragon. The cooperators of 'Mondragon' are equally positive about their own achievements, their self-confidence being typified by the words:

The Mondragon experiment has shown, above all, how workers can create and extend a system of self-management in an environment which is changing rapidly and is becoming more and more competitive; in other words, within a developing economy.... The main achievement of the cooperative approach, indeed the reason for its success, has lain in making the best possible use of these resources.... The way in which it — the Mondragon experiment — ties together workers, cooperatives and the community itself is both the explanation and justification of the experiment.... (Perez de Calleja 1975: 10, 11).

Notes to this chapter may be found on pp. 12-13.

Most writings about Mondragon have been descriptive rather than analytical, and the time has now come for more 'detailed studies' (Oakeshott 1978: 212) on a variety of aspects of the Mondragon experience, as the cooperators themselves like to call their activities. This book is the first study to analyse the 'economics of Mondragon'.[2] A primary objective is to trace its economic history and to discover whether sufficient evidence is available to substantiate the very positive assessments made by so many observers. In doing so, the private sector in the Basque provinces will be examined in order that the performance of the cooperatives may be compared with that of other enterprises functioning under similar general conditions. The second objective is to find the explanation of the observed phenomena in order that lessons may be drawn — as far as the 'economics' are concerned — from the Mondragon experience. Our working hypothesis is that Mondragon can be characterised as a 'system of self-managed enterprises' (Vanek 1975: 30), in the same manner in which a group of Peruvian self-managed enterprises has been characterised as a 'social property' sector.

WORKERS' CONTROL

Visitors to Mondragon have usually been practitioners rather than academics, and they have gone there in the hope of finding lessons that could be drawn for the own situation. For example, the Peruvians went to Mondragon and studied its experience while introducing forms of workers' control in their own industrial sector; indeed, there are similarities in the innovative sector of social property initiated during the Velasco regime (1968-75) and some aspects of the 'Mondragon' model.

Of particular interest are the visits made to Chile by members of Mondragon top management in the period 1970-73, when workers' control was being implemented in part of the Chilean industrial sector under the Allende regime.

But perhaps the most striking factor is the exceptional interest shown by the British. Robert Oakeshott, in particular, 'discovered' Mondragon in the early 1970s; since then, he has contributed much by way of careful descriptive accounts to stimulating interest in Mondragon among social scientists, labour leaders, and various sections of the British political spectrum.[3]

Great Britain

The concepts of workers' control and of industrial democracy have a long history in the British labour movement. Ever since the Industrial Revolution experiments have been undertaken with the aim of giving workers a stronger (or less weak) position in society. The projects and ideas of Robert Owen, and the consumers' cooperatives of the Rochdale Pioneers, are just two examples of this long tradition about which there is an extensive literature. The political system, however, did not allow any drastic shifts in the existing power structure; the workers had first to organise their union movement, a process that lasted several generations. The workers' first priority became to improve wages and working conditions, and to introduce social security legislation.

A long-term objective such as the participation of workers in the own work organisation can only be realised infinitesimal step by infinitesimal step. The pattern has typically been first to increase workers' control on the shop-floor; joint consultation became another instrument with which workers were involved in the functioning of their enterprise. Eventually, the nationalisation of enterprises became a primary aspect of the British labour movement's strategy in achieving the democratisation of economic structures.

The limited success obtained by all these forms is wellknown and it is understandable that, through the programme of the Labour Party, the labour movement has expressed its wish to be involved in the key planning agencies which dominate decision making on industrial structures. This new strategy is conditioned by the crisis in British industry at large, and by the felt need to prevent further industrial decline which would endanger the position of the work force.

During the 1970s the workers' cooperative was also included among the strategic options for the democratisation of economic relationships,[4] implying the turning of a page with respect to the attitude of trade unions towards producer cooperatives (Kendal 1975; Jones 1977a, 1980a; Coates & Topham 1980).

This is all the more surprising because worker cooperatives have so far not inspired any great confidence. They have a reputation, strongly influenced by the writings of the Webbs, of collective egoism, and are assumed to have little long-run potential for economic survival in a hostile capitalist environment. Producer cooperatives supposedly are bound to degenerate into forms of capitalist control, and tend to be less efficient than capitalist enterprises.

The research carried out by Derek Jones, however, has shown convincingly that a new assessment of producer cooperatives is justified.[5] Jones found that some producer cooperatives in Great Britain have survived for several generations, and evidence indicates an economic performance at least equal in efficiency if not superior to that of capitalist enterprises. Finally, he found that throughout the 19th and 20th centuries a few dozen small cooperatives continued to exist and to maintain the cooperative identity. The picture is therefore not as dismal as it is generally believed to be; at the same time, however, it cannot be denied that the impact of the cooperative movement has been extremely limited. There have been periods when only very few workers' cooperatives have managed to survive economically. A new period was reached in the early seventies. In 1974 three large workers' cooperatives were established with strong government support: the 'Wedgwood Benn Co-ops', named after the minister who was instrumental in coming to the rescue of The Scottish Daily News, Kirkby Manufacturing and Engineering, and Triumph Motorcycles at Meriden. This new start, however, has done little to repair the negative image of producer cooperatives. Already by 1979 two of these firms had met with such economic difficulties that closure was inevitable, while the third had considerable trouble in avoiding bankruptcy (Bradley & Gelb 1980).

A notable example of worker involvement in planning the future of a company is that of Lucas Aerospace.[6] In 1968, faced with the threat that the work force would have to be reduced from 18,000 to 12,000, the workers set up a 'Combine Committee' which, on the advice of Wedgwood Benn, drew up an employment plan for all 17 associated plants of the conglomerate. That plan had three objectives: to maintain and possibly to create jobs; to start the manufacture of other products of greater interest to the general public; and to achieve a breakthrough in the enterprise's hierarchical non-democratic organisation. The Committee's 1979 report on *Turning Industrial Decline into Expansion*[7] gained a great deal of attention. Earlier, in 1978, the workers at Lucas had gained the backing of the trade union movement and of the Labour Party.

It seems logical to conclude that the work force of Lucas Aerospace has made some advance towards workers' control for the protection of employment and for the achievement of self-management in the enterprise.

Perhaps the most fascinating aspect is that, in spite of new setbacks, the labour movement continues to explore new forms of workers' control, even including national self-management as a main element of future labour relations strategy. We may mention here the interest shown by the trade unions in supporting workers' cooperatives in depressed areas, such as those of Wales. 'A Mondragon for Wales?', headline of a newspaper report, vividly illustrates the optimism which British labour representatives feel with respect to the Mondragon model.[8] This sort of interest in the Mondragon group is understandable when it is realised 'that the discussion of industrial democracy is only just beginning, and that it is liable to feed upon its failures, which will provide matter for further analysis and further development of its ideals' (Coates & Topham 1980: 140).

The Netherlands

Another country where the attitude of trade unions towards cooperatives is changing is the Netherlands, where the history of cooperatives shows the negative characteristics mentioned earlier. By the early 1950s the cooperative movement had almost entirely disappeared, but then new workers' cooperatives started up and a national association was established, which now publishes its own journal. Several dozen workers' cooperatives were established during the 1970s, including a large building company.[9]

The realisation gradually grew that government policies are of critical importance, the odds against successful performance being great if strong supportive structures are lacking. By the middle of the decade the time seemed to have come for careful analysis of the potential to survive in a mixed economy. If producer cooperatives, whether individually or collectively, were to be a domain for the exercise of workers' control in the future, then it was essential to know which conditions would be likely to contribute to success or failure.

The research foundation of the national trade unions therefore made an exploratory survey of the cooperative phenomenon in the Netherlands, with field study trips to Britain and France. In its study of the relevant literature, the report of that survey gives a detailed account of 'Mondragon', emphasising the significance of the 'vertical integration' between various types of cooperatives that is found there (SWOV 1979: 98). The report concludes that a worker-managed sector can be strengthened within the perspective of a transformation of society. Mondragon is called an 'inspiring example', where forms of coordination among cooperatives have been introduced which have partly neutralised the negative consequences of competitive markets (Ibidem: 319).

A national congress of producer cooperatives was held in 1980, attended by the top leadership of the national unions as well as by Members of Parliament. One statement made at that congress was that 'Cooperatives are islands in a capitalist society, from which much can be learned'.[10] It was recognised that the labour movement and the socialist party do not have clear strategies for 'transition', and that lessons from the new workers' cooperatives should therefore be welcomed.

A LABOUR-MANAGED ECONOMY[11]

'Mondragon' is difficult to categorise. Is it a case in which a high degree of workers' participation is practiced in industry? (Loveridge 1980). Does 'Mondragon' fit the characteristics of producer cooperatives? (Jones 1980b). How should one analyse a socio-economic phenomenon that includes factories in which all workers are members of a General Assembly which has ultimate control over work organisation; which includes other organisations such as a bank and educational institutions whose General Assemblies consist of different constituencies; which includes a rapidly growing — more traditional — consumers' cooperative as well as housing cooperatives? Furthermore, each of the principal dimensions — education, factories, and banking — shows a strong tendency to combine an outward-looking attitude with the determination to strengthen and further develop existing organisations. Educational programmes train the cooperators for work in the factories but have also become involved in the development of primary and secondary education curricula for the entire province. The factories do their utmost to be efficient and profitable, but also are active in creating new employment opportunities. Lastly, the bank, the Caja Laboral Popular (CLP), allocates its resources in such a manner that this twofold orientation of the associated institutions, and of the factories in particular, has become a significant aspect of the Mondragon cooperatives.

How should such a complex and dynamic phenomenon be researched? For our purpose – the economic analysis of a group of cooperative factories, linked with a cooperative bank and other cooperative institutions – Vanek's work is particularly helpful.[12]

Vanek uses two criteria with which to identify different forms of economic systems and types of productive organisations. In his view, there are great similarities between all 'capital-controlled' systems. The main dividing line between different systems of socio-economic organisation is determined by whether workers in the organisations can exercise control over the many problems related to production, whether at the micro, meso or national level. The second criterion is concerned with different forms of 'ownership'.

Vanek's categorisation of socio-economic systems is illustrated in Table 1. The first order distinction regards whether control in the productive organisation is vested exclusively with those who work; the pure model furthermore assumes that all who work in the productive organisation exercise rights of control. We thus have the extreme form of self-managed work organisations as opposed to those that are capital-controlled. In reality, of course, mixed forms are more common.

Table 1. *Categorisation of economic systems and types of productive organisation (arrows mean 'corresponds to')*

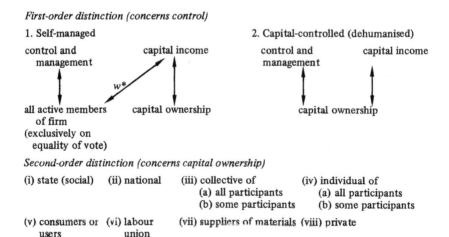

First-order distinction (concerns control)

1. Self-managed

2. Capital-controlled (dehumanised)

Second-order distinction (concerns capital ownership)

(i) state (social)	(ii) national	(iii) collective of (a) all participants (b) some participants	(iv) individual of (a) all participants (b) some participants
(v) consumers or users	(vi) labour union	(vii) suppliers of materials	(viii) private

Taken from Vanek (1975): 14. w^* = worker-management.

The difference between labour-management and worker-management is of criticial importance. Labour-management is that form of self-management in which the working people view the means of production as capital that belongs to society. For the use of buildings, land and equipment, they need to pay a scarcity rent, whereas they are under an obligation to maintain the value of the borrowed capital goods. Worker-management is that form of self-management in which the working people have a narrower perspective of the ownership and use of capital goods. They realise that the factories belong to 'the state or society', but are under no obligation to pay a scarcity price to the owner. At a later stage, when evaluating the economic performance of the Mondragon group, we shall return to this problem, which has major policy implications. Worker-managed firms, for instance, are typically found in Yugoslavia, and Vanek argues that many of the problems faced by the Yugoslav system of self-management derive from the fact that pure labour-management has not been adopted.

Capital ownership – the second criterion – is found in many forms, each of which has its own implications (eight types are listed in Table 1). These range between such extreme cases as state ownership through nationalisation and private ownership by way of shareholdings. This variety of forms of ownership, and of combinations of elements of the first and second order criteria, allows the design of many different models. For instance, consumers' cooperatives – a second order criterion – are most commonly 'capital-controlled'; producer cooperatives, on the other hand, under a variety of ownership forms, could be worker- or labour-managed, dependent on the actual control situation in the productive organisation and on the manner in which capital incomes are allocated. In Mondragon some cooperatives are fully 'self-managed', i.e. each person has a vote, while others, for example the CLP and the education cooperatives, have more complex structures with General Assemblies consisting of different categories of voters. The ownership factor in Mondragon is complicated in that it represents a combination of individual and collective ownership, the balance between which has shifted with the passing of time.

Operational Design

Various characteristics can be listed which, on theoretical grounds, are necessary conditions for an 'optimal and viable self-managed economy (or, implicitly, of an isolated self-managed firm)' (Vanek 1975: 33). First, in any labour-managed situation, production must be arranged in such a way that ultimate control and authority are vested with those who work in the specific work organisation. Second, ownership of capital resources must be such that it does not entitle 'control' – but merely the receipt of a scarcity price.

Third, there should be a 'shelter' organisation which serves partly as an 'investment fund', and whose main tasks are to safeguard an adequate flow of financial resources towards self-managed enterprises, and to promote the development of the self-managed sector or to strengthen the national self-managed economy. Fourth, the sheltering organisation needs to undertake some planning functions which, together with market mechanisms, determine the manner in which economic decisions are coordinated. Educational programmes and political democracy are also necessary ingredients or preconditions for an efficient system of self-management which should be looked after by the shelter organisation.

A fifth criterion has been elaborated by Horvat with respect to issues of equity. The distribution of earnings should just compensate for the work performed by cooperators; sharing of the surplus then becomes a reward for collective performance. To the extent that earnings do not cover the needs for 'the development of individual capabilities' there needs to be provision of non-market goods by way of collective consumption in six directions: 'education, medical care, social welfare, culture, physical culture and environmental conservation and creation' (Horvat 1976a: 36-37).

The first two of these characteristics refer to the categorisation of socio-economic systems (see Table 1). The following three are main principles of operation and dynamic development. Lastly, the objectives of such work organisations have to be formulated. In a narrow sense, maximisation of income per worker rather than profit maximisation per unit of capital might be expected. In a broader sense, the objectives of worker-controlled factories may include maximisation of income for the collective of workers rather than per individual worker; the continuity of the enterprise and a variety of other objectives ranging from environmental policies to active employment creation, may also figure prominently. The objectives of the Mondragon cooperatives will be analysed and evaluated within this wider perspective.

In this study theory is not regarded as a 'straightjacket' in which hypotheses have to be tested. It has provided us with insight into the key themes of productive organisations in which workers have a considerable degree of control, as is the case in Mondragon, and also helps in the integration of analyses at the micro-, meso- and macro-levels. Questions about macro-conditions for micro-transformations can be formulated with the aid of tools provided by economic theory.

This is the way in which the experience of Mondragon will be evaluated in this study. Does the Mondragon model offer scope for transformation? If so, in what direction?[13] We shall go further than a mere investigation of Mondragon's economic record — its successes and weaknesses and its comparative performance — and shall hope to provide answers to these basic questions.

PLAN OF WORK AND THE MAIN FINDINGS

In Chapter II we summarise the cooperative history of Mondragon as it unfolds from 1943 onwards, giving an overview of the main themes in order to provide a background to the specific themes that will be analysed in subsequent chapters.

We start with the historical trends — industrialisation, Basque nationalism and cooperativism — which later played a role in Mondragon's development. The history of the Mondragon group can be divided broadly into four distinct periods. First, the *years of preparation* from 1943 until 1956; during which the only 'activity' was the establishment of a school for technical training. The years 1956 to 1960 represented the *period of formation*, during which foundations were laid. Strategic choices then had to be made with respect to the organisation of the factories, the rules of distribution and of accumulation, and the manner in which the credit cooperative bank, Caja Laboral Popular (CLP), would establish its links with so-called 'associated cooperatives'. Then followed a period of extremely *rapid expansion* which lasted until the end of the 1960s. By that time the Mondragon group had proven its economic viability and had started to devote more time to planning in order that its achievements might be consolidated and new structures designed for the challenges of the 1970s, being concerned particularly with the worsening economic situation: years of *consolidation*.[14]

The research design derives mainly from two sources: theory on the economics of self-management, and the already extensive literature on 'Mondragon'.[15]

In Chapter III we study aspects of work and training. *Employment creation* — from 24 in 1956 to 15,672 in 1979 — has been impressive, and has had three principal causes. Firstly, the cooperative enterprises have expanded, achieving average work forces of about 225 members. Secondly, the Credit Cooperative Bank has always played an active role in establishing new cooperatives. Finally, existing private enterprises have linked-up with the Mondragon group; in a process of 'association' they are transformed into producer cooperatives. A rise in cooperative employment during the 1970s contrasts sharply with a strong fall in provincial employment in industry.

Absenteeism — an important indicator of labour relations — is markedly lower in the cooperatives than in private enterprises in the province of Guipúzcoa.

Considerable attention is given to the *education* cooperatives which form one of the most fascinating aspects of the Mondragon experience. Programmes of recurrent adult education, a special cooperative for the provision of research and development (R&D), and a cooperative in which students work part-time in order to combine work and study, are among the outstanding features of an educational structure which supports the entire Mondragon group.

The *distribution of work* among the cooperators is the final aspect to be analysed in relation to the work situation, and proves to be largely similar to that found in private enterprise.[16]

Credit cooperatives and savings banks have achieved success in many countries. Caja Laboral Popular, the *credit cooperative* that was established in Mondragon in 1959 and which is the subject of Chapter IV, is thus no exception in cooperative history. By the end of the seventies CLP had become the fastest growing financial institution in the province of Guipúzcoa, accounting for about 13 per cent of total deposits held at all banks. Over a period of 20 years it developed into a modern bank, differing in two important aspects from private commercial banks. Firstly, it is controlled by a General Assembly and a Supervisory Board. And secondly, it has a strong *management services department* whose work is mostly oriented towards strengthening the cooperative factories. To an important degree, this explains how the Mondragon group functions: the linkage between a credit cooperative and a group of cooperative factories is an innovation in cooperative history.

In Chapter V we examine *the growth record* in terms of sales and of value added, of exports and investments. Particular attention is given to comparing Mondragon's economic performance with that of private enterprises. Moreover, a distinction is made into pre-1973 and post-1973 performance in order to discover whether the economic behaviour of the cooperatives reacted to fluctuations of the business cycle, and whether or not their performance was similar to that of private enterprises. This task was unfortunately hampered by the almost complete lack of information on the performance of the provincial economy and of private enterprises at large.

Cooperative factories — starting from a very small base — have grown rapidly, accounting for about 10 per cent of industrial production in Guipúzcoa by the late 1970s. *Investments* have consistently been strong, while *export* figures clearly indicate the dynamics of these cooperatives: at the end of 1980, about 20 per cent of their total sales were to other countries, compared to about 10 per cent a decade earlier, when it had been realised that saturation of the national markets would force the cooperatives to sell abroad if they were to maintain the rapid expansion that had taken place during the boom years of the late 1950s and 1960s.

The use of ratio analysis enables us to make a comparative study of efficiency, defined as the value created by the joint 'resources' of people and capital.[17] The finding is conclusive that the cooperative enterprises have made considerably better use of their available resources than have private enterprises.

Our analysis also extends to *the various branches* of economic activity in which the cooperatives are engaged, and comes to the important finding that cyclical behaviour between sectors shows considerable variations. A further aspect to be investigated in this chapter relates to the *size* of cooperatives and to the relationship between size and economic performance. Finally, we shall examine the financial structures of the cooperatives and their capital intensity of production.

In Chapter VI we analyse the *distribution* of earnings and of capital incomes. Many observers have reported on the famous Mondragon *three-to-one formula* as well as on the so-called *alpha-coefficient* by which surplus is distributed between collective reserves and individual accounts of the members.[18] A brief historical record is presented of the debate that takes place each year on aspects of distribution, in an attempt to discover which issues play a role in the discussions on this crucial aspect of economic decision making. Various aspects of 'equity' are elaborated, and the complex phenomenon of incentive structures is also discussed.

This exercise has proven very rewarding in that it has clarified some of the problems which a group of cooperatives has to face when it is connected to the labour market at large.

Data on earnings show that the Mondragon cooperators have been successful in preventing differentials from exceeding a three-to-one range between highest and lowest earnings; also, the system by which surplus is distributed forms the basis for the strong financial position of the cooperative factories.

Social security provisions are also studied. Cooperative law in several countries — the situation in the Netherlands is a good example — puts cooperators in a rather unfavourable position since they are considered to be self-employed; as a result, they have to make their own social security arrangements. The Mondragon group has dealt with this problem by establishing a separate cooperative to deal with all problems of social security and welfare.

Whether all the cooperative activities add up to a *labour-managed sector* is the subject of Chapter VII. Our conclusion is that 'Mondragon' partially meets the condition outlined in this chapter. This offers scope for some comparison with other cases of partial transformation of the economy — the social property sector in Peru and the Kibbutz economy in Israel being theoretically the most important. A comparison with the Yugoslav economy also enables important lessons to be drawn.

It is after such an examination that the possible *limits* of Mondragon become apparent. Can a labour-managed sector continue to expand? Can it first reach a position in which it controls 15 to 20 per cent of the provincial economy; then move forward to attain even more power in the economic structures with which it is so closely interwoven, and on which it can exercise increasing influence?

Our concluding chapter puts our findings into a wider perspective and focusses on a number of issues that are of particular relevance to underdeveloped countries, to countries with underdeveloped regions, and to countries that have an interest in stimulating cooperatives, for instance as a means with which to combat unemployment.

NOTES

1. See, e.g. *The Economist* (3 May 1975, 11 December 1976, 8 January 1977); *The Times* (7 and 14 April, 29 December 1977); *The Guardian* (28 October 1977); *Industrial Management* (May 1974), 35-40; *Personnel Management* (March 1979).

2. The following authors have dealt with some economic aspects of the Mondragon cooperatives. Aldabaldetrecu & Gray 1967, Aranzadi 1976, Ballesteros *et al* 1968, Desroche 1970, Garcia Quintin 1970, Gorroño 1975, Gutierrez Johnson & Foote Whyte 1977, Oakeshott 1978, and Trivelli 1975. Each of these has given a multidisciplinary account of Mondragon's history, including an introduction to the economic dimensions. Gorroño's study was the first to include specific data on economic performance, and the work of Gutierrez Johnson (1978) has provided useful information on the distribution of earnings. The latter's work focusses on the 'sociology of Mondragon'; the field study undertaken by Bradley in investigating the sociology of the work organisation in a few cooperative factories, should also be mentioned in this respect.

3. See in particular, Oakeshott (1973): 'Spain's Oasis of Democracy', reprinted in Vanek 1975: 290-96, and his book on workers' cooperatives in which he gives an excellent description of the historical context of the debate on producer cooperatives in Britain. Comparisons with Italian and French cooperatives are helpful for a good understanding of the cooperative phenomenon.

4. See, e.g., Derek C. Jones (1977a); also, a paper by Paul Derrick presented at a conference of the International Cooperative Alliance held in Rome in October 1978. Specific information may be found in *Job Ownership* (November 1978); also, in the Report of the Working Group on a Cooperative Development Agency (1977), and in the Cooperative Development Agency Bill (1978). See Stan Windass (1981) for interesting details of recent cooperative initiatives and community ventures.

5. For a review of Jones's research into producer cooperatives, see Jones (1980a).

6. Coates & Topham (1980), as well as the Dutch journal *Zeggenschap* (April 1981) have given attention to this important new trend of workers developing their own ideas about technology and products. If 'human capital' is not valued adequately by management, the workers themselves are ready to prove their own value.

7. Lucas Aerospace Confederation Trade Union Committee (1979). An important aspect of this study is the emphasis on the company's international dimensions. Loss of jobs in Britain is compensated by employment expansion elsewhere.

8. See Steve Vines, *The Observer*, 8th February 1981, 'A Mondragon for Wales?' This study is being financed partly by the British government and represents a constructive trade union response to the crisis in Wales. The Wales TUC has signed a broad collaboration agreement with the Caja Laboral Popular covering possible joint areas of interest for closer future relations. There are a number of cogent reasons why cooperatives can be successfully introduced in Wales, was the conclusion of a Wales TUC delegation after a week's visit to Mondragon and discussions with CLP executives, factory workers, trade union and political representatives.

9. *Werken in Kooperatie* (SWOV 1979), a study commissioned by the national trade unions, gives comprehensive information on the history and actual practice of producer cooperatives in The Netherlands.

10. National congress organised by the Associatie voor Bedrijven op Cooperatieve Grond-slag (Association for Firms with a Cooperative Basis, Utrecht, 1980); statement by Member of the Netherlands Parliament.

11. This section is derived in particular from the work of Vanek and Horvat; for a survey of the literature on the economics of self-management, see in particular Steinherr (1978).

12. Vanek (1975: 11-16). The usefulness of Vanek's theory lies in the fact that it includes both micro- and macro-economics, and is therefore very appropriate for a case in which the micro-economics of the firm play a dominant role. Horvat (1972) gives an additional per-spective of the political dimensions at the national level.

13. It is fully realised that 'economics' is just one of the dimensions that play a role in a process of wider societal transformation: the sociological and political dimensions will also be determining factors.

14. This chapter gives a bird's-eye view of the broad historical and organisational trends of the Mondragon cooperatives and therefore partly overlaps with earlier accounts mentioned in Note 2 supra.

15. See Notes 1 and 2. Information on the data used for each of the problem areas in this study will be provided in subsequent chapters.

16. The organisation of the enterprise, of course, is quite different as regards the control structure.

17. We shall discuss the various aspects of 'efficiency' in a labour-managed sector in Chap-ters V and VII.

18. Cf. in particular Gutierrez Johnson (1978) and Trivelli (1975).

II

AN HISTORICAL AND ORGANISATIONAL OVERVIEW

INTRODUCTION

Three factors need to be taken into account in any attempt to understand the background of the Mondragon experience. Firstly, the degree of industrialisation that was to be found in the Basque Provinces in the 1930s. Secondly, a labour movement which, on balance, showed positive inclinations towards the cooperative phenomenon. And lastly, Basque Nationalism, and the tension between the Basque Provinces and Spain's central government. These themes will be introduced in the following section of this chapter.

Subsequently we shall give a bird's-eye view of the main periods into which the Mondragon experience can be divided, between 1943 and 1980, and shall also consider the wider socio-political and economic context of each of these periods.

A number of aspects which are not singled out later as focus of research will also be discussed briefly in this chapter in order that the reader who is not familiar with the broad outlines of the Mondragon experience may gain some understanding of its historical and organisational developments. We shall examine the role of its founder, Don José María Arizmendi-Arrieta, and the problems that had to be faced during the early years in selecting the products to be made and the technologies to be introduced. Particular attention will be given to fundamental principles with regard to economic matters and to the organisation of the cooperatives. An interesting factor in this regard is that most of these principles, which were to be of such significance to the Mondragon experience, were introduced during the initiatory period.

THE BASQUE NATION: STRUCTURAL CHANGES

The present territory of the Basques, on either side of the French-Spanish frontier, is a result of the ebb and flow of history. In classical times the Basques had

---

Notes to this chapter may be found on pp. 39-41.

made the Pyrenees their home, spreading as far south as Burgos in Spain and northward to Bayonne in France in times of peace, and retreating to their mountain fastnesses in times of war. The Basque nation has never become fully integrated into the Spanish state, a fact which, given the survival of a distinctive culture and a difficult language, causes problems to the present day.

During the Middle Ages maritime trade and fishing provided the Basques with a major source of wealth which was vital given their limited agricultural resources. By providing Castile with an outlet to the sea they became important in the wool trade, selling Castillian wool to Flanders. In the 14th century they were able to open their own consulate in Bruges. The Basques also played an active part in voyages of discovery, and in the establishment, administration and commerce of the American colonies.

This economic structure changed over the centuries until, by the end of the 19th century, the minor nobility had become ironmasters and traders, and were increasingly university-educated. Iron ore, the region's most important resource, was now privately rather than communally owned and exploited as had earlier been the case. The usual class division gradually emerged into an industrial proletariat and a capital-controlling bourgeoisie, which was quick to realise and to seize the advantages of integration into the Spanish market and the greater protection that this offered against foreign competition. Economic growth on Spain's periphery – the Basque Provinces and Catalunya – was rapid, stimulated by the introduction of new production techniques associated with the Industrial Revolution. Foreign demand for the region's iron ore increased steadily in that it was well-suited to feeding Bessemer furnaces. Exports of low-phosphorous hematite ores from the Basque region rose from one million to six million tons per year between 1877 and 1900. Welsh coking coal and external financing became essential elements in the conversion from artisan industry to modern factory-scale production in the Basque economy.[1]

The process of rapid industrialisation caused tension among the Basques, whose capitalist oligarchy had close links with Spain. Through the efforts of individual workers, attempts were made to set up trade unions and political parties. From small beginnings in 1870, the Bilbao Federation of the First International expanded until, in 1882, it numbered seven sections with 525 members. The most enthusiastic supporters of trade unionism were the Bilbao miners, closely followed by the metallurgical and transport workers. Guipúzcoa, the province in which Mondragon is located, also underwent the transition from small-scale to factory production and the corresponding working class organisation also took place, albeit less quickly than in the neighbouring province of Vizcaya and with a lesser overall impact.

The trade union federation Solidaridad was set up following a general strike in 1910 which was led by the Union General de Trabajadores.[2] Solidaridad's appeal was founded on two distinct platforms: social catholicism and love for the Basque country.

The trade union position, before the Civil War, was ... complex. There were the specifically Basque trade unions, federated as the Eusko Langileen Alkartasuna-Solidaridad de Trabajadores Vascos (ELA-STV) — which incidentally emerged victorious in the first trade union elections in the Basque provinces early in 1978. But for the rest it was the conventionally socialist Union General de Trabajadores (UGT), rather than the anarchist Confederacion Nacional del Trabaja (CNT) which was strong among Mondragon's working people up to the defeat of the Basques in the Civil War; but the CNT was unambiguously libertarian; the UGT solidly bureaucratic (Oakeshott 1978: 169).

By the 1930s Solidaridad's membership had grown to rival that of the Socialist trade unions, but for our present purposes the most important influence of the labour movement is its advocacy of cooperativism as a model for society, rather than its political goals.

At the first Congress of ELA-STV (or Solidaridad) held in Eibar in 1929, a call was made for the establishment of a workers' bank, and when the second Congress was held in Vitoria the delegates approved motions calling for a campaign for cooperativism. These motions in effect represent the programme which the Basque Nationalist Party, which had gained its first seat in the Spanish Cortes in 1916, decided to implement:

1. to set up consumers' cooperatives in each town where there was a Basque workers' organisation;
2. to create regional Federations of Basque consumers' cooperatives, in order to buy goods in significant quantities and thus to reduce the costs of essentials;
3. to create a credit cooperative to give all banking services necessary for each and every federated cooperative;
4. to create a Savings Bank within the credit cooperative to collect and direct small savings;
5. to create industrial, agricultural and fishing producer cooperatives and to establish a proper relationship between these and the Regional Federations of consumers' cooperatives, with consequent economies for the producer and consumers' cooperatives due to the removal of the intermediary (de Larrañaga 1977: 207).

ELA-STV had opened an Industrial School in its Bilbao headquarters as early as 1921, and various consumers' cooperatives had also been set up together with a cooperative factory. The latter, *Alfa* in Eibar in Guipúzcoa, achieved considerable fame, and was principally the creation of Toribio Echeverria, a self-taught socialist of considerable drive and astute initiative and clerk at the municipal hall who, when a local arms company got into difficulties, successfully converted it into a cooperative. Not content with this rescue operation, he advocated a change in its product range. Echeverria realised that dependence on distant and competitive markets for firearms produced under a Smith and Weston licence was a less attractive proposition than the production of useful goods for the domestic (and hence protected) market. At that time Singer, the USA corporation, held a virtual monopoly of the Spanish sewing machine market with annual sales of about sixty thousand. Alfa now set up in competition (incidentally, without a foreign licence), and gradually increased its production from 1750 in 1927 to 12,000 in 1936. By then the cooperative had 201 workers and paid out yearly dividends on a capital of six million pesetas.[3] The cooperative became famed, and the young José María Arizmendi(Arrieta), born on a farm in Marquine of which Eibar is the market town, would undoubtedly have known of it.

These historical events, described so briefly above, form the backdrop to Mondragon, a small town in a mountainous district, halfway between Eibar and Vitoria, and some 50 kilometers from the Biscay coast.

THE FORMATIVE YEARS OF THE MONDRAGON EXPERIMENT 1943-56

Following the end of the Spanish Civil War (1936-1939) and the defeat of the Second Republic in 1939, and with the almost immediate outbreak of the Second World War, life for the Basques was wretched indeed. It was under these conditions that Don José María Arizmendi came to Mondragon in February 1941. The son of a farmer, he was born in April 1915 and died in Mondragon in November 1976, after having devoted 35 years of his life to the people of that mainly working-class town. At the age of 12 he had started to study for the priesthood during the turbulent period when Spain was under the dictatorship of Primo de Rivera. From a posthumous analysis of his papers, it seems that Arizmendi was a seminarist with a strong social conscience.[4] During the Civil War he worked as a Basque Army journalist and as editor of the Basque newspaper *Eguna* in Bilbao. When that town fell, he was captured by Franco's troops and tried summarily for military rebellion, which carried the death penalty; he was found 'not guilty' on a technicality. He returned to study theology at the Vitoria seminary, where he was ordained priest. In 1941 his bishop sent him to Mondragon, his first and only parish. He was sent there in part because he was conversant with social problems and because Mondragon was an industrial town.

On his arrival in Mondragon, Don José María found that many of the community's natural leaders had either died or were in exile. Having been appointed counsellor to Acción Católica, an organisation with a broad social bent, he channelled his energies into training young people. Study groups on Catholic social doctrine were set up to impart a Christian, human and social education, values that now would be termed Christian Democracy. Today, the younger cooperators are motivated rather by nationalist and socialist ideologies. Don José María was an eminently practical person, a realist with vision. He described himself later as never having acted 'under the influence of dogmatic enslavement', but rather as having 'contrasted doctrine with reality' (Aranzadi 1976).

The Starting Point: Education

At that time, Mondragon was dominated by one industrial company, the Unión Cerrajera, which had been founded in 1905 and had grown into a medium-sized company. Don José María began to teach at the Unión's apprentice school which admitted the sons of employees plus twelve outsiders: all in all about 15 per cent of the local eligible youth. The priest tried but failed to persuade the management to admit more apprentices, even though he promised to help raise the necessary funds.

He then proposed that a technical training school should be set up for the wider community, seeking support for his idea among the people of Mondragon. Ballot boxes were placed at street corners for those who wished to indicate that they would give assistance to the project, whether in cash or in kind. Some ten per cent of the population as well as some local firms reacted positively, but Unión Cerrajera and the Town Hall notably abstained. The 'zealous guardians of the established order' were suspicious. Support was sufficiently adequate, however, to allow the Technical Training School to be opened in 1943 with an initial enrolment of twenty. The involvement of the students was high: they not only studied, but also engaged in continuous fund-raising activities for their School. By arranging cultural events, concerts, etc., the community was encouraged to identify closely with the school and its aims, and a bond of trust was established.

The first students passed their qualifying examinations in 1947. Arizmendi arranged for eleven of them to continue their studies in the evening at the Zaragoza School of Engineering, while still working in Mondragon in the daytime. It was this successful progress of the Technical Training School which led to the formation in 1948 of a new institution – the League of Education and Culture – which gave legal status to the school and to other educational programmes.

Speaking at an ecclesiastical conference in Valladolid in July 1951, Don José María clarified his ideas about the role of education and its integration into the world of labour:

We must not devalue work. This temptation must not be put before new generations, particularly in a country in which we are at saturation point with speculative careers or bureaucratic employment. The road to self-improvement has to be open to all classes, but through a normal, social channel, that of serious and constant work. That is why we advocate technical training in stages because, while giving access to the truly talented, this will not hinder but will rather give practical help in the placement of others.[5]

In 1952 the eleven students obtained their qualifications from the Zaragoza Engineering School and took up responsible jobs as foremen or section heads in factory workshops, some becoming representatives of workers to senior management. They were all highly motivated by a desire to democratise the workplace and also to change the attitude of management towards its workers: a position that was not popular with Spain's established hierarchy.

With total selflessness and integrity they worked in the hub of many companies, hoping to be able to promote their evolution and change, at least to the extent to which the various antagonistic elements could live together and engage in a dialogue. By one side they were called colleagues; the other side tolerated them less with each day that passed, forcing them to clash with attitudes that were inflexible and intransigent, even in matters that were peripheral to the structure of the enterprise and to its fundamental development – a phase that lasted until 1954 (Arizmendi 1966: 7).

Five of the eleven graduates then decided to set up on their own, as only then would they be able to put into practice their ideas on 'the primacy of labour among factors of production'. This resolute action was to push their ideals to a practical level.

THE EARLY COOPERATIVES 1956-60

Once General Franco had firmly established himself as the leader of post-war Spain, a new technocracy guided the national economy into a programme of modernisation. This process consisted basically of dismantling the old, autarchic structures in favour of a judicious mix of corporatism and the free play of market forces. At the same time Europe was being rebuilt and prosperity was spreading, causing a demand for traditional Spanish exports of fruit and wine. Attracted by a cheap and intimidated labour force, foreign investment began to flow into the country. In the late 1950s a Stabilisation Plan reduced the hourly wage rates of the majority of workers in an effort to promote rapid industrialisation.[6]

Two Basque banks, of Bilbao and Vizcaya, together with the Banco Urquijo, Spain's largest industrial bank, helped to finance the creation and consolidation of national industry, sometimes in collaboration with foreign capital, but always tending to reinforce oligarchically-owned industries rather than to develop the new high-growth sectors: precision engineering, electronics and electrical goods industries, advanced chemicals, large machine tools, etc., all calling for high technology and for trained and experienced labour in new factories. Such industries did arise but found their growth limited by lack of access to capital. In the province of Guipúzcoa, e.g., there was no adequate finance market, but the booming economy nevertheless caused an increase in the demand for consumer goods and created a good business climate in which to take entrepreneurial initiatives.

The Founding Enterprise: Ulgor

Together with Don José María, the five young men studied the Spanish 1942
law on cooperatives and decided that, at first glance, it was not adequate for
their purpose. Thus it was that they formed a limited liability company called
ULGOR – an acronym of the initial letters of their names: Usatorre, Larrañaga,
Gorroñogoita, Ormaechea and Ortubay – and in 1954 purchased a small workshop near Vitoria.[7] They were then able to start manufacturing – the requisite
licence went with the premises as part of the deal. In April 1956 Ulgor started
to construct a new factory, the chosen location being Mondragon. The article
produced by the previous ownership of the workshop – a paraffin-fired cooking
stove – was now considered inadequate and an alternative was sought. One of
the five founders brought an Aladdin space-heating stove from France; it was
dismantled and copied, with no attention being given to patent rights. This
heater complemented the paraffin cooking stove in similarity of construction
and in market area – both were domestic products relying on controlled com-
bustion.

The method by which Ulgor was set up was not, as some may have thought,
part of a general, carefully thought-out strategy, but was rather part of a desire
to find a vehicle through which to express an aspiration. Jesús Larrañaga, one of
the five founders, recalls: 'This was no ambitious and well-considered project;
what we needed was to start with something, to wake up, and to see what would
be the outcome.'[8] Don José María continually pondered on the legal, economic
and financial framework that would be needed if the demand for a partnership
on a new basis for capital and labour was to be satisfied. It took more than two
years and the help of two independent legal experts before an enterprise statute
could be worked out within the prevailing legislation on cooperatives which was
to embody many of their ideals.

The influence exercised by Arizmendi and the founders in the formative
period and the early years of this first cooperative proved decisive. Indeed, Don
José María was to declare with pride some ten years later, recalling the events of
1956-58:

In effect, formulae were found by which our enterprise's essential basis could be brought
into line with current legal precepts, enabling the first industrial cooperative to be set up in
Mondragon.... To do this, we had to overcome more than legal difficulties ... from the beginning we bore in mind the needs of a modern enterprise, and a formula was adopted which
would make its development viable from all points of view: economic, technical, social and
financial; not as a second ranking entity suitable only for a limited field of activity, but one
which would be appropriate across a wide sector of the economy. (Arizmendi, cited in
Ballesteros 1968: 187 *et seq*).

Backing for Ulgor came from the people of Mondragon and its surroundings:
eleven million pesetas were raised from well-wishers who put their faith in the

ability of the Technical Training School's prestigious graduates. Some of the 96 people who advanced loans were relatives, others were known to sympathise with the ideals of Ulgor's founders. Loan capital (and some equity) was thus obtained from the community against a specific commitment to provide jobs for new workers. Operations were commenced in 1956 with a total of 24 employees.

The Spanish patent rights for the British-designed Aladdin stove were sought and purchased. Usatorre also designed a new model, the *Doroty*. The lessons of excessive dependence on one-product profits were quickly learned. Ulgor began to diversify, licencing a new line in electrical products from Germany, while in March 1958 a casting shop and foundry were added, thus reducing dependence on outside suppliers and further increasing profitability. In 1958, too, butane from liquifiable refinery off-gasses reached the Spanish market, and Ulgor quickly realised the consequences of this technological development.

The Italian company, Fargas Spa of Milan, granted Ulgor a licence for the manufacture of butane-fired cookers. A new factory was set up for their production under the brand name *Fagor*. The manufacture of butane cookers and heaters also brought the first assembly lines.

While expansion was taking place within the Ulgor cooperative, others were springing up in the Leniz Valley. *Comet* (later known as *Ederlan*), an iron and steel foundry situated in Escoriaza, was created out of the merger of two private companies which had become convinced of the superiority of cooperative principles. *Arrasate* started up at the same time in Mondragon, producing lawn mowers and stamped blanks, and was later to become one of Spain's premier machine tool manufacturers (Gorroño 1975).

Close ties developed between these cooperatives. As independent entities they had problems in common which were not always directly related to production and marketing difficulties. Their very status as cooperatives, and consequently that of their members as self-employed, was a constraint to their aim of rapid growth. As self-employed, the cooperative workers had to make their own provisions for such eventualities as sickness, injury or death, being barred from participation in the Spanish social security system. More important from the cooperative point of view were the restrictions placed on their collective access to finance for expansion. Outside sources of loans could not be offered adequate guarantees in the form of collateral or equity participation, as both were legally proscribed: prospects for expansion were therefore limited. Lastly, the mutual aims of rapid expansion in output required a certain degree of coordination and periodic access to managerial expertise at a high level, which was difficult for modest cooperatives to provide for themselves. The solution to these problems proved as simple as its effects were to be stimulating.

A Support Organisation

Don José María was confident that a way out of these dilemmas would be found. Under Cooperative Law it was permissible to establish what were termed 'second degree cooperatives', i.e. organisations that were not entirely worker-owned and controlled but which also had associated cooperatives as institutional members. Such a support organisation could attract the savings of the local community (which were high by normal standards) and invest them in the associated cooperatives. Loans could then be advanced and their allocation could be coordinated by a team of suitably qualified experts. Ulgor, Arrasata, Funcor – another cooperative in Elorrio – and the consumers' cooperative San José then formally associated with each other for the purpose of constituting the *Caja Laboral Popular* – their own support organisation. The statutes of the CLP were approved by central government on 16th July 1959.[9]

The People's Savings Bank (CLP) began to operate in 1960 as the source of additional investment funding and of professional expertise at the service of its associated cooperatives, and intended to render financial, technical and social assistance to artisan, professional and producer cooperatives which apply for and are granted association.

Apart from the pension fund provisions and the deposits and investments that were required by law to be made with other branches of the Spanish financial system, the initiation of CLP meant that all financial resources captured could now be dedicated to the reinforcement and spreading of cooperativism. This necessitated the checking of loan proposals and a high degree of managerial integrity and expertise, both within CLP and between it and the associated cooperatives who were the sole beneficiaries of its funding and planning activities. In order to benefit from CLP's loans or advice, a cooperative had to associate formally with it by signing a Contract of Association containing a statement of principles. Given the importance of a legal framework for determining the rights and duties of members, and the overall limits set upon the permissible conduct of a cooperative as a legal entity, such rules and statutes are of critical importance.

The Contract of Association puts special emphasis on those aspects that differ from conventional commercial and business practice. Sections on Economic Relations and on Operational Relations regulate the links between associated cooperatives and the CLP. Article 3.1 of the section dealing with *Economic Relations* states that capital of an associated cooperative shall be made available to CLP, the exact amount of an individual cooperative's financial resources which is to be pooled being determined by the Bank's General Assembly. Hence, the member cooperative surrenders not only some degree of autonomy on association, but also is required to transfer equity. The reason for this is said to be to ensure that CLP will always be able to meet the requirements of the Central Bank with respect to the percentage of own resources held against the total amount of deposited accounts.

In addition, up to a quarter of the initial contributions of any associated cooperative, made upon entry by new cooperators, is required for CLP's third party guarantees — an arrangement which considerably increases the Bank's solvency.

Article 4 on *Operational Relations* sets out the conditions that have to be met by an associated cooperative in the conduct of its business. The previous year's Balance Sheet has to be made available to CLP, together with the annual budget, in a standard format with monthly statistics that show details of performance against this budget. Such a system of financial control and general management information, of course, is standard practice for any holding company. As a counterpart, CLP undertakes to provide periodical reports on its budgetary planning, together with broader information that is considered relevant concerning other cooperatives and the wider technical-economic environment. Such a *reciprocal exchange* brings obvious benefits to management in the movement as a whole and in individual cooperatives, ensuring as it does a high standard of professionalism, a uniform system of reporting, and a constant monitoring of performance. In addition, the operations of any associated cooperative are subjected to audit at least once every four years. Such an audit is comprehensive, covering 'economic, social and business development', and forms the basis of a report containing 'recommendations to correct any existing or potential problems that may have come to CLP's attention'. Additional audits can be carried out should either CLP, the General Assembly, Watchdog Committee, Management, or the Social Council of the cooperative, or 10 per cent of its members, feel that circumstances warrant it. All banking and financial operations should be conducted through CLP which, according to Article 4.3 of the agreement, will offer credit and may expect its associates to deposit with it any surplus monies that they may have available.

Finally, operational relations between associated cooperatives are based upon the 'principle of inter-group loyalty and mutual assistance', which effectively means that unless the 'interests or autonomy of the cooperative itself' are affected, CLP should have a say in operational decisions intended for the support of all cooperative institutions and for optimisation of overall group business efficiency.

BASIC ECONOMIC PRINCIPLES

Each cooperative, on signing the Contract of Association, undertakes to comply with a set of basic principles regarding employment creation, capital ownership, earnings differentials, distribution of surplus, and democratic organisation.

The 'Open Door'

'Membership of the cooperative shall not be restricted but shall be open to all those whose services are appropriate.' A member joins voluntarily, and agrees to abide by the rules and to accept the responsibilities entailed by membership.

The 'open door' principle implies that cooperators have no intention of becoming a local élite. It could perhaps be said that because workers are screened as regards general suitability, this in effect detracts from the 'open door' principle, and the fact that each new cooperator has to pay an initial contribution in cash could also be seen as detracting from the ideal. In practice, however, 'all those whose services are considered appropriate' can raise the money for that contribution, if necessary by borrowing from CLP. The job creation record of the associated cooperatives year in year out (see Chapter III), shows that these initial contributions in no way form a stumbling block to new entrants. Selection criteria are an inevitable corollary of a specialized world; cooperatives employ their own criteria for recruitment — criteria that are authentic and also effective.

Ownership and Distribution

The Contract of Association, while dealing with general guidelines, is quite specific with regard to ownership of cooperative organisations, and to the manner in which earnings and surplusses may be distributed. These latter issues will be discussed in Chapter VI.

The initial capital contribution that has to be made by all new cooperators represents their capital stake or share in their enterprise. In part, each contribution finances the cost of the new workplace that is created; maximally 25 per cent of it is non-returnable. Each year, the value of the individual member's capital stake is adjusted upwards to compensate for inflation. Under normal circumstances, these individual capital accounts cannot be cashed or withdrawn, emphasis being placed on capital accumulation for expansion of employment.

The earnings structure of an associated cooperative is governed by principles which establish a suitable range of wage differentials to enable members to participate in its income, both as regards the payment of wages, considered as an advance, and the distribution of surplus (for which the same differentials are used).

Consideration of the solidarity principle brought the early cooperators to the decision that the maximum range of earnings differentials should be set at three-to-one. In other words, the gross earnings of the highest-paid cooperator can never be more than the three-fold of those of the lowest paid. Only in exceptional circumstances can the differential be rather larger for extra hours worked, continued absence from home on business, etc. Ulgor's decision to pay average

wages more or less in line with the two most important Mondragon employers –
Union Cerrajera and Elma – must be understood in the perspective of maximal
creation of new jobs. Solidarity with the neighbouring area was thus an operative
principle to enable the promotion of employment. The practical mechanism is
complicated but the effect is broadly to make the lower paid cooperators earn
slightly more than their equivalents in local factories; middle-range wages and
salaries are about the same, while upper management and directors earn far less
than their counterparts elsewhere.

The interest to be paid on the capital account of each member is determined
each year by the General Assembly. Under no circumstances can it exceed the
base or inter-bank rate of interest set by the Bank of Spain, which prevails for
the largest period of that year, by more than three percentage points. Interest
payments on capital contribution can be cashed up to six per cent maximum.
    In times of inflation this rule effectively means that the cooperatives can
protect their capital base, can preserve their capability to expand by further new
job creation, or can endure reduced profitability and poor cash flows during
adverse conditions.

Surplusses and Losses

A minimum of 30 per cent of any surplus (net profits) is allocated jointly to the
Reserve and Social Funds, with the provision that the Social Fund allocation is
set minimally at 10 per cent. At most, depending on actual profitability in a
given year, 70 per cent is allocated to individual capital accounts of cooperative
members. It follows from this that 90 per cent of net profits remain within the
cooperative movement, either as collective reserve or allocated to individual
capital accounts.
    Losses are borne according to a similar formula, being booked against the
Reserve Fund and against own capital accounts of cooperators. In the most dis-
advantageous cases, cooperators may be called upon to make new capital contributions.

ORGANISATION

All the industrial cooperatives of Mondragon are organised internally along
similar lines, the principles being laid down in the Contract of Association.
Details are elaborated in the Statutes and Internal Rules, which are based on the
Ulgor regulations and are applicable to all cooperatives.
    The Democratic Principle of the Contract of Association states that all
authority is ultimately conferred by the democratic votes of all the members of

a cooperative. Those who are ultimately responsible for administering the cooperative are elected and are accountable to the membership, although the use of the ballot box is confined to the selection of Supervisory – or Control – Board Members and management is in fact appointed by this Board. Managers derive their authority from their ability to conduct the affairs of a cooperative successfully. In the last instance democratic authority and sanction rests with the General Assembly.

To ensure equity between members and their full commitment, all workers are members of their respective cooperative. Only in exceptional circumstances will a cooperative hire other workers, but their number may never exceed five per cent of the total membership. Such cases usually concern persons with special skills or knowledge, whose services are required for a limited period.

The contract also lists a 'cooperative spirit' and flexibility in working relationships. The members generally, and management in particular, are expected to demonstrate a positive commitment to cooperativism through proper professional behaviour, social involvement, and responsibility in furthering its promotion and development.

Spanish law prescribes three organs of government for all industrial cooperatives: the General Assembly of Members; the Supervisory Board – a governing, non-executive board – and the Watchdog Council. In addition to these mandatory bodies, associated industrial cooperatives also have Management as the executive organ, and two other bodies: the Management Council and the Social Council. This basic organisation is shown in Diagram 1, which outlines the relationship between the institutional and managerial bodies in the conduct of an industrial cooperative's business.

The *General Assembly of Members* meets at least once yearly in ordinary session and can be called when necessary for an extraordinary meeting. It is empowered in an ordinary session to examine and approve the accounts and balance sheet of the previous financial year. It is also empowered to deal with matters concerning initial capital contributions of new members; with any requirement for further capital contributions or with rights issues; with the approval of Internal Rules; and with the establishment and modification of organisational norms for administering and carrying-out the different services within the cooperative.

When a new cooperative is set up, the General Assembly elects those cooperators who are to serve without pay on the Supervisory Board, and who can be dismissed if they are considered incompetent in the performance of their duties. The Supervisory Board is normally comprised of a Chairman, Vice-Chairman, Secretary and six ordinary members. In the normal course of events, each Board member in an established cooperative is elected for four years; half the Board must step down or stand for re-election every two years.

Extraordinary Assemblies may be convened for such purposes as: to under-

Diagram 1. *Organisational Structure of the Cooperatives*

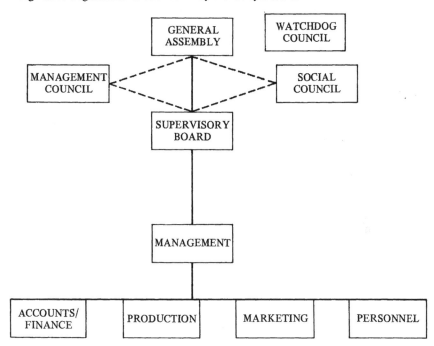

take some other form of association between the cooperative and other cooperatives or bodies; to name persons who are to be appointed to the Supervisory Board or the Watchdog Council, and to deal with all major questions which fall outside the competence of the Supervisory Board or which the latter deems convenient to put before the Extraordinary Assembly for discussion and judgement.

A meeting of the EGA can be convened either by the Supervisory Board, which must place a specific agenda before the members, or by petition by one-third of the cooperative's members, who are equally obliged to specify the subject of the meeting.

The *Supervisory Board*'s nine members must meet at least once a month, or at the request of the Chairman or of two of its members. Decisions are taken by vote, with the Chairman having the casting vote in the case of a tie.[10]

The cooperative is represented legally by the Chairman of the Supervisory Board, who is empowered to delegate specific tasks to others. He also has the authority to convene the General Assembly and the Supervisory Board, over both of which he presides.

The *Management* of a cooperative may consist of one person, or it may be a collegial body of managers with the executive function of running the cooperative as a productive unit. Appointed by the Supervisory Board, management is responsible and accountable to the Board and, through the Board, ultimately to the cooperative's membership gathered in the General Assembly, a structure that avoids some of the problems of authority and responsibility which have plagued other workers' self-managed cooperatives. This indirect accountability of management has proved to be one of the strengths of the Mondragon cooperative formula. As Sidney and Beatrice Webb have indicated, directly elected managers cannot in practice exercise the necessary control of the workers under them.

Members of management can never belong to the Supervisory Board, but may attend its meetings 'with a voice but without a vote', at the Board's discretion. Managers are appointed for a minimum period of four years and cannot be dispensed with except in the case of some grave fault which is duly denounced by the Board and sanctioned by an Extraordinary General Assembly. Should management consist of more than one person, a meeting attended by a member of the Supervisory Board will be held at least once weekly, and minutes will be taken.

Management is directly responsible for all those administrative tasks which are typically carried out by managers and middle level executives in private sector enterprises. Responsibilities include the commercial and financial aspects of cooperative performance; implementation of production plans; coordination of the programmes and plans of the various divisions, sections and workshops in accordance with the general plans outlined and approved by the Supervisory Board; and keeping the latter fully informed on progress in output and administration. The Supervisory Board determines the appointment of each manager and his conditions of employment, leaving it to the discretion of Management to select candidates for subordinate roles in the cooperative, provided there is no conflict with Internal Rules. This system has led to the formation of highly competent and successful management teams, whose devotion to the development of cooperative values is a major motivating force.

The *Management Council* is an advisory and consultative body, reporting to both Management and the Supervisory Board, and is made up of managers and high executives (i.e. heads of departments) of the company, plus any outsiders who may be contracted for their special experience and skills. Those executives who are not elected members of the Supervisory Board and who belong to the Management Council may attend the meetings of the Board, again 'with a voice but no vote'. The Management Council meets at least once a month.

The *Social Council*, reporting both to Management and to the Supervisory Board, is the elected voice of members of the cooperative, and has wide prescriptive and advisory powers in all aspects of personnel management. Social Council decisions are binding in such matters as accident prevention, work safety and work hygiene, social security, wage levels, administration of Social Funds, and welfare payments. Representatives are elected for three-year terms and can offer themselves for re-election, with one-third being required to step down each year. Each worker votes for a representative at section level, with whom meetings are held at least once a week, and each cooperative must hold a general plenary session of Social Council section-representatives at least once every three months.

The ultimate safeguard in ensuring the correct running of a cooperative's affairs is the *Watchdog Council*. As its name implies, the Watchdog Council exists for the purpose of controlling and inspecting the overall conduct of management, the Supervisory Board, and the two advisory Councils. It consists of three members of the cooperative who are elected directly by the General Assembly for a four-year term, and who are charged with providing any information or opinion from cooperative members which the meeting may require. The Watchdog Council may ask the advice of experts of CLP on specific problems, in order to strengthen its position.

THE DECADE OF EXPANSION 1961-70

At the beginning of the 1960s the bulk of Spanish industry was in dire need of rationalisation due to its fragmented structure and low level of inter-sectoral linkages. Census data collected from 1958 indicates that industrial firms were on average rather small: enterprises employing between one and five workers amounted to 82 per cent of all industrial firms, 12.5 per cent employed between six and 25 persons, and only 0.07 per cent over 500 workers (Pinillos 1967). By the mid-1960s, however, the rise in consumer spending associated with real growth in national income caused the restructuring and consolidation of existing enterprises, and the rapid creation of new ones. There was ample room for expansion into new product areas, given that tariff protection was high and that the government planned further increases in real incomes.

Excessive reliance on foreign patents and technology, however, effectively limited expansionary scope to the domestic market. As a result, Ramón Tamames wrote about the over-riding need for industrial concentration and rationalisation, and for greater capital investment as a *sine qua non* for an increase in international competitiveness (Tamames 1965). In a later book he also stresses the inherent dynamics of the traditional industries of the Basque and Catalan provinces (Tamames 1976), and it is against this background that the performance of the Mondragon cooperatives should be viewed.

Growth and Diversification

Ulgor became a full cooperative in 1959, and was in a position to grow now that its marketing policy had a firm basis. In doing so, it could count on the support of Caja Laboral Popular, forming as it did part of the more extensive group of CLP-associated cooperatives. CLP expanded rapidly until it had 54 branches in 1970, with approximately 80,000 account holders. The industrial cooperatives also increased in numbers, another 34 being accepted as associated members of the Group between 1960 and 1970, and membership rising to 8570 by 1970.

In 1960, Ulgor added a water heater of the gas-geyser type to its products, having obtained a licence from Bulex Contigea of Brussels. The following year it diversified further into the hotel and general catering markets, which enabled it to adapt its accumulated in-house knowledge of domestic cookers and ovens. In the same year, given their internal needs for electronic components and the buoyant Spanish market, the cooperatives also obtained a licence from Semikorn of Nuremberg, Germany, for the manufacture of such components (Larrañaga 1979-80).

Arrasate was by then moving rapidly out of simple part-blanking and lawn-mower manufacture to become a leading producer of industrial equipment such as sophisticated mechanical presses, shears, and transversal and longitudinal cutters. Comet became the associated cooperative Ederlan ('Good Work') in 1964, and moved away from aluminium injection moulding and castings to more sophisticated foundry work which could serve the machine tool industry. *Copreci* was formed to continue the policy of entering into the component market, making measurement and control instruments for domestic appliances. Taking advantage of the captive Ulgor market for thermostats, valves, programmers etc., this cooperative was even able to enter the European market.

In 1964 four cooperatives joined together in a group called *Ularco*, which had an internal, organic rationale, but no legal status. The Ularco set-up had four basic advantages. Firstly, a common sales, marketing and purchasing organisation; secondly, it enabled closer planning and coordination which, since each cooperative traded part of its output with its fellows, was especially beneficial; thirdly, pooling made sense given that fluctuations in the cash flow of individual cooperatives could thus be offset; finally, but of critical importance, Ularco provided a means with which the growth of Ulgor, undoubtedly the pace setter and prime mover of the cooperative group, could be slowed down while still benefitting from the dynamics of current market opportunities.

By 1964 the rate of association of new cooperatives had become about three per year. These were mostly small operations located in towns and villages throughout Guipúzcoa and, to some extent, Vizcaya. By the middle of the 1970s nine of these small cooperatives had become medium-sized enterprises, in itself no mean achievement. The range of products now included metal frames, earthmovers, scaffolding, furniture, components, coach bodies, heavy machinery, pipe fittings and lifts.

To consolidate Ularco further, the decision was taken in 1966 to convert

Ulgor's electronics section into an independent cooperative. This followed the handing-over, in the previous year, of the entire foundry and casting operations of that company to Ederlan, which integrated them within its own operations. The mutual support group Ularco then began to develop a more rational structure and its own inherent dynamic. The general association of cooperatives centred upon CLP also experienced its most rapid expansion at the time, based upon the decisive role played by CLP in providing finance and some degree of coordination for all initiatives. These industrial cooperatives were engaged principally in the traditional mechanical engineering sector associated with the Basque country although, as we have seen, some were in the emergent and expanding electronics industry. Some cooperatives, however, were formed in the primary sectors of agriculture: milk distribution, processing farm products including timber, and fishing. This latter development is of significance because the cooperative concerned, *Copesca*, has been the only failure experienced by the group to date.

A Primary Sector Cooperative

Copesca was the result of a CLP attempt to intervene constructively in an important sector of the Basque economy, where a certain degree of cooperation already existed. The attempt started in 1965 and had finally to be abandoned in 1973, after much frustration. Copesca was another second degree control or support organisation, consisting of 24 fishing cooperatives with as many boats, each cooperative employing on average eighteen crew members. The aim was clear:

This body had as its principal objective the establishment of an orderly and accountable administration which would at all times make evident the financial and economic situation of the fishing cooperatives and would imbue the necessary spirit and managerial understanding for the type of undertaking that was being formed (Erdocia 1979-80: 50).

Fishermen, although they work together as a crew at sea, see themselves as individuals rather than as members of an enterprise. Moreover, their incomes are seen as coming from the proceeds of each catch, so that they take an essentially short-term view to the organisation of their activities. In the climate prevailing in Spain in the mid-1960s it was extremely easy to purchase fishing vessels, with the use of very soft government loans repayable over a long period. Subsidies amounted to 80 per cent of the cost of a boat overall; in Copesca's case, the State advanced 71 per cent and CLP another 24 per cent. The fishermen thus found it possible to retain the greater part of the value of their catch, raising their incomes while ignoring the need to pay off their long-term capital debts. It was very difficult to inculcate a different spirit, especially when the men found that over-exploitation of fishing grounds was leading to stock depletion, smaller catches and financial losses. A cooperative approach required a different mentality, but the fishermen were in the main incapable of adopting such new values. In 1973 CLP proposed buying from the State, at a fair price, the eight or ten boats which were financially worse off in order that they might be put on a sounder cooperative basis. On being refused by the State, however, the bank withdrew, somewhat chastened but reinforced in its belief that cooperativism needed sound preparation and a change in values if it was to be successful. Copesca was then wound up as CLP could not continue to put its depositors' money at risk.

Some experience has been gained in farming and forestry, in which a tradition of cooperative values originated in the early, pre-historic clearing of land for settlement and cultivation.[11] For instance, CLP provided capital and expertise for *Lana* in the Deva valley which produces and markets dairy products; the breeding of dairy cattle and fatstock, and the management of forests for timber are two other primary sector activities.

FURTHER DEVELOPMENTS:

EDUCATION, CONSUMERS AND SOCIAL SECURITY

In 1966 the idea of combining vocational training and the inculcation of a cooperative spirit resulted in the founding of *Alecoop* a cooperative factory run by students of the technical training school, who combine five hours of daily study with five hours of work in this cooperative factory (for further details see Chapter III).

In 1968 *Eroski* was founded as the result of the amalgamation of nine consumers' cooperatives in Guipúzcoa. Retail cooperatives play an important role in cooperative history, and it was thus no surprise that CLP wanted to promote consumers' cooperatives; San José, which has been mentioned earlier, was a consumers' cooperative among the founding organisations of CLP.

Observers have commented favourably on the performance of this modern consumers' organisation:

Eroski is a highly dynamic retail cooperative, aggressively seeking to extend its market penetration throughout the Basque country. Its pricing policy is very competitive, achieved through a constant search for higher productivity and better buying.... The cooperative retains its commitment to cooperative principles by distributing 10 per cent of its profit in Social Benefits, with a spectacular success in making members and in involving them in the running of the Society. Clearly Eroski shows that the dividend-on-purchase system is not essential to member involvement; but that local assemblies and local communities, in close contact with managers and other employees and given effective powers to influence the progress of their shop, will attract widespread interest and support (Royal Arsenal ... 1979).

The need for welfare provisions, including pensions and health care, having been one of the motives for the establishment of CLP, the expansion in the numbers of cooperators led to various organisational structures being adopted to this end. From 1959 to 1966 the welfare needs of members were covered by CLP's Social Security Services, which charged members a premium according to their wage level plus a method of saving for further cover, if desired, by means of a Special Savings Book. Cover extended to pensions for retirement, widows and orphans, funded by individual special provisions (see further Chapter VI). During 1967-1968 the cooperators' social security needs were met by affiliation with the Independent (i.e. self-employed) Workers' Friendly Society, an act suggested by the Ministry of Labour.

Lagun-Aro was created as a separate legal entity in 1970, and registered under the 1941 law on Pawnshops and Friendly Societies, which was adequate but far from satisfactory. The services provided by Lagun-Aro (a Basque neologism for Friendly Society) included preventive medicine, hospitalisation, health and safety at work, disablement-invalidity compensation, psychological services and the usual pension benefits.

YEARS OF CONSOLIDATION 1971-79

Economically, the early part of the 1970s saw a continuation of the growth experienced in the previous decade in Spain and in the rest of the industrialised world, although on a somewhat lesser scale — less than five per cent as compared to more than six per cent in the 1960s.

The Basque Country continued to develop its industrial potential until the middle seventies when, as a result of political uncertainty and of the recession, the economy entered a crisis.

As the recession deepened, output declined in the iron and steel industry, and in heavy engineering including shipbuilding. The fishing industry went into a crisis that is as yet unresolved. Overall, some spectacular collapses occurred.[12] Unemployment rose rapidly, indicating the magnitude of the crisis.

In the Basque economy this recession was heightened by political developments.[13] Following the death of Franco in November 1975, the Basque situation and the demand for autonomy became world news, ETA in particular becoming familiar to many as a revolutionary organisation. ETA continues its armed struggle against the Spanish state, thus exacerbating the crisis since many Basque businessmen have left the area, investment has been reduced, and capital has been transferred away from Euskadi. Violence and counterviolence are regrettably still part of the political process in Spain, which has yet to secure a transition to the resolution of conflicts through the ballot box rather than by the bullet. As a result, an already difficult situation is worsened and has its repercussions on the CLP cooperatives, causing economic and socio-political tension.

The Factories

The rapid expansion of the 1960s transformed Mondragon and its environment into an area of prosperity and industrial sophistication, the Leniz Valley being dominated by the factories of the Ularco group. By 1979 the number of cooperatives had increased to 135 (74 industrial, 1 retail, 5 agricultural, 36 educational, 14 housing and 5 service cooperatives). The construction of houses and flats was a new initiative, being considered an appropriate field for CLP since it provided not only employment and a broader field for productive investment, but also had broader social considerations. Land speculation had been rife in the narrow valleys characteristic of the Basque Country and many people had difficulty in finding a decent home. Hence, CLP considered that housing construction would be a socially-responsible example of 'how things could be arranged in a better way'.

The industrial cooperatives are still principally in the engineering and domestic consumer goods sectors, in which some diversification can be seen into such lines as furniture, printing, packaging, mouldings, bicycles, etc. New patent acquisitions have facilitated entry into electro-domestic markets with highly profitable lines, such as improved cookers and more modern washing machines.

There are five basic ways in which cooperatives are formed under an association agreement.

(1) The original Ulgor model, by which a number of founding members get together and, having studied the markets accessible to them, establish an enterprise and subsequently develop it.

(2) A hiving-off of divisions of an expanding cooperative in order to avoid the problems of giantism, while yet maintaining the new and independent cooperatives within the group. This process is analogous to the cell division of a natural organism and was first pioneered by Ulgor.

(3) An opportunity for the establishment of a new cooperative is identified by CLP's Management Services Division, and a feasibility study is undertaken by economists, engineers and other relevant specialists. Those who set up such cooperatives frequently do so after having requested assistance from CLP for their initiative; at other times CLP is the prime initiator.

(4) It is not uncommon for existing cooperatives to contact CLP and to request association. They may do so after having experienced the drawbacks of independence, either in terms of liquidity problems, or of the inability to finance desirable investment because of restricted access to outside credit. The sacrifice of some degree of autonomy may well seem advisable in exchange for security and access to more comprehensive financial and management services.

(5) An existing capitalist enterprise may be converted into a cooperative, a method which is particularly current during the present financial crisis. If problems are very severe — usually involving managerial incompetence — there is a genuine desire to adopt CLP rules; even if there is no immediate crisis, those rules are seen to offer a better long-term future.

In 1979, for example, the CLP Annual Report noted that two cooperatives had associated; four erstwhile capitalist companies had been converted into cooperatives by the Bank; two new cooperatives had been launched by the Management Division; and a further eight were being studied.[14]

A Strike

One particular dispute which arose in 1974 shook Ulgor, the founding cooperative, and challenged one of the key premises upon which the whole movement had been based: that there was a meaningful system of workers' self-management and an identity of interest between all members of every enterprise. The ostensible reason for the disruption was job revaluation, whereby some workers found that their jobs were downgraded in terms of the rate paid for particular tasks. It was made clear by management that only new entrants to these job areas would in fact receive the lower rates. Some felt, however, that although existing workers' pay would not be affected, they could not accept downgrading. Rather than use the normal channels for the discussion of their problems, the dissidents then called for a strike which lasted eight days and involved 414 cooperators. Ulgor's Supervisory Board exercised its authority, ordering the dismissal of 17 workers and disciplinary measures against 397 others who had been involved in the dispute and the subsequent strike action. This was challenged at an Extraordinary General Assembly, held in an acrimonious atmosphere replete with mutual accusations, but the Board's decision was endorsed by a majority vote of 60 per cent.

One of the factors identified as being partly responsible for events getting out of control was the sheer size of Ulgor, which then had a membership of 3250, causing inadequate communications and leading to worker alienation. Since that time, the general policy is to keep unit sizes as small as possible.

Several years after the 1974 strike some cooperators suggested that those who had been dismissed should be reinstated. After a momentous debate, however, a decision was taken against re-admission on the grounds that failure to abide by the rules rather than conformity with management decisions on workplace evaluation was the real issue.

Another factor was Taylorism, i.e. scientific management. Study teams examined Scandinavian methods of assembly operations carried out by autonomous work groups, with maximum discretion as to how individual members undertook their part of the overall task. Despite the favourable report brought out by the study teams, however, Ulgor workers were unhappy about such an innovation and expressed a preference for the assembly line. Their reservations were due in part to uncertainty about the transferability and the cost of the new methods.

Innovations

Ikerlan, the research and development cooperative and a services-providing institution, was a result of the struggle to meet the challenge of the 1970s. This R&D centre, which cost over two million dollars, researches such fields as machine tools, electronics, and home comforts. Its researchers have investigated the use of computers in process automation and control, the design and application of robots, the various solar energy products already available and their susceptibility to improvement as part of programmes in the general areas of electronics, thermodynamics, mechanical engineering, and informatics. In following this path, the cooperatives are adopting the successful Japanese model of moving from copying to innovation as a means of carving-out a niche in the international economy.

The *ikastola* educational cooperative movement has developed since the death of Franco in response to a demand that more consideration be given to Basque as a language and as a cultural vehicle. An ikastola, or school, is a bilingual institution which gives Basque parity with Spanish up to the lower secondary level. Thirty-six ikastolas at present receive financial, legal and organisational assistance from CLP. In addition, through its Teaching Service, the Bank proffers advice on bilingual education to the Bilingual Technical Office of the Basque General Council, the administrative body responsible to the Basque Government. Over 26,000 pupils are currently enrolled in ikastolas; parents and others who support the schools total almost 18,000; and 1159 teachers are employed. CLP has intimated that this activity should not be the specific responsibility of a private body but rather of a public or semi-public entity. In the meantime, however, it continues to support the schools until alternative arrangements can be made.

Two further service cooperatives have been created during the seventies. *Club Arkitle*, located in a central Bilbao avenue, is a sports and social club, well-decorated and with an impressive swimming pool. Another more unusual development which has found its imitators in Britain is *Auzo-Lagun*, which provides employment for women, primarily those whose family commitments necessitate flexible hours or part-time work. The major activities in which Auzo-Lagun members engage include the preparation of canteen meals, laundry, general office cleaning, and subcontract work.

Caja Laboral Popular

After the rapid increases in the numbers of its depositors, and a strong drive to open new branches throughout the Basque provinces, CLP thought it necessary to consolidate its existing network and to improve its efficiency, notably by computerising branch and control operations, while awaiting the results of new legislation on the position of cooperative banks.

The bank continued to expand in step with the concentric spread of associated cooperatives away from Mondragon. Its Management Services Division was set up in 1969 to promote cooperativism throughout the Basque Country and to ensure the continued advance of existing cooperatives, while ensuring the best use of CLP's financial and human resources. Its tasks are as follows:

1. *Promotion*: industrial and agricultural initiatives; teaching and education in general; research into products and their markets; exports.
2. *Engineering*: town and land use planning, product engineering, industrial building; housing construction.
3. *Counselling*: auditing and inspection services; legal advice; organisation and office mechanisation; personnel matters.

Modern managerial techniques have been employed in order to determine the direction which the Mondragon group of cooperatives should follow. Since 1972 longer-term plans have been prepared which run in conjunction with the yearly management plans prepared by each cooperative. A consultative and reiterative process determines the targets and the obstacles to success with which each cooperative can identify.

NEW STRUCTURES FOR THE FUTURE

The 1978-80 plan called for further experimentation with cooperative groups or federations, such as Ularco. As a result, a more complex structure is now emerging as a pattern for the future, with interrelations between cooperatives which have more in common with each other than merely their physical location and adherence to CLP's Contract of Association. The basic philosophy behind the new idea of Cooperative Groups is to capture economies of scale without destroying the spirit of workers' self-management based upon high levels of participation and managerial decisions which are given democratic endorsement. In a world that is increasingly dominated by multinationals and with growing industrial concentration, some response is needed if the cooperatives are not to fall behind in wages, technology, productivity, capital accumulation and expansion. The first Cooperative Group since Ularco was launched in March 1979: *Biharko* (literally 'Tomorrows'), located in the Urola area and made up of five furniture manufacturers.

Cooperative Groups will reflect the structure of individual associated cooperatives. Policies will be determined by a General Assembly made up of all members of their Supervisory Boards and Managements, who will express the collective wishes of component cooperatives. Simple majority voting suffices in the determination of policy, the approval of budgets, on the admission of new members, or on the sanctioning of member cooperatives for infraction of the norms. Individual cooperative votes, in fact, are stock votes: the cooperative with the smallest number of members has ten votes and the largest 30 votes.

Integration of the activities of member cooperatives requires that Central Services be established; that personnel be transferrable between cooperatives; that priority be given to inter-cooperative deliveries and supplies when necessary; that open or covert competition (with other cooperatives) be abandoned; and that provision be made for redistribution of the net surplus.

Up to 70 per cent of the net profits (pure surplus) are to be pooled, entailing the need for complete harmonisation of accounts and for criteria for resource allocation in order to determine the surplus and the consequent distribution of 'dividends' to individual members. By amalgamating the trading activity results of each cooperative in this way, greater Group cohesion, strength and commitment should be attained. The process begins gradually with only 20 per cent of the pure surplus being pooled in the first year, rising annually by 10 percentage points until the upper limit of 70 per cent is reached.

Two categories are seen to be emerging within the generic concept of Cooperative Group, i.e. Social Groups and Industrial Groups. The former are defined as those whose common link is geographic location, and whose attention is directed to the socio-economic balance and long-term problems of their area by means of planning and promoting development. The latter are based on technological and commercial convergence or communality between cooperatives in the same sector of economic activity.

The preoccupations of the Cooperative Groups indicate a more panoramic vision than that which characterised the emergent Mondragon Group more than two decades ago. They reflect the consequences of maturity, of efforts by numerous cooperatives to try to find the right balance between centralised control and the independence of individual cooperatives. They also reflect different dimensions to the questions posed many years earlier by Don José María: how do you build up a nation? how do you develop an individual to his full capacity and also serve the broader community, while avoiding the manifest disadvantages of liberal capitalism or state socialism?[15]

NOTES

1. The role played by British capital and Welsh coking coal was particularly notable. From 1876 to 1914 maritime trade between Bilbao and the United Kingdom stood at record levels, far surpassing the trade with other European ports and exceeding even Spanish port traffic. Basque capitalists made alliances with British and other partners. For example, Ybarra, a Bilbao industrialist, formed Orconera Iron Ore Ltd in 1873 together with Dowlais Iron Company, Consett Iron Co., and Krupp, and in 1876 the Société Anonyme Franco-Belge des Mines to Somorrostro (Espagne) with the Belgian steel interests including Cockerill.

2. Policarpo de Larrañaga, author of a history of ELA-STV, or Solidarity, was one of the so-called 'propagandist priests' who promoted 'Christian Social Unionism', together with other influential nationalist priests in the Basque Nationalist Party (PNV). He was particularly concerned to stress that Basque culture historically had an answer to social conflict, provided by the medieval guilds: 'These armourers' guilds, whose constitutions, methods of government, behaviour and development were of great interest, constituted true producers' cooperatives with an admirable system of obtaining contracts from almost all European governments while working above the class struggle [associated armourers could be either merchants or workers]. These guilds continued to function until half a century ago. The guild of gunsmiths, united in a closed shop with obligatory apprenticeships, succumbed only 30 years ago, before the doctrines and workings methods imposed by economic liberalism' (de Larrañaga 1977: 16).

3. Jakin: *Koperatibak* (1973) gives an extensive account by Imanol Laspiur of this Eibar cooperative, from its origins to the present day. Echeverria, who went into exile after the Civil War, died in Caracas in 1968. He was clandestinely in contact with Don José María, through a cousin in Eibar who sent him letters, and passed on his request for some of Arizmendi's writings on the Mondragon cooperatives. Direct contact between the two was established in October 1966, Echeverria being fulsome in his praise when he wrote: 'I am following with real interest the work you are carrying out in that locality [i.e. Mondragon], which has radiated so profitably throughout that region where industry flowers. I believe it is the best thing that has been done in suffering Spain in these 25 years' (Letter dated Caracas, 2nd May 1967). And: 'I have received your magnificent book on the cooperative experiment in Mondragon in the Leniz Valley ... I believe your excellent work represents a true social revolution, having purged this word of its bloody reputation given it by certain literature and limiting it to its substantive meaning' (Letter dated Caracas, 2nd October 1967).

4. Mendizabal (1978 Tomo I: 6) notes that between 1932 and 1936, Arizmendi took numerous cuttings from the nationalist paper *Euzkadi* on such topics as social advance, cooperativism, farmhouse economics, work safety, the Fishermen's Benefit Societies, Solidarity, etc.

5. Ibidem: 155. Arizmendi went on to outline the manpower planning imperatives of locating the various types of vocational training in the right places, bearing in mind future employment prospects and the need to offer as broad an education as possible, resisting the modern de-skilling pressures exercised by industry.

6. Ansola (1971: 88 *et seq*). In this book, which was banned for many years, Ansola analyses the period of rapid structural change and of further industrialisation. A salient point of Ansola's argument is that the Spanish state de-capitalised Euskadi, taxing the workers and the employers to promote growth outside the region.

7. Based on an interview with Don Alfonso Gorroñogoitia Gonzalez, one of the founders.

8. Recounted in *T.U. Lankide*, No. 223-224 (December 1979-January 1980).

9. The credit for inspiring others with the ideal of a financial intermediary or deposit-taking bank is exclusively Don José María's. An early arrangement whereby the Guipúzcoa Savings Bank held deposits collected by the founders of Ulgor at two small offices, served a useful purpose as a catalyst. Under Spanish law, 'workers' savings' received an extra half-a-percentage point above that given to ordinary depositors.

Gorroñogoitia recounts how the priest brought up the subject of a 'Bank' in 1959 during a sudden visit in which he disrupted a fraught Ulgor Board Meeting. The unanimous reaction was to dismiss him angrily: 'We told him we were very busy and that we thought his suggestion was unrealistic, had nothing to do with our area of knowledge, our origin or ways of thinking; [we were] totally apart from the world of banking and finance, which seemed to us to be spooky and a bit Mafia-ridden, given our total ignorance of it.' Don José María smiled, attempted to bring the subject up on other occasions, and continued to draft statutes. One day he presented these to be signed by 15 persons, and without further ado departed for Madrid to set in train the necessary bureaucratic processes. The People's Savings Bank was the product (one more!) of his vision and single-minded perseverance.

10. The competences of the Supervisory Board are as follows: (1) admission of new members; proposing the level of, and earnings on, initial capital contributions; distribution of economic surpluses; fixing of labour indices for members; coordination of external capital borrowing and voluntary contributions; establishment of labour rates. (2) Nomination of Management and Department Heads for technical, economic, commercial and labour management. (3) Study and approval of Internal Rules for submission to the General Assembly. (4) Study and approval of general plans for the management and growth of the cooperative. (5) Creation of financial reserves, opening of current accounts; administration of assets; allocation of funds; and negotiation of loans. (6) Expulsion of members or suspension of their rights. (7) Decisions relating to legal action. (8) Clarification of Statutes and Internal Rules and rectification of omissions, giving due account to the General Assembly.

11. In the Basque country there is a traditional form of obligatory cooperation on a communal basis between families on the farms in a particular neighbourhood (*hauzoa*). They work for each other for the common good – *hauzo-lan*. This involves all the farms in a specific territory, which is identified by a proper name and is distinct from the village nucleus. Farmers who form part of a *hauzoa* have their land scattered throughout its area and not merely around their own farmhouses. Social and economic interaction is mainly within the neighbourhood, with farmers building and repairing neighbourhood roads, ensuring the supply of water and electricity, and in many cases the upkeep of a chapel. Organisation is the responsibility of a 'steward' who is appointed on a rotational basis. See Douglass 1970.

12. See IKEI (1979: ch. 2) for extensive coverage of the current structure of the Basque economy.

13. The reintroduction of democracy and the restoration of political freedom is as yet incomplete in Spain, In February 1981 King Juan Carlos faced an attempt by the Right to overthrow the precarious governmental coalition after the first democratic premier Suarez had resigned. Neither the Right nor the Socialists have an overall majority in the Congress or Lower House of the bicameral *Cortes*, in which the Basques are represented by: Nationalists (PNV) 7, Socialist Party of Euskadi (PSOE affiliate) 6, Pro-ETA Left Herri Batasuma 3, Moderate Left (Euskadiko Eskerra) 1, who have no common ideology with each other or with the 34 Catalan and eight Andalusian deputies. The PNV is the majority party in the reinstated Basque Parliament under President Karlos Garaikoetzea, a businessman from Navarra. Commenting on the current dilemma, Gerry Foley wrote in *Intercontinental Press* (18 December 1978):

In the Basque Country, the failure of the radicalised nationalists to develop a political alternative for the masses and their continued support of a suicidal guerrillaist course enabled the Basque Nationalist Party to re-establish itself as the main representative of the national aspirations of the Basque people.... But the Basque Nationalist Party still faces the pressure of a population that has mobilised again and again in the struggle against Spanish rule, and in general strike after general strike. Moreover, despite the recent rise of the moderate Basque party, the radicalised nationalist groups and revolutionists still have a powerful voice.

14. As we have seen, cooperatives are an accepted form of organising production among the Basques. Thus, although those associated with CLP are the most dynamic and stable, they do not, numerically speaking, represent the totality of cooperatives in Euskadi. Closures and crises have recently produced a spate of worker-owned enterprises. In the early 1970s Inaki Gorroño contrasted the CLP-associated and independent cooperatives; his re-

search shows clearly that the former were more robust in view of the greater number of workplaces that they offered, as in the following table.

Basque Cooperativism and the Relative Incidence of CLP-Associated Cooperatives (1972)

Provinces	Industrial Cooperatives			Workplaces		
	CLP	Total	% CLP	CLP	Total	% CLP
Alava	3	23	13	290	850	34.1
Guipúzcoa	35	82	30.5	9,005	10,178	88.4
Navarre	1	30	3.3	39	1,953	2.0
Vizcaya	10	58	17.3	884	5,380	16.4
Basque Country	49	193	25.4	10,218	18,361	55.6

In Guipúzcoa cooperativism was clearly synonymous with 'Mondragon', i.e. the CLP with its head office and associated cooperatives. But penetration was far less in Vizcaya (Gorroño 1975).
15. Ormaechea (1979-80: 61 *et seq*). A film that currently introduces the Mondragon Cooperative Movement to English-speaking audiences is called, significantly, *Herrigintza* (Making a People), a suggestive title that harks back to the first attempts to mobilise the community.

III

COOPERATORS: WORK AND TRAINING

INTRODUCTION

The first aspects of the labour situation to be studied in this chapter is that of employment creation, a fundamental factor in the evaluation of a cooperative group such as that of Mondragon. Economic dualism, for example, may isolate privileged workers in self-managed enterprises from those who are unable to gain access to work. There seems to be little guarantee that associations of workers will offer much employment. Jones argues for the need to study growth and size 'because of the arguments that not only are producer cooperatives smaller than capitalist firms, but if they grow at all, they will do so more slowly', in his listing of principal areas in need of research (Jones 1980a: 143). We shall therefore examine the data on aggregate employment as well as on distribution of employment among the cooperatives, and shall compare the cooperative record of employment creation with the development of employment throughout the province.

Absenteeism has a negative impact on total work hours; in several countries, work hours lost in this way amount to more than 15 per cent. The rate of absenteeism also tells us a good deal about labour relations in factories, and as such, is one of the few indicators that are widely used. Such information is rarely published for cooperative enterprises, an exception being the Chilean study by Espinosa and Zimbalist in which the authors find that during the three-year span of worker participation in factories absenteeism dropped significantly (Espinosa & Zimbalist 1978: 143-46). The availability of data on absenteeism in the Basque provinces in general and of comprehensive statistics on cooperative absenteeism irrefutably show a significant difference in this respect between the Mondragon cooperatives and industry at large in Guipúzcoa province.

We shall then pass on to skill formation, the supply of 'human capital'. One characteristic of cooperative history is the emphasis given to programmes of edu-

---

Notes to this chapter may be found on pp. 73-74.

cation and training. Any list of the main principles of the cooperative movement would certainly include intensive and continuing education of the cooperative members as one of the most important phenomena. The Workers' Universities in Yugoslavia, the courses on cooperative principles in the international cooperative movement, the apprenticeship schemes for the acquisition of specific skills such as were introduced on a large scale in Chile in 1970, all show that education can be emphasised in various ways. Vanek argues that 'At all times, but especially in its early stages, the effort of introducing self-management, must be accompanied by an educational effort', and includes education among the necessary conditions for successful development of a labour-managed firm, sector, or economy (Vanek 1975: 36). Education, thus, serves many purposes. It can increase workers' knowledge about the environment and about the functioning of the own enterprise within society. The critical factor, however, is the supply of skills without which no factory is able to utilise even unsophisticated equipment and tools. Education plays a dominant role in the history of the Mondragon group. Its founder devoted most of his energy to this aspect, and his stimulating dialogues made him an outstanding teacher, contributing a great deal to the solution of innumerable problems over a long period of time. In Mondragon, education involves a range of objectives; furthermore, with the passing of time, it has become oriented more towards the community at large and not only to the manpower and staffing needs of the cooperatives.

The last aspect to be examined is that of the division of labour. Education prepares future cooperators for a wide range of jobs, implying a considerable division of labour. We shall examine in particular the manner in which this division of work is linked with a point system, representing the evaluation of a great variety of jobs. We shall concentrate on the way in which the job evaluation system leads to a job hierarchy. A range of indices, running from one to three is the base of the earnings structure, an economic problem of the greatest importance which will be studied in Chapter VI.

EMPLOYMENT CREATION

We have already noted the rapid expansion of the Mondragon group, and also that its statutes include a so-called 'open door' policy, entailing that each cooperative must make it a major objective to create new jobs. Data on the employment situation as it has developed from 1956 until 1979 are presented in Table 1, showing figures for the cooperatives and for the Guipuzcoan economy as a whole.

Ulgor's employment figures are given in Column 1. In 1956, 24 cooperative members started-up a small workshop where employment doubled within a year to 47 members. Ten years later Ulgor had become a large enterprise with almost 1000 workers, and by 1970 it had a labour force of 2400, with no indication of a slow-down in the expansion of employment. Ulgor had grown beyond any expectations, despite a deliberate policy of establishing new cooperatives, even to the extent of 'hiving-off' complete departments: the start of *Fagelectro* in 1966 and of *Fagindustrial* in 1974 resulted from such action. This explosive development was then halted, it being felt that large enterprises create major problems of communication, thereby frustrating participatory processes. On the other hand, few options were available in a competitive and dynamic economy. Either Ulgor would have to continue to grow in order to maintain its leading position in the market for consumer durables, or it would have to limit its rapid expansion and run the risk of losing its competitive edge. The deep economic crisis of the mid-seventies, for which Ulgor was ill-prepared, forced the issue. In 1976 the work force expanded to 3460 cooperators distributed over several plants, and it was planned that 3855 cooperators would work in Ulgor by the end of 1979. Further conclusions cannot be drawn regarding the importance of economies of scale, but it is clear that the cooperative response to the crisis was to defend its market share rather than to experiment with smaller plants. This is understandable since failure by Ulgor to maintain its leading national position would have jeopardised the future of the entire Mondragon group. The risks involved can be understood if we look at Ulgor's main competitor in the Spanish market, Orbaiceta, a strong capitalist enterprise located at Pamplona in the province of Navarra. In 1971 Ulgor gained first position in the national market of refrigerators, cookers, and washing machines, followed closely by Orbaiceta. In 1976 the positions had changed. Orbaiceta had absorbed smaller enterprises through mergers whereas Ulgor wished to slow down its employment growth. Orbaiceta's sales now exceed Ulgor's by a small margin (7800 million pesetas as against 7500 million pesetas); its value added was less than that of Ulgor (1800 as against 2283 pesetas). Orbaiceta showed a preference for relatively capital-intensive technology; as a result, its work force increased from 2775 in 1971 to 3000 in 1976, whereas Ulgor expanded from 2945 to 3460.

   Column 2 shows the aggregate employment of enterprises which later joined together in 1964 to form a group, Ularco. Figures for 1956 and 1957 were identical to those of column 1, but from 1958 onwards other enterprises joined and the group grew rapidly. In 1964 these cooperative enterprises already employed 1350 workers and since then employment has risen rapidly to almost 6700 in 1979; only during one year, 1975, did a slight fall occur. The figures tend to under-emphasise the total employment impact because Ularco stimulated other cooperatives in their own expansion in preference to absorbing smaller firms through mergers. Ulgor has a dominant position within the group which initially comprised four and later six enterprises.

   Further insight into employment creation is obtained from the pattern in 22 cooperatives between 1965 and 1979 shown in the third column of Table 1. Total employment was 3178 in 1965, increasing to 7227 in 1971, and growing further to 10,780 in 1979. Ten of the 22 enterprises report increments for all years (1965-71, 1971-72, and so on); the other twelve show a slight drop in one or more years. Only one firm had fewer members in 1971 than in 1965, and two small ones had slightly fewer in 1979 than in 1971.[1] Thus, excluding the enterprises of the Ularco group, 17 enterprises with a total employment of 1535 members in 1965 expanded to 4100 in 1979. If we compare 1979 employment figures with those for 1965 we see that Ulgor's employment increased by 350 per cent, that of other Ularco firms by 305 per cent, and of the 17 just referred to, by 165 per cent.

Column 4 gives aggregate employment figures for all industrial cooperatives associated with Caja Laboral Popular (CLP). In 1960 the movement consisted of eight enterprises, of which Ulgor took the lion's share with 228 out of 395 members. In 1964, when Ularco was formed, total employment in 27 cooperatives amounted to 2620; Ularco accounted for half of total employment, and Ulgor for 31 per cent of the aggregate figure. Aggregate employment has grown without interruption either through the expansion of associated cooperatives or by the admission of new cooperatives. Using 1965 once more as a base year, we find that total employment in 1979 was 360 per cent higher than that of 1965.

Column 5 gives data on numbers of industrial cooperatives which have associated with CLP from 1960 onwards. During the early years expansion was rapid, mainly due to the association of existing capitalist or cooperative enterprises. This process slowed considerably during the latter part of the decade, expansion depending increasingly on the promotion of new cooperatives by the CLP. The present objective of CLP's Management Services Division is to add ten cooperatives to the movement each year, six as a result of transforming existing capitalist enterprises and the remaining four as new productive entities.

In 1978, the average size of all industrial cooperatives, excluding Ulgor with its 3599 members, was 170 workers; the 22 enterprises which draw special attention – column 3 – expanded on average, again excluding Ulgor, from 110 workers in 1965 to 304 workers in 1978. Eight cooperatives, not included in column 3, had only 217 members in 1965, making an average of 27 workers. These eight enterprises, as well as another 40 subsequently associated, reached an aggregate employment of 4693 workers in 1978, or an average of 98 workers per enterprise.[2]

'Cooperative performance' can also be compared with employment creation in the entire province of Guipúzcoa. Column 6 covers all industrial cooperatives located within this province. The cooperative share of all industrial employment had grown to 12.5 per cent in 1979.[3] An analysis of employment expansion is revealing. As against a fall of jobs in provincial industry between 1973 and 1979 of 19,000, the cooperatives have expanded with 3756 places: if

Table 1. *Employment in Mondragon industrial cooperatives*

Year	Employment in Ulgor (1)	Employment in Ularco enterprises (2)	Employment in 22 cooperatives (3)	Employment in all industrial cooperatives (4)	No. of cooperative enterprises (5)	Employment in industrial cooperatives in Guipúzcoa (6)	Cooperative employment (6) as % of total industrial employment in Guipúzcoa (7)
1956	24	24					
1957	47	47					
1958	143	170					
1959	178	215					
1960	228	265		395	8		
1961	316	358		520	12		
1962	429	498		807	16		
1963	600	904		1780	24		
1964	816	1350		2620	27		
1965	858	1643	3178 (22)	3395	30		
1966	940	1931		4202	31		
1967	1000	2253		5082	37		
1968	1800	3301		6418	38		
1969	2030	4038		7703	40		
1970	2400	4131		8570	40		
1971	2945	4700	7227	9423	43		
1972	3406	5400	7968	10329	44		
1973	3243	5700	8198	11141	45	9862	7.7
1974	3284	5900	8785	12063	46	10604	8.3
1975	3191	5800	8970	12543	50	10897	8.3

1976	3460	6300	9640	13493	57	11702	9.8
1977	-	-	-	14517	61	12615	11.3
1978*	3599	6550	9983	14676	66	12753	11.6
1979**	3855	6680	10780 (22)	15672	70	13618	12.5

* In December 1978 there were 16,022 cooperators in 72 cooperatives (including 3 agricultural: 213; Eroski: 554; and two service cooperatives: 579). Data on other than industrial cooperatives are elaborated on in Chapter VII.

** The 1979 figures are estimates made during May of that year by CLP.

Sources: Martinez & Ramos 1976: 139-43. *Estructura Industrial* 1976: 20, 21. *Económia Guipuzcoana* 1971: 27; 1975: 31; 1976: 33. Documents and internal information provided by Ulgor, Ularco, and CLP. IKEI 1979: Cuadro 15.

it had not been for the Mondragon cooperatives, aggregate industrial employment would have fallen by 22,750.

A point of reference is the development of employment in the two major enterprises in Mondragon itself. Union Cerrajera and Elma, once the major employers in the area, have long since lost that position. In 1976 employees in Union Cerrajera had decreased to 1640 and in Elma to 950; in 1971 Union Cerrajera had employed 1798 and in 1974 Elma had had a work force of 990.

From the provincial perspective, cooperative performance is of increasing importance as regards employment creation. In 1976, for the first time in many years, there was net emigration, following many years of rapid expansion due to immigration. Unemployment increased. Numbers of workers who were either fired or suspended in Guipúzcoa rose from 2136 in 1973 to almost 8000 in 1976, with total employment of 217,962 in 1975. Official figures indicate that unemployment reached 25,660 in 1979.[4] This development reflects the economic malaise in the four Basque provinces: Basque unemployment as a percentage of aggregate Spanish unemployment rose from 3.7 per cent to more than 7 per cent between 1976 and 1979 (IKEI 1979: Cuadro 17). This development is also reflected in the cooperatives. In 1976 more than 25 per cent of the cooperators were of non-Basque origin, a percentage that had fallen from a peak of 28.2 per cent in 1974; in one new plant, for instance, the percentage of immigrant worker cooperators declined from 40.6 to 33.6 per cent over the same period.

The Mondragon group has taken several steps in response to these adverse economic conditions. Some diversification has taken place: more attention is being given to three agricultural cooperatives which had an aggregate employment of 213 in 1978; at the same time, the consumers' cooperative Eroski has expanded rapidly to reach 554 jobs in 1978, and 700 by the end of 1979. Cooperators who, under adverse conditions, would face unemployment in a 'capitalist environment' can be given assistance, for example by being shifted to other enterprises. Also, with the assistance of CLP, possibilities of moving into other product lines can be investigated at a very early stage should difficulties arise. Available evidence suggests that labour turnover, whether by resigning or by taking up work in another cooperative, is very low: in 1976, turnover in the Ularco group was reported at less than two per cent.

Job security is almost guaranteed, at least in the view of those who have joined a cooperative or of non-cooperative workers who see that cooperatives continue to expand and to create employment on a large scale while the province as a whole shows a dismal picture. The data presented here give gross figures of employment creation from the provincial viewpoint, since many small cooperatives were established through the transformation of existing enterprises. At the same time, it is clear that the prime motive for firms to join a cooperative has been lack of capital: in the normal run of things this would have caused them to become bankrupt and jobs would have been lost in provincial industrial employment.

The figures given in Table 1 show clearly that cooperative employment has largely been created in industry, with the exception of the rapidly expanding activities of CLP which, by late 1979, employed about 900 cooperative members in its headquarters and branches. In the tertiary sector the consumers' cooperative Eroski also expanded, while the Educational Cooperatives may contribute to employment creation in the future.

Many insights have been gained from this close investigation of employment statistics. Our main conclusion must be that the cooperatives have continued to increase employment under adverse economic conditions, whereas industrial employment creation on the provincial level has fallen strongly. The growth of aggregate employment can be traced to more than one cause. Firstly, there is the expansion of cooperatives, after they have associated with CLP: Ulgor, the cooperatives that form Ularco, a sample of 17 factories and another group of eight cooperatives — all considerably increased their average size in terms of work places over a relatively short time span. There is thus a potential to grow, irrespective of size. Secondly, CLP plays a major role in the process of employment creation. In addition to providing credit for the financing of investment plans of associated cooperatives, CLP actively engages in associating enterprises. Some such enterprises may already exist and seek assistance which they cannot find outside the cooperative group; others result from promotion by CLP's own Management Services Division.

ABSENTEEISM

Absenteeism — the number of work hours lost as a percentage of total work hours — is not a very precise measure with which to gauge the degree of alienation of workers with respect to their work, or, to put it positively, the extent to which workers feel loyalty and commitment to their own enterprise.[5] In the field of industrial relations, however, absenteeism is often used since it is a powerful indicator on which it is relatively easy to obtain information. This has also been the case in our research project.

Absenteeism obviously has a negative effect on total work hours. It may also be assumed that considerable absenteeism in a cooperative will reflect personal traits as well as objective conditions regarding work in the factory concerned.

Information on the Mondragon cooperative movement is summarised in Graph 1. The outcome is favourable, even taking into account the rising trend in recent years. Between 1965 and 1972 cooperative absenteeism averaged about three per cent, i.e. aggregate absenteeism due to illness, accident, conflict, childbirth, or otherwise. This compares with an average of over ten per cent during the same period in non-cooperative enterprises. From 1973 onwards, absenteeism in the Ularco enterprises rose quickly to 8.33 per cent in 1975, followed by a drop in 1976 to 7.69 per cent; a mid-year report in 1979 indicated a further fall to 6.84 per cent for average absenteeism in all cooperatives. During the same period, absenteeism in capitalist enterprises averaged about 15 per cent. An important point is that from 1974 onwards, a new category of absenteeism – 'due to conflict' – is included in the reports.[6] For 1974 this amounted to .73 per cent; in 1975 it reached 2.71 per cent, and in 1976 it was 1.86 per cent. Recently, a 'solidarity aspect' has also been included: during the political upheavals when Franco left the political scene, the General Assemblies decided that the cooperatives, in an organised and well-planned manner, should join solidarity strikes throughout the Basque region or even Spain as a whole.

A study of job satisfaction at Ularco focussed on various causes of absenteeism. Generally, it was found that the incidence varied considerably among individual cooperatives. Of the many variables investigated, three explained a higher incidence of absenteeism: a 'lower' level of job in terms of skill content; not belonging to the Mondragon area; and being a woman. That study concludes: 'Absenteeism is definitely a personal response and the variables that influence human behaviour are many and diverse. It is therefore a phenomen that is hard to analyse, although systematic tendencies can be observed.' The researchers are convinced that 'ultimately absenteeism is rooted in lack of a sufficiently strong motivation with respect to work and the enterprise.' This must be the point of departure for further analysis.

Data on absenteeism due to illness and accidents only are available for the Ularco enterprises and for the entire movement. Graph 1 shows that the absenteeism trend due to illness for all cooperators is slightly higher than for Ularco enterprises which, excluding Ulgor, have an average work force of 568. It seems that those enterprises which got together at an early date and have since formed the basis of the movement, in spite of their larger size have experienced slightly less absenteeism in the period under study. This is an interesting finding because a study by the San Sebastian Chamber of Commerce on absenteeism during the years 1965-71 showed that it increased rather than diminished with the size of the enterprise.

A report on absenteeism 'due to illness' for 2500 workers in non-cooperative enterprises (see Graph 1) shows that this is about twice as high in capitalist enterprises as in cooperative firms. For 1965 a percentage of 2.05 in Ularco compares with 4.33 per cent in capitalist enterprises, this relative position being maintained up to 1976 when the percentages were 3.63 for the cooperatives versus 8.65 for others. 'Other factors' – mainly conflicts – are an almost equally important reason for the high rates of absenteeism in capitalist enterprises.

Graph 1. *Absenteeism in Cooperative and Capitalist Firms*

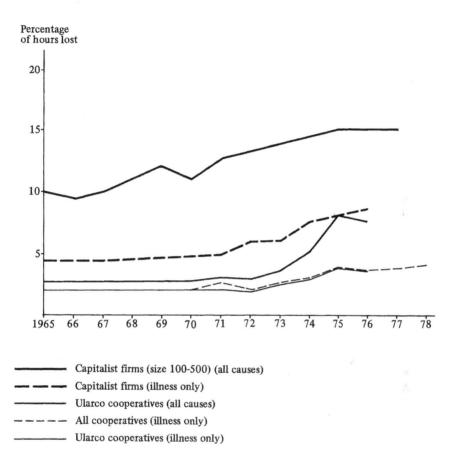

Percentage
of hours lost

—————— Capitalist firms (size 100-500) (all causes)

— — — — Capitalist firms (illness only)

—————— Ularco cooperatives (all causes)

— — — — — All cooperatives (illness only)

—————— Ularco cooperatives (illness only)

Source: Lagun-Aro, 1979; an internal report by Ularco's personnel department contains information on absenteeism in the enterprises which form Ularco and on absenteeism due to illness among 2500 workers in non-cooperative enterprises. A summary of a study by the Camera de Comercio de Guipúzcoa on absenteeism has also been consulted for the years 1965-71.

Precise data for the last few years are not available, but an observation made
by the general manager of Ularco regarding 15 per cent absenteeism due to illness in Union Cerrajera and some 20 per cent in other enterprises, suggests that
the very favourable cooperative figure, in spite of some increases, has hardly
changed.

This has also been observed by doctors in Mondragon who see 'absentee' pa-
tients belonging both to cooperative and to non-cooperative companies, and who
notice a significant difference between the two. Under the state social security
system many cases of absenteeism are in no way justified, but the cooperative
social security system gives an entirely different picture, in the sense that absenteeism occurs to a much smaller degree.

This brief exploration of absenteeism has thus produced two findings. Firstly,
that absenteeism in cooperatives is very low in comparison with Guipuzcoan
standards and with international data. Secondly, that cooperative absenteeism
rather suddenly jumped to a higher level in the mid-1970s: performance is still
good but is less impressive than previously.

EDUCATION: AN OVERVIEW

The start of the first producer cooperative in 1956 was preceded by thirteen
years of education and this has continued to be a distinctive characteristic of the
Mondragon cooperative group.[7] Arizmendi, a charismatic educator, has thus
made a lasting imprint on the Mondragon cooperatives. Due to his vision, technical education at the lowest level was introduced in Mondragon during the
1940s; due to his persuasion, a technical training school was not only established, but was upgraded to be able to play a dynamic role in the expanding
cooperative movement. Later, Arizmendi argued for a combination of work and
training in a 'study-and-work' cooperative (Alecoop), for the introduction of
permanent education, and for opportunities for girls to take up professional
careers. We shall follow the institutional developments from 1943 onwards, gaining new insights into the dynamic processes that are characteristic of the Mondragon cooperatives.

It is impossible to give a complete history of education in Mondragon as part
of a chapter; clearly, that needs to be the subject of an individual study. Here,
we shall briefly introduce the most important educational institutions, putting
particular emphasis on their roles with respect to the entire cooperative system,
and giving sufficient details to outline the various aspects of the education and
training programme without indulging in exhaustive detail about curriculum
development, budgetary and managerial aspects. The complexity of the topic
has made it advisable to present the general picture in a diagram; in this the
upper half relates to inwardly-oriented activities and the lower half to the ex-

Diagram 1. *Cooperative Education in Mondragon*

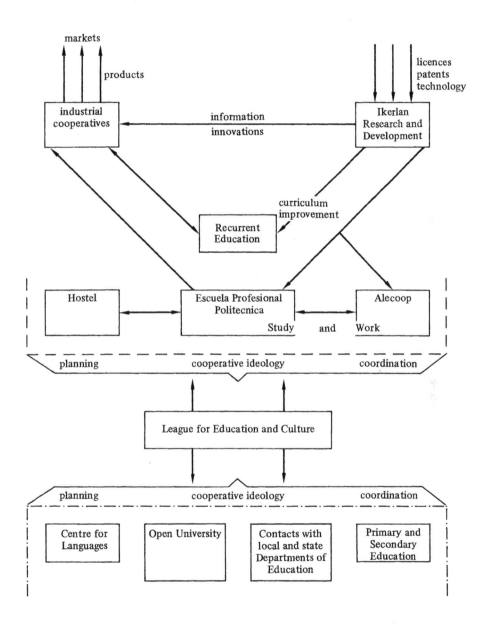

ternal activities of the cooperative educational institutions. At the centre is a small planning nucleus – the League for Education and Culture – which originally focussed all its attention on technical education and on the manpower requirements of the cooperatives. In recent years this has become heavily involved in the promotion of Basque culture, the improvement of primary and secondary education, and in planning for education at local and provincial levels. Particular attention will be given here to the technical training school (EPP) with 1179 students (1978); to Alecoop, the 'students factory' with a capacity of 505; and Ikerlan, the small research and development centre. EPP is the oldest institute, and several of the now independent institutions such as Alecoop and Ikerlan were originally small departments of EPP. The relationships between them are indicated on the diagram by means of arrows.[8] The cooperative preoccupation with primary and secondary education, with an open university at Vergara, and with planning for the district, will also be discussed briefly.

The diagram illustrates the dependent and open character of the cooperatives. On the one hand we find a dependency on the market economy of which the industrial cooperatives form a small part. On the other hand, there is an open attitude towards the community to which the cooperative movement wants to contribute, beyond its own immediate needs for technical education.

Escuela Profesional Politecnica (EPP)

On his arrival in Mondragon in 1941, Arizmendi found that the small technical school run by Union Cerrajera, the big local factory, was insufficient to meet the needs of the people of Mondragon. He therefore took the initiative to start a small technical training school. Starting with 20 pupils in 1943, the first batch graduated successfully in 1947. One obtains a clear idea of the views of Arizmendi on education from the contents of a speech he gave in 1945 to an audience of youth leaders:

Good education should be both theoretical and practical. As for the theoretical aspects, emphasis must always be laid on methods and a general understanding. Students should understand in the first place the most fundamental problems, such as ownership, work, capital, salary, and the relationships between capital and work, the duties of employers and employees, their rights and professional morals. Next they must understand the meaning of such concepts as production, consumption, banking and markets. But side by side with a deep understanding of socio-economic realities, students should be educated in a practical manner, which is far more difficult. There is a need to study the concrete realities of one's own town and neighbourhood, and to define problems or projects which can be solved or undertaken. Above all, once one has identified a line in which a productive activity can be undertaken, one has to study the production, marketing, etc. etc. of that specific product, because every productive activity has its own difficulties that one needs to master step-by-step. But all the time, while one is almost completely absorbed by such practical problems, one should have a utopian vision through which one can then adjust projections and plans (Arizmendi in Mendizabal 1978: 19-22).

In 1948 it was felt necessary to establish an organisation — the League — which would provide the school with a legal position, and which might be instrumental in promoting other educational activities which the technical training school was unable to provide. The school's staff needed to devote all their attention to meeting the standards set by a degree-granting institution at Zaragoza. Having obtained a subsidy from the Ministry of Education, the school moved to a new location, which was planned to accommodate a thousand pupils. By this time enrolment had risen to 170, in no way sufficient to make use of the school's huge capacity. Some wonder was expressed about Arizmendi's judgement since job prospects in Mondragon were minimal.

While emphasising technical education, Arizmendi was convinced that a more just society would never be achieved unless industry were to be shaped by people with vision. He considered that 'through mastering technology it would be possible to develop and generate processes that would permit a more human and social development.' This is worthy of mention because elsewhere cooperatives have not given such high priority to innovation, to research, and to technical education. As a result, in France, in the United States and to a lesser extent in Britain, cooperatives have been involved in rather labour-intensive lines of production.

In the early 1960s further buildings were added to the schools, including facilities for sports and physical education. Local fund raising was a decisive factor in this expansion and consolidation; the technical training school then offered courses in mechanics, electricity, electronics, welding, design and automation. In 1968 a landmark was reached when it was given official recognition as a school for technical education. New buildings were planned, again far in excess of existing enrolment. The educational programmes were continuously adjusted to product and technology developments in the cooperative factories and their levels raised to the highest grade possible. In 1976 the Ministry of Education recognised the school as a polytechnic institute. By that time a complete programme of technical education at three levels — low, middle and higher professional training — was functioning efficiently, catering for a total enrolment of more than 1000 students. Table 2 shows enrollment in recent years.

Table 2. *Students enrolled at the Escuela Profesional Politecnica*

	1969/70	1972/73	1976/77	1978/79
Lower technical education	455 ⎫	492 ⎫	539 ⎫	516 ⎫
	⎬753	⎬724	⎬1029	⎬920
Middle technical education	298 ⎭	232 ⎭	490 ⎭	404 ⎭
Higher technical education	191	208	300	259
Total	944	932	1329	1179

Source: see text and footnotes

It is hardly surprising that EPP enjoys a monopoly position in technical education in Mondragon and its immediate environment. Enrolments reached a peak in 1976-77 with 1329 pupils, declining to 1179 in 1978-79. A gradual shift in emphasis towards higher levels of technical education has now been made. It seems that EPP has stabilised itself at the capacity reached in the late 1960s; from 1943 onwards, enrollment has accumulated to about 6500 students.

Courses at various levels respond directly to the manpower needs reported to the school by the cooperatives. Its curriculum also adjusts frequently to long-term developments at the highest technological level of the cooperatives, and to the specific requirements of the University of Valladolid, to which the EPP is accredited by order of the Ministry of Education.[9]

EPP has always had a 'community orientation', although it was intended principally to educate young people for employment in cooperative enterprises. Some small capitalist enterprises, which for several years have given the school financial support, are institutional members of its General Assembly, on which seats are also reserved for the community at large.

EPP is organised as a cooperative with the exception that its General Assembly includes three categories of members: teachers, pupils and parents, and supporting institutions. This applies also to the Supervisory Board which allocates quota to each category of interested parties; the occupation of seats is decided by vote in the General Assembly. A further adjustment of the organisational structure is the existence of two Social Councils: one for the teachers of the school, and the other for students and parents. This structure is related to the financial interest which the parties have in running EPP: about 30 to 40 per cent of the budget should be subsidised by the central administration in Madrid; pupils and enterprises, mostly cooperatives, who are the direct and indirect beneficiaries of educational efforts, provide at least 20 per cent each; and finally, 20 per cent has to be found by 'self-financing'. In reality, however, state subsidies do not exceed 20 per cent, whereas the Funds for Social Projects — mainly from Ularco and *Amat*, another large cooperative — provide almost 40 per cent of budgetary needs.

EPP has played a central role in the development of cooperative education, and most likely will continue to do so, because students from elsewhere come for technical training and to learn about cooperative principles. Practice and theory are equally important in the educational programme of EPP, as they are in another educational institution of a highly innovative character, Alecoop.

Alecoop – Study and Work

In 1966 EPP realised a plan for the better integration of work and study than by giving them equal importance in its own programmes: *A*ctividad *L*aboral *E*scolar *Coop*erativa (Alecoop), a working enterprise run by pupils of the school. The idea for Alecoop had been Arizmendi's, who himself wrote its statutes. Resistance to his plan had been great. According to a senior manager: 'we felt that for the first time Arizmendi had become very impractical.' His reasoning had been, firstly, that many pupils could not afford education unless there was an opportunity to earn money with which to pay fees and hostel costs; secondly, and even more importantly, only through actual experience could pupils be prepared adequately for work in cooperative enterprises. Arizmendi wanted to design an educational system in which the balance would shift gradually from study to work. By the time they obtained employment, students would be fully prepared to contribute towards production and towards strengthening the cooperative, but would still be motivated to continue their education in evening courses and programmes of recurrent education. This was needed in order that they could be fully informed about product innovations and new techniques.

The early years of Alecoop were extremely difficult, even to the extent that in 1970 it was asked whether a money-losing experiment should be continued. Students made a special plea, however, and succeeded not only in keeping open the factory in which they spent 50 per cent of their time, but also in making it financially successful.

In 1970 Alecoop became an independent cooperative rather than a department of EPP. 1971 was the last year in which it recorded a loss – of almost three million pesetas. Since then positive results have been recorded, reaching net profits of about eight million pesetas in 1974 and 1975, over 13 million pesetas in 1976, and about 40 million in 1978. A healthy financial situation has been reached in which own resources fully cover the fixed assets; profit rates amounted to about 20 per cent of total sales in 1977, while capital yield in 1978 surpassed 30 per cent.

During the formative years of Alecoop, any money-earning project had to be accepted. The industrial cooperatives were hesitant to give it their orders, fearing that regular supplies of good quality would not be forthcoming. As a result, Alecoop had to undertake such activities as digging ditches and making balcony railings. Gradually, it began to establish a reputation for reliability and, as a result, orders came from the industrial cooperatives. As the level of education at the school rose, the situation improved. One product that had been abandoned by a cooperative became a commercial success at Alecoop, the breakthrough being caused by a steel bar-feeding machine. In particular, the production of didactic equipment for technical education, such as testing devices, has acquired a stable market; such equipment is purchased in large quantities by the Ministry of Education in Madrid, and export orders, for instance to Venezuela, have materialised. Sales revenue increased sharply once successful products had been identified: a rise of sales value to 100 million pesetas, a considerable part of which is paid out as earnings to pupils, proves that Alecoop has become a viable cooperative. The success in marketing products meant that work places could be increased from 216 in 1971 to 505 in 1978, and further expansion to 800 is envisaged. Work is in two shifts – students work half-time in Alecoop and the remaining time in the EPP; about half the work places are in a separate building to the school, and the remaining jobs are found in Ularco cooperatives to which students are transported by bus.

The expansion of work places is obviously linked to the possibilities of placing the students in a cooperative factory after completion of their studies. The minimum condition for entry is completion of the first level of technical education, which implies that students can 'work themselves' into future jobs. After the highest level of technical training, in particular, all pupils can easily find employment. Alecoop is an independent cooperative, however, and the industrial cooperatives have no obligation to recruit its pupils; neither can Alecoop guarantee that it will succeed in finding jobs for the pupils. It seems to be a good system of micro-manpower planning: intake closely follows the demand for skills by the industrial cooperatives, and the curriculum changes accordingly. An overall trend has been that the level of technical skills has risen considerably in response to demands by the cooperatives; in turn, this has had a favourable impact on opportunities to sell products, to the extent that Alecoop now exports part of its production.

Alecoop's General Assembly and Supervisory Board consist of three categories: students, staff, and supporting institutions. A council of students and a council of staff both elect representatives to the Supervisory Board, while the supporting institutions nominate their representatives in relation to their 'financial stake'. An interesting phenomenon arises with respect to 'ownership of the means of production', over which students have considerable voting power. At any time, a statutory majority of members could decide to liquidate the enterprise and to reap the benefits of accumulated capital. At the end of 1978, own resources exceeded 160 million pesetas, forming about 70 per cent of total resources available. So far, however, this problem has not been discussed in Alecoop's Social Council, which devotes particular attention to fair earnings-cum-scholarship levels.[10]

The rapid changes have not occurred without growing pains. At one moment absenteeism rose, carelessness increased, and personnel policies did not adjust to the higher number of jobs. In short, a healthy organisation in which study and work could go hand-in-hand in one factory had not been designed. The demands of educational processes required a different rhythm from the running of a factory, making the planning of activities particularly complex. Economic survival determined the boundaries beyond which 'educational concessions' could not be granted. This was diagnosed at an early stage, however, and proper measures were taken, ensuring that this cooperative would continue to play a role of critical importance and would also serve as an example for new 'Alecoops' in other cities.

At this moment, it is not possible to make a general evaluation, but the fact that very positive comments are made in the factories about the competence and motivation of the students can be taken as an indication that, after a dozen years, the experiment has become an important characteristic of the entire co-operative movement. The staff of Alecoop put it very modestly:

We make sure that technical education at EPP reaches a very high level because EPP pupils get work experience in our factory. Pupils and teachers are not technically superior to those of similar institutions elsewhere; the factory is not very special, it just has to make ends meet in order to survive. Of course, the fact that we know all students extremely well, as workers in teams, helps in finding the best place for a student and in assisting cooperatives to find the best people for their needs. And, of course, it is a good thing if engineers who, later on, will never again do routine jobs, will at least have gone through that experience.[11]

Alecoop has become an important element in the cooperative educational system and may need to be subdivided into smaller cooperatives, either along product lines or on a regional basis, when the cooperative movement starts to spread more quickly through Basque country.

Ikerlan: Research and Development

The industrial cooperatives themselves do a certain amount of research, but most innovations as far as technology and new products are concerned have been introduced after obtaining licenses and patents from elsewhere. The founding of a separate institute for research and development (R&D) came about gradually. EPP had become more involved in problems of research, to the extent that a department for R&D had been set up which played a useful role with respect to technical education, but which could not provide the necessary dynamic force for the entire cooperative group. The economic crisis of the mid-1970s for instance, had caught Ulgor, the largest cooperative, when its technological know-how was inadequate. Limits had been reached in several markets, and new technologies, particularly in the field of electronics, automation and micro-processing, had been introduced in international markets. There was thus an urgent need to invest in these areas and to obtain first-hand knowledge by doing their own research. In 1977, CLP, the Ularco companies and some of the smaller industrial cooperatives took the initiative of jointly establishing an R&D centre (*Ikerlan*). This was thought preferable to leaving all cooperatives to finance R&D budgets of relatively small proportions.

The objectives of Ikerlan, in the engineering, consumer durable goods and electronics branches, are:

(1) to become thoroughly familiar with specific technological developments and

their application in the field of production and training in order to safeguard a permanent flow of marketable products;

(2) to promote the highest degree of adaptation to new developments in those
branches in which the cooperatives are active;

(3) to ensure that, at various levels and through different channels, the members
become prepared for such new developments; and

(4) to make the best use of knowledge obtained, including sales to third parties
of licences and patents.

In its statutes and bylaws, special articles protect the interests of the various
enterprises which promoted Ikerlan: each industrial cooperative is independent,
after all, and may even compete with other cooperatives when searching for the
most profitable lines of production in domestic or foreign markets. Members of
Ikerlan, i.e. the cooperating enterprises, its staff, and members of cooperating
enterprises, need to be cautious since disclosure of certain kinds of information
could greatly harm the interests of some or benefit the position of others. Owing
to the delicate character of the services rendered, the Supervisory Board reflects
the various interests that are involved: two seats for cooperating institutions,
four for representatives of Ikerlan staff, four for cooperating institutions whose
technologies are closely associated to research activities undertaken by Ikerlan,
and two seats for cooperating institutions which are not active in areas researched by Ikerlan staff. In 1977, Ikerlan was linked to 32 cooperatives.

Research for new products or techniques naturally benefits the cooperative
or non-cooperative enterprise by which it is commissioned. If new innovations
of commercial interest are spotted through independent research, the information is passed on to all member institutions. In case of conflict, in the sense that
more than one firm takes an interest, the Supervisory Board will decide who gets
the right to introduce the innovation. If no interest is expressed, the news is
made known to 'the public'. In the short time during which Ikerlan has been
operating, its staff of 43 full-time and 18 part-time specialists has concentrated
on establishing contacts with some 20 centres throughout Europe. EPP engineering students may participate during their final year, thus providing a stimulus for
independent research by Ikerlan.

Considerable resources are involved: during 1979 income and expenditure
amounted to about 80 million pesetas,[12] the initial investment of 200 million
pesetas being largely financed by Caja Laboral Popular. The annual budget is
provided partly by supporting cooperatives, particularly the large ones, the remainder being funded by CLP and by self-financing. Ikerlan adheres to normal
regulations as regards amortisation, payment of interest, and repayment of the
outstanding debt in an agreed period of years.

Ikerlan is located centrally, next to the new CLP headquarters and to those of
the League of Education and Culture. It has three spacious offices: one department for consumer durables, one for engineering and thermodynamics, and one

for information systems. In 1979 R&D orders were received from more than a dozen cooperatives, independent research was undertaken, and general assistance provided in the field of technology to the entire cooperative movement. This is somewhat reminiscent of the situation in the late 1950s when 'the school' had huge excess capacity, but with one difference: little imagination is now needed to predict that the three departments will soon be used to capacity.

Within a short period of time, Ikerlan has become a strong centre with a clearly formulated R&D policy. Much time is devoted to the design of new components for existing products, to the study of competitors' products, and to keeping in touch with developments all over the world, particularly Japanese innovations which are the most threatening in the branches covered by the Mondragon cooperatives. Ikerlan's activities feed back into CLP's Management Services Division, into EPP's curriculum development, and directly into the cooperatives, influencing their decisions on products to be developed and techniques to be used.

EPP: Other Involvements

Two other activities of EPP concern a hostel for students and a department for permanent education. The hostel, Colegio Menor Viteri, was set up in 1965 and plays an important role in inculcating 'cooperative values'; it also functions as a cooperative.

The Colegio is part of EPP and caters for about 350 students: 50 per cent at higher technical and 50 per cent at middle technical level. Admission is part of a long-term strategy: 'We have a preference for selecting in such a manner that it stimulates the creation of new associations of workers in response to interests that in due time will come forward in those communities', according to one document. This implies a strategy in which a large group of students from a specific town undergo training and work experience in the Mondragon area, after which they may become the nucleus or growth pole of a cooperative enterprise in their own town. During 1975, for instance, 38 students came from the town of Guernika and 33 from Marquina, both located about 50 km from Mondragon. A short-term objective is to let the small staff of the hostel organise workshops and conferences in strategic towns and villages in order to inform parents, relatives and friends of the students about the Mondragon cooperatives. They also explain the need for dedicated and competent workers: EPP students have a hectic daily schedule of ten solid hours of study and work in factories, laboratories and classrooms. It is expected that capacity will expand, but also that emphasis will be placed on qualitative change. In particular, discussions with students about problems of their villages or towns, about work conditions and about control mechanisms will play an important part, similar to those held by Arizmendi in the late 1940s and early fifties when he prepared the first group of students from whom the founders of Ulgor originated.

The EPP set up a department for permanent education in 1971, as a final step towards building a comprehensive micro-educational system that would provide manpower with the required skills and desired cooperative background for a rapidly expanding group of cooperative enterprises. On the one hand it is necessary that those workers who were trained in EPP should be further educated and, on the other hand, that new and sometimes immigrant workers should be made familiar with cooperative principles. Efforts by Mondragon's educational experts to convince people that technical training is a permanent affair are backed-up by a study of French law on recurrent education.

A programme of permanent education would obviously be of unique value for the long-term survival of the Mondragon movement as a dynamic cooperative system. Programmes of continuous education will teach older cooperators about new products and techniques, thus encouraging them to adjust to new circumstances, and possibly safeguarding the dynamic and pragmatic response to new situations that so far have been the hallmark of the Mondragon cooperatives: a hallmark that might otherwise disappear if, in another 15 years or so, the average age of the cooperators is much above the present one of about 36 years.

The League for Education and Culture[13]

Arizmendi's long-term vision about education is also reflected in the League for Education and Culture. In his view, technical education would not be sufficient to meet the educational needs of the community, and a supporting organisation was therefore required which would later play a much wider role. Until the late 1960s the League – a very small organisation – devoted all its efforts towards promoting vocational education and other activities closely linked with the EPP. It served as a source of new ideas: Alecoop, Ikerlan, the hostel and the department for recurrent education would not have developed if the League had not given strong support. The staff of EPP would never have been able to set aside sufficient time for reflection on such long-range strategic issues. During the 1970s, the League for Education and Culture became involved in a range of new activities, as if in implementation of the ambitious goals of Arizmendi, who continually repeated the words: 'Knowledge is power; socialising knowledge implies the democratisation of power.'

The annual report for 1976, the year of Arizmendi's death, states that the existing institutions 'offer an extraordinary platform on which to initiate a new phase in which we shall press forward towards ambitious goals.' This new phase would be characterised by open attitudes towards the community.

The League, with a permanent staff of four members: director, secretary, accountant and education specialist, is located in the same building as Ikerlan under the name Central Educational Services. It has a fullfledged cooperative organisation with a General Assembly and a Supervisory Board. Members of the

General Assembly include educational cooperatives, cooperating industrial enter-prises, other institutions such as public authorities, staff of the League, members of associated cooperatives and, finally, individual members of other Mondragon cooperatives. Detailed regulations are now and then revised to take into account new developments, and to establish a democratic forum in which interested parties can meet and share responsibility for the work of the League. These regulations also specify the financial contributions expected from members of the General Assembly. An important task of the General Assembly is the trustee-ship of resources allocated by the cooperatives to the Fund for Social Projects.

During 1978-79 total expenditure amounted to about 300 million pesetas, of which 37 per cent was funded by pupils and parents, 33 per cent came from the state education budget, 7 per cent from various sources, and the remaining 23 per cent from the Fund for Social Projects.[14] The League monitors 13 centres of education: three nursery schools, three primary and lower secondary schools, two senior secondary and preparatory university schools, and five for various levels of technical education. In 1978-79, total enrolment at these centres, including EPP which consists of three centres, was 6000 pupils; the staffs totalled 234, and there were 188 classrooms.

The League plays a supporting role, stimulating and developing new ideas and plans. It forms a loose federation of the 13 centres which, if they so wish, may become fully independent while still maintaining membership of the General Assembly. There are also many schools — educational cooperatives — which are associated with CLP and are not monitored by the League.[15] A great deal of attention is given to the district system of primary and secondary education, and Basque language, culture and history are actively promoted. The bylaws (art. 11) state:

Basque culture: Taking into account the characteristics of the people with which it is con-nected, the League strives, in cooperation with local provincial and state authorities, for the use of Euskara [Basque language] and for studies of Basque culture at all levels of education; at the same time to promote knowledge about socio-political and economic realities, there-by contributing to the formation of people who identify with the Basque nation, and serving as a means to integrate the local and immigrant populations in a single bi-lingual community to serve the country.

The cooperative group considers that these subjects can be promoted proper-ly only in schools that are run by the community rather than by the state or religious organisations. It has therefore started to finance primary and secondary education throughout the region and to draft a standard cooperative statute and bylaw which will apply to all 'cooperatives of education'. The community, teachers, parents and pupils together form General Assemblies which have ulti-mate responsibility for the affairs of a particular school. The results are im-pressive: enrolment in primary schools run by the community rose from 24 per cent in 1975 to 35 per cent in 1977. An average of 40 per cent of classes use Euskara as medium of instruction.

Concern has been expressed that teachers' salaries are too low and should be tied to average cooperative earnings so as to prevent jealousy and frustration. On the other hand, teachers should also work the same number of hours as other cooperators and should have only one month's vacation each year.

The League for Education and Culture has gradually undertaken a planning role which benefits the entire community. From 1975 onwards, for instance, comprehensive and detailed statistics are available for the first time for the entire district with its 67,000 inhabitants for all levels of education: from nursery schools to the cooperative polytechnic institute.[16]

The data given in Table 3 illustrate the impact of the League on the educational system of the district in which Mondragon is located.[17] The League monitors about 38 per cent of nursery education, 20 per cent of primary and lower secondary education, 35 per cent of higher secondary and pre-university education, and almost 50 per cent of lower, middle and higher technical education.

Table 3. *Education in Guipúzcoa (1978-79)*

	Province of Guipúzcoa	District in which Mondragon is located	League for Education and Culture
	(1)	(2)	(3)
Nursery schools (3-6)	41,000	3,600	1,350
General primary and lower secondary education (8-14)	106,000	10,500	2,250*
General higher secondary education (15-17)	20,000	1,400	500
Technical education (15-17)	20,000	3,500	1,700

* In addition, 36 schools with 26,000 pupils are associated with CLP

Sources: see Notes 13 and 17.

If we add to these activities the *Centre for Language Studies*, at which over 800 students took courses during 1978-79, and the manifold contacts with local, provincial and state educational authorities, it is clear that the League more than lives up to Arizmendi's dreams. In 1977 it was reported that 'the fundamental preoccupation of the League for Education and Culture has been to study the educational structures of the district ... in order to adapt them to the demands of the new times, i.e. to serve the country as they should.' As specific objectives were mentioned:

1. participation of the community, together with parents and teachers, in the promotion of education;
2. a coordinated effort to develop the Basque language and culture; and

3. access to education for all without discrimination, with a true community reorientation.

Through the issues that the group raises it exercises an ideological, conscientising influence on pupils and students, as well as on the community at large, far beyond the immediate environment of Mondragon.

An example of the role played by the education group is the increased consciousness regarding the position of women. Several planning documents express concern that women have not yet acquired access to the higher job strata in the cooperatives. Less than one per cent of all women were employed in the top ranks in 1976 as against 9.5 per cent of all men.[18] This relates directly to the educational system: out of a total enrolment of about 500 students from Mondragon in the various levels of EPP, only 17 are girls: 14 in lower technical education, three in middle technical education, and none at the highest level of engineering education. It is recognised that discrimination is exercised between boys and girls, and that such training for girls is under-valued. Parents prefer their daughters to stay at home rather than to go to technical training school; as a result, 'Girls are filling jobs in offices and factories which demand the least skills.'

An important document states clearly:

The lack of schooling of girls must be recognised as a problem in our district. The causes are many and include the following:
– little importance attached by parents to girls' education;
– preconception that girls do not have real competence for work in industry;
– failure of technical training programmes to adapt to the special qualities of girls;
– undervaluation of factory work and the existence of a social class of office workers.
If we continue with this system of education, we shall create a female class of industrial drudges and low skilled office workers. (Liga de Educación 1976a: 10, 11).

It seems that, while the industrial cooperatives are facing economic difficulties, the education projects of the cooperative movement have now entered their most dynamic phase. In about a third of a century, spectacular developments have taken place in the field of cooperative education. First, an innovative group of institutions was created step-by-step, focussing in particular on the staffing needs of the industrial cooperatives. More traditional institutions, such as a school for technical training and a hostel were set up, as well as innovative projects such as Alecoop, Ikerlan, and the Department for Permanent Education. Emphasis has gradually shifted towards making their educational experiences available to the wider community in Mondragon and its surrounding district. The League for Education and Culture, established in 1948, has assumed more responsibilities and has become an important intermediary institution in making various cooperative resources available to the public educational system of the Basque Provinces.

DIVISION OF LABOUR AND WORK

Lastly, an important dimension of the labour situation which should be given considerable attention is the division of work. Cooperative factories that compete in markets have to organise their work efficiently. In the first instance, the Mondragon cooperatives adopted existing technologies; in fact, they could hardly have done otherwise. Even though relatively less monotonous technologies may be preferred to achieve greater job satisfaction, one is still bound by the division of work and labour that is implicitly given by the available processes of production.

Job evaluation is of great importance since it relates directly to the distribution of work among cooperators and to earnings differentials, and the cooperatives have invested much time and effort to laying down precise regulations in this regard. The result of a complex pattern of consultations, committee work, checks and balances, is that every person is allocated a job with a certain number of points.[19] The Social Council supervises the procedure and has a decisive vote when changes are proposed.

Each cooperative is free to design its own system of job evaluation and procedures for reaching an agreement, provided that the final earnings differentials adhere strictly to the 'three-to-one' rule. In practice, cooperatives have fairly similar committee structures which, in the large enterprises, include a personnel department and a personnel director. Frequent consultations with CLP enable 'economies of scale' in the sense that experience gained in one cooperative is transmitted to others. In all cases the job evaluation manual has to be endorsed by the management and approved by the Supervisory Board. The general pattern is that, with increasing size, the personnel director has final responsibility for implementing all approved procedures, several of which specify participatory aspects. For instance, the fact that a job evaluation committee always includes two alternating members from the shop floor is valuable in channelling information 'two ways'. The committee analyses each job periodically, taking into account feed-back from other departments, protests, and suggestions, to ensure that the evaluation is fair and generally accepted. Several cooperatives have a permanent CLP delegate 'with a voice but without a vote'. In all cases, the permanent members of this important committee are appointed directly either by the Social Council or by management after approval of the Social Council has been obtained. Departments nominate representatives to such committees in free elections. Much thought has been given to designing systems that can help to reduce potential sources of conflict.

Job Evaluation

The complexity of job evaluation procedures is immediately apparent when the various characteristics of each job are listed: knowledge and experience; intricateness; decision making and managerial aspects; relational skills; physical, mental and visual demands. All ranks, irrespective of blue or white collar work, seniority, or importance of position, are covered in a single manual. For each job, from cleaner to managing director, points with different values are given to each factor. These weights have changed over time, sometimes even spectacularly. A striking example is the value − 20 per cent of all points − given to 'relational skills' in the 1973 manual although earlier manuals allocated less than 10 points to this aspect. The purpose was 'to change the individualistic attitude in manual jobs into a more social one', according to an explanatory note. Theoretical knowledge has been always given a high score, close to 20 per cent; in 1973 it was raised to 25 per cent. As a result one may find 25 per cent allocated for theoretical knowledge, 25 per cent for experience, 8 per cent for decision making, 7 per cent for leadership, 20 per cent for 'relational skills', and a mere 15 per cent for (physical and visual) stress.

Following this allocation of points, intervals are made and a structural index decided upon, in the 'one to three' range. In CLP's job evaluation, the points run from 123 to 383.5. The lowest index 1.15 is given to all jobs which have more than 122.5 and less than 129.5 points; index 1.20 is given to the interval 130-137 and so on up to the highest index 2.80, which covers the interval 370 to 383.5 points, which is for department directors.

Individuals are thus given a job index and credit is given for performance in a particular position. During the 1960s, the principle was strictly adhered to that the demands of the job should almost exclusively determine a person's index. This has not been maintained, however. Subjective personal elements are now also included in each person's index.

Members, particularly new ones, may not immediately be awarded the index that normally corresponds to a specific job because their knowledge and experience is insufficient. Equally important is the fact that an additional element can be added to the index for extra performance. During the 1960s it was made possible to add as much as one-tenth of a point to the index. More recently, the range has been expanded to include values from .1 to .2 for 'above average performance'. This opens-up considerable scope for 'wage drift'; during the late 1960s, for example, 80 per cent of the members received .075 and the remaining 20 per cent the full .1 as bonus for good performance. A final correction relates to special difficulties which are not otherwise taken into account, such as heavy noise, and danger. We thus get a system in which

Index of Work = Structural Index - Apprentice 'Penalty' + Performance rate + Compensation for Hardships (noise, danger, etc.)

Humanisation of Work

It is frequently said that grading and evaluation systems can only be changed after the organisation of the work itself has changed. Recently, enterprises have been actively encouraged to substitute teamwork for conveyor belt work. Experiments with autonomous workgroups at Volvo, Olivetti, Saab, and so forth, are followed with great interest and the cooperators like to learn from 'humanisation of work' developments in other industrialised countries. They realise that such solutions may be too technological and that more needs to be done before work can really be humanised. In some cooperatives whole 'layers' of supervision have been done away with in order to encourage participation. In one case, a team without a supervisor which had performed badly was split into two groups: this enabled solution of the personal and organisational problems. In another case it was decided that a coordinator should be shared by a number of teams, while in yet another it was decided to elect a foreman who would continue to work as a member of the team. The continuous challenge is to 'turn a formal democratic structure into real participatory enterprises', in the words of a policy document; 'human relations' are considered so important in making organisations work effectively that Social Councils no longer meet outside work hours but as an integral part of work. As a senior executive remarked: 'first we solved the problems of technology and organisation, and it is only now that our attention can be given to the personal and human aspects of work.' This is of critical importance if the new organisational concept of teamwork rather than conveyor belt labour is to succeed. The goal is 'to build a participatory organisation by objectives' instead of the wellknown 'management by objectives'.

Job evaluation is becoming progressively more difficult and heavy demands are made on supervisors who grade the performance of team members. Most members still think that the only purpose of the exercise is to raise wages. To combat such ideas, workers are educated in cooperative values and their rationale. This is a continuous process since new members join each year, many of whom have had no education in the cooperative schools and understand little of the underlying philosophy. A frustrating conflict occurred in one big cooperative for example, when productivity rose by more than 20 per cent following the substitution of autonomous work groups for the conveyor belt. As a result, production targets were raised, which gave rise to protests. The following year was a poor one due to adverse national market conditions, and so the cooperative had to learn that external demands are heavy and that one can never rely on existing structures and targets to guarantee future success.

The attitudes of direct supervisors and of higher ranking directors are of great importance in creating an atmosphere of trust, an atmosphere in which readiness to experiment increases. Leaders can stimulate initiatives to enrich jobs and to rotate work, short-cut lines of communication, and so on, or they may feel threatened and prefer to leave things as they are. A radical departure from traditional forms of work organisation in the Mondragon group has been made at a new furniture factory where all work is planned as teamwork. The idea is to allocate points in the usual manner but to allocate the performance index to the entire team, which will then decide how these gains should be distributed among its members. One such team on the shopfloor decided to grant the entire group allowance for high performance to one outstanding and highly experienced colleague on condition that he would teach all the other members to acquire the same skills.

Hierarchy

In Table 4 the outcome of the allocation of workers to the index structure (one to three) in Ulgor enables us to obtain a realistic picture of the situation.

Table 4. *Job-evaluation of men and women in Ulgor, the largest cooperative* (percentages) (1976)*

	Men	Women	Total
1.00-1.25	1	8	2.5
1.25-1.50	36.5	77.5	45
1.50-1.75	40	12	34
1.75-2.00	13	2	11
2.00-2.25	5	.5	4
2.25-2.50	2.5	0	2
2.50-2.75	1.5	0	1
2.75-3.00	.5	0	.5
Total	100	100	100

* Own calculations, based on data of internal report.

Indices are grouped in eight intervals, each covering one-quarter of a full index point. The great majority, 79.5 per cent, fall into a small range of indices in the interval 1.25 to 1.75. Only a small percentage is found in the lowest interval, whereas 7.5 per cent of all cooperators are given indices greater than 2.00.

The data show that men and women have different job opportunities and promotion prospects. Only one per cent of all men are found in the lowest interval as compared to eight per cent of all women, while the lowest two intervals cover 37 per cent of all men and 86 per cent of all women. As for the interval ranging from 2.00 up to 3.00, only three women have reached the higher ranks as compared to 276 men, a ratio of 1 to 92, whereas the ratio of employment is about one to four.

The close relationship between education and division of work is shown clearly in Table 5. There is no perfect correlation between the two distributions but it is obvious that a cooperator's level of education is a determining factor with respect to his or her future career in one of the cooperatives.

Table 5. *Division of work in Ularco cooperatives (percentages) (1976)*

Education		Work categories	
Primary education	62	Production line	65
Lower technical education	22	Skilled and administrative work	21
Middle education	9	Supervisory work and staff function	9
Higher technical training	7	Middle level work	4
		Technical and economic experts and senior jobs	1
	100		100

Source: Ularco document 1977.

The potential for upward mobility therefore needs to be assessed realistically, as in any organisation of considerable size. Available information shows that in 1976 approximately two per cent of cooperators were promoted to jobs of higher value, but the distribution is rather uneven, with less than .50 per cent mobility for category 1, and 3, 8 and 5 per cent respectively for categories 2, 3 and 4. If, at some point in time, the rapid expansion will slow down, then the possibilities for promotion will be further reduced.

All this reveals a fundamental problem of cooperative organisation. While it may be true that upward mobility is slightly higher than in capitalist enterprises, this does not mean that Mondragon cooperatives are able to offer on a huge scale less monotonous and more interesting work than elsewhere. The cooperative group is aware of this and at times explores other ways of distributing work, but existing technologies severely restrict the experiments that can be undertaken in this respect. The necessity to compete in national and international markets leaves insufficient space to implement alternative manners of work organisation on a large scale.

CONCLUSIONS

In any analysis of economic systems, considerable attention is given to the capacity of 'a system' to create full employment, the achievement of which is a fundamental objective in socialist systems. 'Planning the labour force' implies that attention is given to education and on-the-job training of the type found widely in the Soviet Union and China, and that labour specialisation is given high priority (Ellman 1979: 151-77; Schrenk et al. 1979: 244-85). We have seen that Mondragon displays important features in each of these three dimensions – employment, education, and division of work. Obviously the scale of problems faced in Mondragon is different; moreover, considerable emphasis is given to decentralisation and participation 'from below' rather than to planning 'from above'. Yet the behaviour of the Mondragon group can be better compared with the socialist systems than with that pertaining in capitalist countries.

Our findings have shown that the Mondragon cooperatives, collectively and individually, have given much attention to increasing employment. The open-door principle is practiced to a high degree, as has become particularly clear in recent years. With employment in private enterprises falling, the cooperatives continue to give high priority to safeguarding existing jobs and to attempting to expand as quickly as is feasible. In marginal terms, and taking the indirect employment impact into account, the Mondragon Group has had a strong impact on the employment situation in the entire province during the 1970s.[20]

The worsening economic climate has had a considerable impact, as we shall see in our analysis of economic performance in Chapter V. The cooperators are well aware of the increasing risks. In some 80 interviews held in 1977, security of employment was consistently mentioned as a great advantage of belonging to the Mondragon group (see Chapter VII). In a series of interviews held more recently in 1980, the fear was frequently expressed that the cooperatives would face major problems in protecting even existing jobs.[21] Further expansion in new production lines, creating work for young and well-educated cooperators, is to be expected, but guaranteed work for those who are reaching seniority is no longer almost absolute. This was made painfully clear in 1980 when the cooperative social security system, Lagun-Aro, decided to introduce an unemployment insurance which would help cooperators in the event that cooperative factories would face closure.[22]

From the viewpoint of comparative evaluation, an important aspect is that in Mondragon all workers are also cooperators with full rights; the only exception is the temporary employment of highly skilled experts who are employed for short periods. The phenomenon of second class citizens, or 'the hired labour dilemma' discussed by Barkai in his study of the Israeli Kibbutzim, does not exist in Mondragon (Barkai 1977: 221).

From a comparative perspective, our analysis of absenteeism has produced some very positive results with respect to the Mondragon cooperatives. Yet during the 1970s absenteeism rose considerably in comparison to earlier years. We have emphasised the quantitative aspect of absenteeism in relation to the employment situation. The evidence suggests that the cooperating factories face many internal problems which cause withdrawals from work for varying periods of time. The percentages found, although highly favourable, are nothing more than averages, implying that considerable differences exist between the cooperative factories. In a few exceptional cases the percentage of absenteeism is as high as in private enterprises; in others, the percentage is as low as two or three per cent.

As in the case of employment, analysis of the roles that educational and training programmes play in the Mondragon group shows a community orientation. A network of institutions forms a supporting structure for the cooperative factories; but also and increasingly in recent years, funds are made available to spread educational and training achievements among the community of the district in which Mondragon is located. Since 1975, developments in this respect have been impressive. An infrastructure has been created, including in particular the League for Education and Culture, which has great potential for promoting a dynamic relationship between education and wider community participation in the Mondragon group.

Mondragon's education is very innovative; and a comprehensive evaluation cannot yet be made. The merits of institutions such as Alecoop and Ikerlan, which respectively emphasise the need to combine practice with theory, and the promotion of research and development, will not be proven fully for another five to ten years. Even in their initial phase, however, those merits have become clear. Perhaps the most difficult task will be to build a system of lifelong recurrent education. If that should not come off the ground, tensions will emerge sooner or later between the older generation and the younger cooperators who have undergone better and more advanced technical training. If the programme is successful, then Mondragon's education will have written a new chapter in the cooperative movement.

The last and most complex issue studied in this chapter was that of division of work and, implicitly, organisation and hierarchical relationships. Work distribution is the foundation for efficiency and equity, the dimensions of which will be taken up in the analysis of economic performance. Work distribution will be the focus of further analysis in Chapter VI.

Several issues have been mentioned only in passing. For instance, the skill content of jobs was briefly touched upon with regard to the job rotation and enrichment projects that have been introduced in some cooperatives. We have also seen that the familiar hierarchical pyramid has been a common organisational feature. The indications are that a real break-through in the organisation of work relations will be a mammoth task. The need for such a new orientation has been well put by Nutzinger:

... there can be no doubt that any strategy of industrial democracy aiming at increased workers' participation in decision-making and earnings must contain humanisation of the work conditions as an essential component.... Co-determination and self-determination of the working man is not exhausted by measures of democratic control and legitimation; it has to be experienced personally in everyday work. For this reason, humanisation of working life, combined with changes in labour law, co-determination and collective bargaining, is an essential element of any realistic and meaningful strategy of democratic socialism (Nutzinger 1980: 146).

In each of the areas studied in this chapter, the Mondragon group has found pragmatic solutions guided by long-term objectives. In some aspects — employment creation and education — remarkable results have been achieved; in others — absenteeism and the division of work — fundamental problems are faced by a cooperative group that operates within a mixed economy.

NOTES

1. Ballesteros *et al* (1968: Anexo 1, 257), give some details regarding location, product and employment for 22 cooperatives in 1965. The same 22 factories have again been selected in an investigation of the employment record from 1971 to 1978.

The aggregate series for all industrial cooperatives — column (4) in Table 1 — in some years during the 1960s may also include employment in other cooperatives mentioned in this section. During the 1970s a downward trend occurred due to the fact that a number of new cooperatives were not integrated into the accounting and reporting system during the first year of association with CLP. This also applies to the number of cooperatives given in column (5) of Table 1. CLP is not a central organisation which holds all information and keeps records of the past. Associated cooperatives are encouraged to adjust to the 'mould' of reporting, but it takes several years before they learn the new routine. This is why employment data reported by various observers differ slightly, and also why data published by CLP do not always refer to the same base, i.e. either of all associated cooperatives, or of the industrial ones only.

2. The association of existing enterprises makes it impossible to compare employment creation exactly from year to year: the base expands continuously. Several observers have disregarded this phenomenon and have only reported the rapid expansion in aggregate employment.

3. Censo Industrial de España (1978) puts industrial employment at 111,063 in 1978 as compared to 110,300 given in IKEI (1979: Table 1, Cuadro 15).

4. For population and employment statistics see the sources mentioned for Table 1; Luis C-Nuñez (1977) and Servicio de Estudios (1978). CLP (1976a, 1977) are good sources of information on labour in the Basque Provinces. Unemployment in Spain rose from 434,000 in 1974 to about 800,000 in 1977. OECD (1978), IKEI (1979: Cuadro 17).

5. The discussion on absenteeism is based on an internal study made by Ularco's personnel department.

6. During one of our meetings with a senior manager in Ulgor, he apologised for a ten-minute absence in which he voted on a strike for a Basque political cause.

7. For this section use has been made of articles published in *Trabajo y Union* (various years), of statutes and bylaws of the institutions analysed, and of planning documents.

8. The design of this diagram owes much to a 'private tutorial session' kindly given to us by Sr Javier Retegui, Director of the League for Education and Culture.

9. During 1979 the University of the Basque Country at Bilbao took over as accrediting university.

10. Continual de-capitalisation takes place in Alecoop since the accumulated accounts of students are transferred to the cooperative in which they go to work when they leave the polytechnic. For this reason, the rules of allocation of profits have been modified: two-thirds are collectivised and only one-third is entered into individual accounts.

11. Interviews with staff of Alecoop (Spring 1979).

12. The lion's share is contributed by Ulgor. The quota for each cooperative enterprise depends on the size of the cooperative in terms of employment.

13. Information on the activities of the League for Education and Culture may be found in Liga de Educacion y Cultura (1976a and 1976b).

14. The League plays a brokerage role, submitting plans to the General Assembly for the allocation of funds. In 1978-79, for example, 52 per cent was allocated to general primary and lower secondary education, eight per cent to general higher secondary education, and

the remaining 40 per cent to the various levels of technical education, including the polytechnic.

15.   Recent initatives of the League for Education and Culture include a centre for the study of languages (since 1973) and an Open University at Vergara (started in 1976). The language laboratory offers courses in French, English and German, and has become particularly important since it also teaches courses in Euskara, an alien language to about 40 per cent of the population of Mondragon. The laboratory is located in the hostel but in due course will have its own premises. The Open University (La Universidad a Distancia UNED) at Vergara, ten kilometers from Mondragon, got off to a quick start with ten staff and 1100 students, expanding to 15 staff and 1500 students in 1978. The significance that is attached to the introduction of Euskara is indicated in 'Previsiones de Evolucion' (1975).

16.   Liga de Educacion y Cultura (1976b) elaborates on the long-term goals of a comprehensive educational programme for the district in which Mondragon is located. The need is emphasised for the involvement of the entire community and for education to become an integral part of regional activities, for which only minor subsidies are required from central government.

17.   For information on education in the Basque Provinces see Servicio de Estudios (1976: Tomo 2, 1-206). Pre-school level (nursery school) is for the age group 3-6 years; General Basic Education (EGB) applies to all children from six to 14 years. A student may then continue with general education and prepare for university (three-year study), or enter the technical stream, which also lasts three years. Cross-linkages permit a shift from one stream to the other. More facts on education in Guipúzcoa may be found in Servicio de Estudios (1977: 75-79).

18.   This problem is analysed in Liga de Educacion (1976a).

19.   This section is based on internal reports produced by the Personnel Departments of Ularco and the CLP. Organisational matters are studied continuously, and this is obviously an area in which much research still needs to be done.

20.   It is regrettable that an input-output table for the province of Guipúzcoa has not been constructed. Such a table is a necessary instrument for any evaluation of the impact of the Mondragon group on the provincial economy.

21.   In-depth interviews were held by Eduardo Kotliroff and Irene Benavente in the preparations for an audio-visual on the Mondragon cooperatives, produced by the Institute of Social Studies (The Hague, 1980).

22.   *Trabajo y Union* (March 1980; No. 226).

IV

THE PLANNING OF FINANCE

INTRODUCTION

To find financial resources for the formation of capital is a fundamental problem for any company, but producer cooperatives have their own peculiar problems to cope with. Firstly, cooperatives rarely have sufficient assets of their own to present as collateral, so that commercial banks are not eager to provide the short, medium or long-term credits which are indispensable for the smooth operation, let alone development, of factories. Furthermore, legal restrictions often make it difficult for cooperatives to obtain credits; for instance, access to a stock exchange is seldom possible. And finally, cooperatives have always been hesitant to apply for extensive credit, fearing that their independence might be put in jeopardy. In Draheim's opinion, therefore, the acquisition of finance is the greatest problem that producer cooperatives have to face, being likely to impede their development and compelling them to remain small and medium-sized enterprises, mostly in labour-intensive branches of industry (SWOV 1979: 25-116; van Dooren 1978: 129-53).

The mobilisation of financial resources also meets a major problem at the theoretical level. Vanek has argued, and this is a cornerstone of his theory on the economics of labour-managed economies, that labour-managed enterprises should preferably be funded entirely by external financing: if such enterprises are dependent on self-financing through generating their own financial resources, major inefficiencies will be unavoidable in the development of a labour-managed sector of the economy. One of Vanek's postulates for the design of such an economy is the existence of a 'perfectly competitive loanable-funds market' (Vanek 1975: 33-36).

A fundamental difficulty is thus inherent in the structure of producer cooperatives that function in a mixed economy. When labour is in full control of the work organisation, not only will it most likely encounter a bottleneck in the field of financial resources, but on theoretical grounds it will not be desirable for it to solve this problem through extensive self-financing.

Notes to this chapter may be found on p. 95.

CREDIT ORGANISATIONS

Cooperative history, on the other hand, shows that a substantial flow of financial resources has been mobilised through credit and savings cooperatives and credit unions. On a worldwide scale, there are more than one hundred million members of such credit organisations; the credit cooperatives take second place, after the consumers' cooperatives, in ranking according to size of membership of the international cooperative movement. Geographically, they are widespread, e.g. 22 million members associated with 20,000 unions in the USA and some 43 million members of credit organisations in India.[1]

These organisations have mostly been oriented towards rural areas and in particular to small farmers. They originated in the 19th century when Herman Schultze Delitz and Friedrich Wilhelm Raiffeisen were the driving forces behind a highly successful movement of credit cooperatives in Germany (Bol 1978: 9-25). Schultze's dedicated work had a huge impact, as can be seen from the fact that in 1890 1,043 cooperatives were united in one national association with the specific aim of furthering 'the interests of the lower classes' who, in times of need, were the victims of usurious practices. The first credit cooperative along lines that Raiffeisen had designed was established in 1864; it grew rapidly and in 1898 'Raiffeisen-credit' organisations comprised about 300 member cooperatives.

Credit and savings cooperatives generally have performed more than one function. Savings cooperatives frequently organise educational programmes for their members; credit cooperatives become involved in the purchasing of raw materials, help with marketing problems, and assist with the solving of production problems.

The Mondragon experience has been highly innovative with respect to the allocation of financial resources, in that it has linked a credit cooperative, Caja Laboral Popular (CLP), with producer cooperatives. This is a new phenomenon in cooperative history which formerly has witnessed only the isolated development of consumers' organisations, credit cooperatives, and producer cooperatives. The linkage is meant to provide producer cooperatives with the financial means for their credit requirements; at the same time, the old cooperative principle of self-financing continues to be of critical importance. Earlier, in studying the general lines of development of the Mondragon cooperatives and their legal structure, we have seen that this linkage, as well as the legal Contract of Association between CLP and the associated cooperatives, is a key feature of the history of the Mondragon group.[2]

A second novel feature is that CLP has assumed the planning of aggregate financial resources. This is a major explanatory variable in the analysis of the Mondragon cooperatives, implying a strong degree of planning 'from above'.

A CREDIT COOPERATIVE

CLP was constituted in 1959 as a credit cooperative, specifically to provide financial, technical and social assistance to those cooperatives that associated with it, and to individual cooperators.[3] This objective, and the need to achieve economic viability, required official permission to open accounts of various kinds on behalf of associated cooperatives and of individual cooperators, and to open savings accounts for the public.

The highest authority in CLP is vested in a General Assembly that meets annually and which may also be convened for special sessions. Much thought went into designing a system of control and accountability which would discourage oligarchic tendencies, so common in financial institutions. Membership of the General Assembly may be on one of three grounds: employment by CLP; association with CLP as a cooperative;[4] or individual membership of an associated cooperative, in which case certain conditions have to be met.[5] The intention is to achieve a broad-based General Assembly that is not easily dominated by a particular constituency; it also gives the right of 'self-management' to staff of the bank and its branch offices. As is the case with producer cooperatives, individual cooperators may exercise their rights only when the full entry fee has been paid.[6] Cooperative factories, through their representatives, can occupy their seats after signing a Contract of Association with CLP. The cooperatives are expected to use the financial facilities of CLP, to keep business information well protected, and to abstain from harmful competitive action. They also make frequent reports to CLP to enable it to fulfil its monitoring role.

Members of CLP's Supervisory Board are elected by the various constituencies of the General Assembly with a four-year mandate. Among the representatives of associated cooperatives, this ensures a system of rotation and of interlocking control which guarantees some degree of authority by producer cooperatives over the bank. On the other hand, the rotating membership prevents any monopolisation. The formal organisation further consists of a Supervisory Board, two Advisory Councils (social and management), a Watchdog Committee, and the Management.

The organisation of Caja Laboral Popular closely follows the structures of the producer cooperatives, but with modifications to suit its special functions. CLP is thus a 'second degree' cooperative in that cooperatives are among its membership.

The fact that cooperators working with CLP are widely dispersed, over almost a hundred locations, creates some problems. In the branch offices an attempt has been made to remedy this fragmentation by establishing regional social and advisory councils and also by placing greater emphasis on education, exchange and conferences. Also, the classification of jobs at CLP headquarters is not the usual pyramidal one: a fairly large number of moderately skilled people work together with many who are highly skilled, in running the bank and providing the expertise of the Management Services Division.

CLP's General Assembly has the full right of control and of initiative, as has been seen frequently during the last few years when the issue of political strikes in solidarity with Basque causes has repeatedly demanded speedy response and action. In its public relations CLP makes a point of stressing how it serves the Basque cause. Courses on Basque culture and language figure prominently in CLP-sponsored educational programmes, which also give an important place to study of the political economy of the expanding industrial cooperatives in the Basque provinces.

During the 1960s, CLP had three departments: economics, management services, and social security. The social security activities, however, became so manifold and diverse that Lagun-Aro, the social security cooperative, moved in 1977 to a building close to the new CLP headquarters. It is anticipated that, in a few years from now, the Management Services Division will also have expanded to such an extent that it will be more efficient to let it become an independent organisation.

As Table 1 shows, employment in CLP's headquarters and branches was expected to reach 1,000 plus by the end of 1980. With regard to the distribution of jobs, there are two key managerial positions, both occupied by founder cooperators of Ulgor. The Management Services Division includes a great variety of experts, mostly in the economic department which monitors all credit operations: 20 per cent in CLP headquarters in Mondragon, and 57 per cent in the branch offices, which numbered 93 at the end of 1979. Finally, there are also the service and technical jobs.

Table 1. *Employment in Caja Laboral Popular (1960-80)*

1960	2
1965	58
1970	240
1971	284
1972	328
1973	414
1974	496
1975	587
1976	641
1977	745
1978	809
1979	892
1980*	1032

* Projected employment.

CLP has expanded by opening new offices first in its own province of

Guipúzcoa, then by moving into the province of Vizcaya, and most recently by penetrating the financial system of the provinces of Alava and Navarra. Numbers of branch offices by geographical dispersion for selected years from 1966 onwards are shown in Table 2; the indications are that the end of CLP's rapid expansion is not yet in sight. As long as it continues to plan new offices, its deposits may be expected to increase rapidly. At present the expansion rate is eight to nine offices per year. Of all branch offices of commercial banks and savings banks in Guipúzcoa, CLP accounts for nine per cent (*Economia Guipuzcoana* 1977: 56). All CLP branch offices are linked to the main office in Mondragon by way of a computerised system which records all financial activities and allows the main office to operate on an equal footing with other banking institutions.

Table 2. *Geographical distribution of branch offices of CLP*

	Guizpúzcoa	Vizcaya	Alava	Navarra	Total
1966	18	8	1	1	28
1968	26	12	1	2	41
1973	35	18	5	5	63
1978	41	28	8	7	84
1979*	43	31	10	9	93

* There are also four mobile offices.

Credit Cooperative vs. Savings and Commercial Banks

The creation of CLP as a credit cooperative reflected a pragmatic solution which, given the constraints of the existing legal system, best suited the needs of the cooperators in the late 1950s. Bank operations are usually heavily controlled by the central monetary authorities. The allocation of assets to different kinds of investments − cash, shares, bonds, fixed assets, debtors, etc. − as well as the structure of liabilities − own resources, creditors, savings received, depositors − is restricted by the State Bank through regulations and bank laws. A credit cooperative, for instance, is not permitted to issue bonds and other negotiable securities or to open special category accounts, e.g. for housing corporations. Such activities may be undertaken by savings banks and industrial banks, however, which are thus in a more advantageous position. Any financial institution needs to obtain official approval before being able to open a branch office and all three categories can thus be stimulated or hampered by the State Bank in their development.

The main purpose of a credit cooperative is to allow credit to its members; it is not permitted, therefore, to grant credits to other parties. This is an important aspect of the relationship between CLP and its associated cooperative enterprises. If producer cooperatives do not invest sufficiently, CLP will have no other outlet for its financial resources than officially-approved bonds, which yield lower interest rates than medium or long-term financial credits to enterprises. CLP therefore has a strong interest in expansion of the aggregate sales of associated cooperatives; otherwise it will not earn sufficient income to enable it to meet its obligations towards those who have invested their savings with it.

The significance of the legal position is also illustrated by the fact that a credit cooperative is not allowed to be an official guarantor for contracts which enterprises or other organisations enter into with public institutions. Financial transactions related to such contracts thus have to be channelled through the commercial banks. Neither is a credit cooperative allowed to keep social security funds. Given the numerous cooperators who participate in the cooperative social security system, huge sums are thus invested elsewhere which could equally well be recycled in the cooperative system, provided that sufficient measures were taken to protect their safe management.

The development of CLP has been pragmatic because cooperative views regarding the role of capital and its control have necessarily had to follow existing cooperative law. This situation has changed considerably in recent years, however. National banking authorities have recognised that savings banks play an important role in mobilising financial resources, and CLP's management has done its utmost to benefit from the improved position which savings banks have thus obtained among financial institutions in Spain as a whole, but particularly in the Basque Provinces. Through continuous bargaining with the central financial authorities, CLP also has improved its position, in the sense of obtaining greater latitude in the attraction and allocation of resources.

One result of these developments is a need for legal expertise that will enable CLP to keep abreast with current issues, to anticipate future trends, and to ensure a creative response to new situations and new challenges which the cooperative movement has to solve. It is beyond the scope of this study to investigate the great diversity of legal problems in further detail. It needs to be emphasised, however, that cooperative law, which is of such importance in drafting statutes and regulations for the enterprises, is of even greater importance for a credit cooperative, all of whose financial operations are closely watched by the State Bank.[7]

INCOMES AND EXPENDITURES

In Table 3 we present data on CLP revenues and expenditures from 1968 until 1979, as well as a breakdown into categories for 1972, 1977 and 1979. Revenues increased from 103 million pesetas in 1968 to 5,038 million in 1979. Four sources of income accounted for at least 80 per cent of revenues: yields of investments in public and authorised private bonds; interest on deposits with other banks; interest on investment financing by the associated cooperatives;

Table 3. *Revenues and expenditures of CLP* (million pesetas)*

	Revenues**	A	B	C	D	E
1968	103					
1969	172					
1970	268					
1971	327					
1972	485	27	13	20	21	19 (1)
1973	616					
1974	954					
1975	1272					
1976	1644					
1977	2414	18	13	26	28	15 (4)
1978	3830					
1979	5038	17	13	28	31	11 (3)

	Expenditures***	1	2	3	4	5	Surplus****	Surplus/ Gross Revenue
1968	75						28	.27
1969	112						60	.35
1970	173						95	.35
1971	212						115	.35
1972	253	26	44	7	5	18	232	.48
1973	352						264	.43
1974	573						381	.40
1975	862						410	.32
1976	1187						457	.28
1977	1829	25	50	4	4	17	585	.24
1978	3023						808	.21
1979	3903	22	56	3	4	15	1135	.22

*   Pesetas of current value are applied in this chapter since this information gives better insight into bank operations; 70 pesetas = 1US$.

**   A: Authorised bonds
      B: Interest received from other banks
      C: Interest on investments
      D: Discounting of bills
      E: Other sources of income; income earned by advice given is shown in brackets.

*** 1: Personnel
      2: Interest on Savings Accounts
      3: Interest on Own Resources (6%)
      4: Amortisation
      5: Other expenditures

**** Surplus during earlier years: 1964 two million, 1965 four million, 1966 seven million, 1967 eighteen million pesetas.

and the discounting of bills for the provision of short-term credit to associated cooperatives.

In 1972, income from the first two sources, mostly investments that need to be made under supervision of the State Bank in Madrid, accounted for 40 per cent, in 1977 and 1979 for 31 and 30 per cent of revenue. Income from 'own' sources, i.e. the industrial cooperatives, rose sharply from 41 per cent in 1972 to 59 per cent in 1979. This was increased by one to three per cent of revenue earned by the Management Services Division, which charges normal fees for advice given to CLP members.

Expenditures from 1968 to 1979 are reported in Table 3, and are broken down into main categories for 1972, 1977 and 1979. Expenditures rose from 75 million pesetas in 1968 to 3,903 million in 1979, leaving a positive margin during all the years investigated; the lowest yield as percentage of gross revenue, namely 21 per cent, occurred in 1978 and the highest, i.e. 48 per cent, in 1972. Salaries and related costs account for about one-quarter of total costs; total interest payments amounted to 51 per cent of total expenditures in 1972, 54 per cent in 1977, and 59 per cent in 1979; amortisation, public relations, travel costs, office equipment etc. account for the remainder.

Amounts left for surplus have largely been used to strengthen CLP's financial structure. until 1979 50 to 55 per cent of annual surplus was usually allocated to funds for reserves and for financial risks; about 10 per cent to social projects, including education, research, culture and health; the remaining 35 to 40 per cent was profit to be shared among the different categories of cooperative members of CLP's Assembly. In 1979 a new law obliged CLP to allocate 10 per cent of its surplus to social projects, and 35 per cent to reserves, thus leaving a margin of 55 per cent for distribution among the members of the General Assembly. This body, however, decided to add about 70 per cent to CLP's reserves, thus leaving a margin of only 20 per cent for distribution to the capital accounts of its members.

All this shows that CLP is greatly dependent on its associated cooperatives for earning sufficient revenue to enable it to meet all its expenditures. In all years, performance has created a surplus with respect to gross revenue which exceeds 20 per cent. These annual yields have been used largely to strengthen the structure of the capital account by enlarging CLP's reserve funds.

LIABILITIES AND ASSETS

An overall view of CLP liabilities and assets is given in Table 4, which reproduces the main data of the balance sheet as at 31st December 1979. Own funds, consisting of individually-held accounts, collective reserves and surplus accumulated, amount to 10.8 per cent of total resources of just over 46,110 million pesetas. Accounts include current accounts (about 10 per cent), savings accounts and term deposits (each of about 45 per cent). Various other sources, including banks and other credit institutions account for the remaining liabilities. Finally, total resources are enlarged by the fact that the cooperative enterprises put a percentage of their own resources at the disposal of CLP, thus strengthening its

Table 4. *Assets and liabilities of CLP (31.12.1979) (million pesetas)*

Cash and bank	5,520	Own funds	4,981
Authorised investments	9,399	Banks	22
Discounted bills	12,864	Accounts	41,107
Investments	14,787	Other liabilities	6,115
Fixed assets	3,587		
Other assets	6,068		
Total	52,225		52,225
Producer cooperatives		Producer cooperatives	
(other assets)	17,201	(other liabilities)	17,201
	69,426		69,426

creditworthiness, and making 'a general total' of 69,426 million pesetas on the liability side.[8]

Assets in order of decreasing liquidity include cash (10.6 per cent); obligatory investments in state and authorised private bonds (18 per cent); commercial receivable bills (25 per cent); medium and long-term credits granted to associated cooperatives (28 per cent); fixed assets (7 per cent); and finally, a variety of smaller accounts, making-up the remaining 11.5 per cent. Again, the additional resources put at CLP's disposal by the cooperative enterprises are included, making a grand total of 69,426 million pesetas.

The composition of this balance sheet implies an important policy objective; namely, it provides a safeguard for credit accounts in that they are balanced by investments that supposedly can be liquefied within a reasonably short timespan.

To enable more detailed analysis of these items, Table 5 shows data on some important variables between 1960 and 1979. Capital and reserves stood at 22 million pesetas in 1965 when sales by the industrial cooperatives totalled 1,900 million pesetas; in 1979, own funds had increased to 4,981 million pesetas and aggregate sales were reported at 57,245 million pesetas. The increase achieved from one per cent of sales in 1965 to 8.7 per cent in 1979 indicates that CLP's financial position with respect to the associated cooperative enterprises has become much stronger. The distribution of ownership — mentioned in Table 5 column 2 — between individual and collective claims has changed considerably during the last ten years. In 1965, 95 per cent of CLP's own funds were owned by the various categories of its General Assembly; by 1979 this had fallen to 38 per cent. Over a period of about 20 years CLP has gradually re-allocated its surplus in such a way that by 1979 60 per cent of its resources had been 'socialised'; under no circumstances, with the exception of the liquidation of the entire cooperative movement, can these funds be monetised. Such a policy is essential to ensure that, when many of the present cooperators reach retiring age, the percentage of individualised capital will have dwindled to such an extent that temporary de-capitalisation will be compensated by the entry fees of new cooperators.

Table 5. *The resources of Caja Laboral Popular (1960-79)*

	Own funds (capital and reserves) (million pesetas) (1)	Individual capital accounts as per- tage of own funds (2)	Own funds as per- tage of total resources (3)
1960	.315	–	–
1965	22	95	5.0
1966	61	93	8.0
1967	73	92	6.2
1968	151	91	9.0
1969	237	90	8.6
1970	312	86	8.3
1971	416	83	7.8
1972	.572	78	7.9
1973	778	67	8.1
1974	1069	61	8.2
1975	1520	58	8.9
1976	1982	53	8.8
1977	2613	53	9.1
1978	3377	52	9.0
1979	4981	38	10.8

	Accounts (current, savings, deposits)* (4)	Total CLP resources** (5)	Surplus/Accounts (6)
1960	5	–	–
1965	374	435	.011
1966	660	766	.011
1967	1016	1181	.019
1968	1450	1684	.019
1969	2359	2743	.025
1970	3204	3745	.030
1971	4669	5328	.025
1972	6355	7286	.037
1973	8390	9569	.031
1974	11351	12991	.034
1975	14699	17001	.028
1976	19351	22490	.024
1977	24784	28831	.024
1978	32233	37500	.025
1979	41100	46110	.028

* About 300,000 at December 1979.
** Includes own funds, accounts, banks and other institutions.

The position of own funds with respect to total resources is given in column 3 of Table 5. With the exception of 1965 and 1967, own funds reached satisfactory levels, ensuring that an official guideline of maintaining eight per cent as own resources could be implemented.

Data on resources mobilised through the rapid growth of account holders are given in column 4. In 1965 CLP reported 374 million pesetas received on 14,051 accounts held in 21 offices. Since then, growth has been most impressive, although early growth percentages could not be maintained. Growth rates of current, savings and deposit accounts fell in nominal terms to an average of 30 per cent between 1976 and 1979, compared to 58 per cent over the previous decade. Given the fact that, from 1976 onwards, accounts still increased annually by 15 per cent, the increments indicate the dynamics of CLP. The pattern of steady growth of resources is, of course, a force that leads to a well-planned design of investments being undertaken each year.

Total financial resources, accounts and own funds, are also given in Table 5, the last column of which provides information on CLP's profitability. Surplus as a share of total resources rose gradually to three per cent from 1970 to 1975; since then it has dropped somewhat but is still at an acceptable level.

Table 6. *Resources of CLP and aggregate sales of associated producer cooperatives (million pesetas) (1965-79)*

	CLP Resources	Sales of associated cooperatives *	%
1965	435	1900	(23)
1966	766	2900	(26)
1967	1181	3350	(35)
1968	1684	4000	(42)
1969	2743	6300	(44)
1970	3745	7100	(53)
1971	5328	8100	(66)
1972	7286	10700	(68)
1973	9569	13200	(72)
1974	12991	17700	(73)
1975	17001	19700	(86)
1976	22490	24800	(91)
1977	28831	34100	(85)
1978	37500	43750	(86)
1979	46110	57245	(81)

* The figures within parentheses give CLP resources as a percentage of aggregate sales.

Sources: See Table 5 supra, and Chapter V, Table 1. Sales of agricultural cooperatives, a consumer cooperative and two service cooperatives are included.

We have now assembled some important pieces towards completing the 'Mondragon puzzle': total resources at the disposal of CLP are linked to the total short, medium and long-term credit needs of the cooperatives. As a percentage of total sales (see Table 6), CLP resources increased from 23 per cent in 1965 to over 90 per cent in 1976, since when a slight fall has been observed. Shortage of capital had earlier been a bottleneck and CLP needed to exercise great care in monitoring the cooperatives to ensure that the most profitable investments would be met first. In recent years CLP has given high priority to promoting new cooperatives and to transforming existing ones because its resources with respect to the level of economic activity of industrial cooperatives are relatively abundant. The growing sales in themselves show the increased need for working capital, to be financed partly by CLP; and also the medium and long-term requirements for investment financing in order to boost aggregate sales.

The objective is to obtain equilibrium between aggregate cooperative sales and CLP's financial resources.

Self-financing

A second major policy issue relates to the level of own funds; i.e. the role which 'self-financing' plays in the cooperative movement. Annual increments of own funds can be obtained in three ways:

(a) Through allocation of pure surplus to own funds. We have seen already that, except for the Fund for Social Projects, the entire surplus is ploughed back; dependent on specific rules the surplus is allocated either to individually-held accounts or to reserve funds.

(b) Through re-valuation of fixed assets, following which the own funds can also be re-valued, e.g. to account for inflation.

(c) Through payment of entry fees by new members of CLP's General Assembly. Considerable expansion of self-financing seems feasible by encouraging account-holders to become associate members of CLP on payment of a minimal entry fee. For instance, if 100,000 account-holders were to become associate cooperators, each paying 10,000 pesetas as capital, this would secure another 1,000 million pesetas of own resources. The advantage to such account-holders would be the higher yield that their accounts would command due to surplus-sharing schemes.

Given the fact that revaluation and payment of new entry fees can play only a modest role in 'up-grading' own funds, the implication of the eight per cent guideline is that the annual surplus *needs* to reach a specific level once total resources for a given year have been projected. If, for example, 25 per cent of pure surplus needs to be set aside for obligatory reserves, another 20 per cent against financial risks, 10 per cent for social projects, and it is desirable that the 'yield' on earnings and interest payments on own capital should amount to 15 per cent, then, given an hypothetical sum of earnings and interest payments of 500 and 75 million pesetas respectively, the following calculation can be made (in which a revaluation of own resources of 100 million pesetas is also considered):

$$.25X + .20X + .10X + 100 + .15(500 + 75) = X$$

in which X is the required level of surplus.

The annual surplus in this imaginary year needs to reach 414 million pesetas, of which

Yield to capital income and earnings (15 per cent)	86.25
Revaluation (100)	100.00
Social projects (10 per cent)	41.00
Obligatory reserve fund (25 per cent)	103.50
Reserve for insolvency (20 per cent)	83.00
	413.75 million pesetas

In our illustration a specific addition has been made to the item 'revaluation' in order to strengthen the own funds without adding to future claims for further income, as would have been the case if the entire amount had been allocated as yield to capital and earnings. The outcome of the calculation needs to be compared with the forecast of eight per cent required for self-financing. If this target is not achieved, further additions to resources have to be made.

If in a given year, therefore, the surplus, although positive, is not sufficient to boost the own resources to the eight per cent level, then additional income will need to be created, for instance, by the profitable selling of some assets; if pure surplus exceeds the target, then a transfer can be made to reserve on special account.

A further implication concerns the balance between current accounts, savings accounts, and term deposits. If, as has been the case in recent years, the trend is towards attracting long-term deposits, then the cash position can be somewhat reduced, permitting more funds to be used for investments; on the other hand, payment of higher interest on the accounts will diminish the surplus.

It should now be clear why CLP is equally concerned about a possible *lack* of resources as about an *abundance* of financial means. The first case will prevent it from providing credit to the industrial cooperatives; the second case will prevent it from creating sufficient income to keep its 'self-financing' resources at a sufficiently high level to meet the eight per cent rule.

Assets

We have seen that a credit cooperative, just as any other financial institution, is bound by strict regulations with respect to the investment of financial means. This is reflected in the data given in Table 7, showing CLP assets from 1965 onwards. The analysis is quite straightforward, following the earlier discussion of the structure of CLP's 1979 balance sheet. Cash, including deposits with other banks and investments in authorised public and private bonds (Columns 1 and 2), over the years has represented an average 33 per cent of invested resources: the yield on these two categories is obviously low, since cash commands little income. It can be seen that, starting in 1971, CLP was confronted rather suddenly with a relative abundance of resources: cash even reached 19 per cent in 1974. From then on, a policy of actively promoting new cooperatives has been successful, and the cash percentage has been reduced to approximately 12 per cent, still well in excess of the minimum percentage of 5.5 that needs to be kept under any circumstances.

Table 7. *Assets of CLP (million pesetas) (1968-79)**

	Cash		Bonds		Bills discounted		Medium & long-term credits		Fixed assets	
	(1)	(%)	(2)	(%)	(3)	(%)	(4)	(%)	(5)	(%)
1968	191	(11)	239	(14)	849	(50)	203	(12)	158	(9)
1969	386	(14)	339	(12)	1290	(47)	301	(11)	239	(9)
1970	465	(12)	615	(16)	1676	(45)	371	(10)	310	(8)
1971	967	(18)	1046	(20)	1714	(32)	1038	(19)	372	(7)
1972	1277	(18)	1557	(21)	2201	(30)	1416	(19)	524	(7)
1973	1697	(18)	2476	(26)	2653	(28)	1751	(18)	671	(7)
1974	2468	(19)	2465	(19)	4097	(32)	2548	(20)	1067	(8)
1975	2694	(16)	3385	(20)	4926	(29)	4078	(24)	1332	(8)
1976	2791	(12)	4811	(21)	6881	(30)	5814	(26)	1598	(7)
1977	3567	(12)	5997	(21)	8046	(28)	8093	(28)	2089	(7)
1978	4753	(13)	7695	(21)	10029	(27)	10896	(29)	2554	(7)
1979	5520	(12)	9399	(20)	12864	(28)	14787	(32)	3587	(8)

* The percentages indicate the position with respect to total CLP resources. (Table 5, column 5).

Source: CLP *Annual Reports* 1968 to 1979.

Cash in hand is kept constantly at a level that is double that required by the Central Bank authorities. This reflects CLP's policy of always having sufficient means at its disposal to meet the needs of the associated cooperatives. It also reflects the fact that savings accounts are largely of very short maturity and can be withdrawn at short notice.

The second column of Table 7 shows the obligatory investments that have to be made in bonds and approved shares. In recent years these have represented about 20 per cent of total CLP assets.

The next two columns give information on CLP's principal earning assets: commercial bills for short-term credits to producer cooperatives, and medium and long-term credits to finance their investment plans. These two kinds of assets together consistently surpass 50 per cent, reaching 60 per cent in 1979. The figures for discounted bills are linked directly to aggregate sales of the producer cooperatives; CLP counts on handling 80 to 85 per cent of aggregate sales, and on maintaining 20 to 25 per cent of that figure at any moment as discounted bills in order to meet cooperative needs for circulating capital. Since 1971 discounting of bills has reached stability at between 20 and 30 per cent, whereas CLP's active promotion policies have caused increased demand for medium and long-term credits (column 4) by the associated cooperatives. Management of the aggregate resources requires great skill: none of the cooperatives can be compelled to expand or to modernise and, in so doing, to demand credit assistance from CLP.

Fixed assets (column 5) account for seven to eight per cent, which is not surprising in view of the eight per cent obligation towards self-financing on the credit side of the balance sheet.

The following benchmarks have been set by CLP as targets for a well-balanced asset structure: cash in hand 15 per cent; obligatory investment 20 per cent; bills receivable 25 per cent; medium and long-term credits 27 per cent, i.e. 12 per cent to industrial, four per cent to housing, and two per cent to the remaining cooperatives, and nine per cent to individual cooperators; and finally, seven per cent in fixed assets and three per cent in various other smaller accounts.

CLP assets policy can be summarised as follows. A major target is to obtain additional earnings for the Mondragon group: earnings which otherwise would be made by commercial banks. CLP aims at reinforcing the financial situation in the Basque Provinces by purchasing bonds that finance projects on home ground, or which are related to the own branch of economic activity. CLP views financial resources as an instrument of transformation, in the promotion and creation of cooperative enterprises. Its policies are bound by legal requirements, self-imposed additional margins, the financial needs of associated cooperatives, and by the need to obtain adequate financial returns.

CLP has been successful in its banking operations and in its provision of credits to associated producer cooperatives. It has thus provided a link between flows of credits and needs for capital formation. Complex planning is involved in the achievement of adequate yields and in meeting needs of associated cooperatives, while complying with legal conditions and maintaining a high degree of self-financing.

PLANNING OF INVESTMENTS

The linkage of a credit cooperative with associated cooperatives is a new phenomenon in cooperative history. Actually the provision of financial resources for the credit requirements of these cooperatives is a principal objective of CLP. CLP aims also at maintaining credit lines to any cooperative in time of need. This is only possible if expert knowledge is available; otherwise the interests of the account-holders would be in jeopardy. CLP's Management Services Division serves to promote the creation of new cooperatives when, as was the case during the 1970s, CLP has abundant financial resources at its disposal. Otherwise it would be compelled to invest beyond the minimum requirements in state bonds and approved shares. At the end of 1978, CLP's Management Services Division employed more than one hundred experts, including engineers, economists, lawyers, urban planners, etc. Although the creation of this division initially added to costs, the intention is for it to become self-supporting and to develop into an independent organisation. Management services are organised into three main activities: promotion, assistance, and engineering. Promotion of new cooperatives is oriented towards industry, agriculture, housing, education and research. Assistance of existing associated cooperatives includes exports, administration and accountancy, management, staffing and commerce. Finally, engineering is focussed on urbanisation, the design of industrial construction, and production.

Aspects of Planning

CLP documents give considerable attention to long-term objectives and values which are strongly oriented towards the wider community. For instance, CLP's ultimate aim is centered on the development of institutions which enable community progress. There is awareness that higher levels of material welfare may discourage solidarity between and even within cooperatives. CLP can stimulate solidarity in different ways: through incomes policies that guarantee the meeting of basic human needs; through concern for the community by developing welfare programmes; through prevention of discrimination between cooperators and others in the community.

Conditions have changed enormously during the past 20 years. In 1960 social conditions were characterised by poverty following the Second World War. At work, social relations were characterised by hierarchical organisational patterns and by employer paternalism. The socio-political conditions allowed almost no scope for the development of new social forces; it was only possible to try to reform the traditional mentality and to change work relations in companies which had merely elementary industrial knowhow. The Mondragon cooperative movement was thus started on an inadequate basis of worker consciousness. Nowadays there is greater scope for reform, and new objectives have therefore been formulated:

- CLP stands irrevocably for respect for human liberty, to which end it will dedicate all its economic and human resources through enterprise reform, to ensure democracy and freedom; through education for all without discrimination; through information to strengthen community consciousness; through health, so that its policies can be pursued in socially optimal fashion; and through authority, so that the CLP can be an instrument used by society in its democratic organisation.
- CLP's area of social and economic development is restricted to the Basque country: a region defined by tradition, language, culture, and economic cohesion.
- CLP will assist in the democratisation of society, whenever circumstances warrant it.
- CLP will promote freedom of expression, freedom of opinion, the achievement of democratic freedom and of a just income distribution.
- CLP will dedicate its efforts to strengthening the economy of the country which it

serves, with the firm purpose of improving the quality of life of its citizens; to this end
it will stimulate the enterprises' collective economy through expansion and technological
perfection, a balanced sectoral distribution of resources and of industrial locations,
which will help to redress the ecological and high-density imbalance caused by the
shortage of land (CLP 1975).

Increased financial resources caused by the rapid growth of deposit accounts has
created an entirely new situation for CLP, which needs to stimulate the credit
requirements of cooperatives with whom it is linked through Contracts of
Association. But it is now also able to diversify into a wider range of investments, thus reducing sensitivity to business cycles in durable consumer goods
and engineering, i.e. the principal products of the cooperative factories.

The construction of apartment buildings and the financing of their purchase
well illustrates this new trend. In the first place, it entails production in a new
branch of activity; secondly, it is closely linked to the demand for consumer
durables; and lastly, it provides scope for the granting of credits to members of
housing cooperatives who can thus finance the purchase of apartments. Housing
schemes, if carefully planned, can be accelerated in times of recession, thereby
contributing to CLP's investment programme at times when industrial activities
are scaling-down.

The need for increased investments and the wish to diversify will cause demands to intensify for the professionalisation of CLP's management services
group. Its involvement in urban planning, and in education and health, also implies strong political involvement since the cooperative group will have a considerable impact on the socio-economic structure of part of the province of
Guipúzcoa.

From the beginning, Mondragon's economic activities have centered on industry,
and strategies in that direction are of the greatest relevance to the group. Favourable markets, in which almost any good product could be sold in large quantities, are a thing of the past. Priority has therefore been given to the development of coherent groups of cooperatives. In addition to the Ularco group, which
has played an important role in the past, geographical groups of cooperatives
must be formed which will enable scale economies to be achieved but without
creating huge conglomerates. This also poses new responsibilities since industrialisation has reached a point of saturation in terms of space and ecological dam-
age.

With regard to new product lines, several constraints influence their selection;
for instance, the statutory rule that new cooperators must pay entry capital,
thus providing about 20 per cent of total investment per work place. This percentage has gradually been lowered since major investments need to be made in
new technologies and competitive machinery. By linking new investments to
entry payments a balance can be struck between the technical and labour aspects

of development. Another constraint is the size of the cooperatives. On the basis of past experience, it seems that the maximum workforce of a plant should be about 500 persons. Even if larger markets become available, technology should still be planned in such a manner that this practical size is not surpassed.

In coming years, the Mondragon group will also concentrate on industrial activities and will produce a relatively small range of products. Extractive industries and primary raw material transformation, as well as capital-intensive chemical industry, will not be entered into. An exception could be raw material industries in the primary sector, such as cattle farming, fisheries and agriculture, in which some chains might be developed, for instance in milk products and vegetables. The food industry in general, however, is organised in consortia which depend for their patents on the international market, and is therefore not suitable for a group of small to medium-sized cooperatives which desire to develop as independently as possible.

This applies also to several mass-produced items. In the past, particularly in the Ularco group, considerable successes have been scored with mass production, but the future marketing situation will be more difficult because of direct confrontation with multinationals. Problems are also likely to arise in mechanical engineering because domestic markets are saturated and the demand is for more advanced designs.

The industrial activities of the Mondragon group will continue to be based on three branches: household consumer durables and house construction, machine tools, and capital goods. Electronics, given its high incidence in these three branches, is a strong complementary branch. The development of an R&D centre which concentrates on such activities and coordinates marketing research, has therefore had first priority.

In this consideration of the long-run strategy of investment planning, issues have been raised that reach beyond the narrow objective of obtaining optimum yield on financial investment. The allocation of capital has a major impact on society at large, and considerable attention is therefore given to values and objectives which are influenced by capital investments. Another aspect of strategy is that of allocation of financial resources in the primary and tertiary sectors, including public goods such as education projects and health schemes. CLP's principal activities, however, continue to be to assist cooperatives and to promote new cooperatives, mostly in a few branches of the secondary sector.

CLP AND OTHER FINANCIAL INSTITUTIONS

CLP is an important financial institution in Guipúzcoa, accounting for 13 per cent of total deposits held by commercial and savings banks at the end of 1977.[9] It ranked second among the nine largest financial institutions in the province in 1976 in terms of growth of deposits, and in 1977 had become the fastest-growing of those institutions. Again in 1979, CLP had the highest growth rate of deposits among savings banks, having capitalised on the goodwill which savings banks generally have with small savers, to whom a 'savings bank is the natural place to go'.

The savings banks represent a curious amalgam of interest and intentions. In theory their chief aim is to finance small entrepreneurs and objectives which are deemed socially desirable. In practice, while this has to some extent been realised, the savings banks have become increasingly important as buyers of industrial bonds, so much so that there is evidence that the price of bonds is in some cases determined by the savings banks. Deposits in savings banks come mainly from the less well-off members of the rural community (Wright 1977: 110).

During the past 20 years savings banks have grown at a spectacular rate, to total six among the 15 largest financial institutions (Rumasa 1977: 97-108). Financial authorities have encouraged this trend, even though the commercial banking oligarchy may have resisted it, because it enabled huge amounts of additional savings to be tapped for the financing of investments during the long boom that started in the late 1950s.

In addition, important enterprises in key branches of industry have obtained direct access to additional finance because savings banks — and thus also CLP as a credit cooperative — are obliged to invest a large percentage of their funds in public and authorised private bonds. In practice, this means that savings are syphoned-off from rural areas to industrialised urban communities; that savings are not invested in the regions where they were collected; and that large-scale industry obtains additional resources although the original idea had been to stimulate small and medium entrepreneurs.

The result is the existence of privileged circuits, low rates of interest, and lack of long-term finance. Small and medium-sized enterprises, in particular, face difficulties in securing financial support for their investment plans. It has now been recommended that savings banks should preferably invest 50 per cent of obligatory bonds and 75 per cent of 'free' resources in their own province. This will imply that more financial resources will be invested in the Basque Provinces than in the past and that Vizcaya will lose in relation to the gains of Alava, Guipúzcoa, and Navarra.[10]

The extent to which the Basque Provinces have subsidised developments elsewhere in Spain is a politically sensitive issue, and little statistical information is available. CLP's Research Department cautiously posits that transfers in the public sector are partly compensated by a net inflow in the private sector, leaving a net outflow of about 18 per cent of gross capital formation in the Basque Provinces (CLP 1978: 11-24).

The mobilisation of savings has become an issue of highest priority in the Basque Provinces, where industries have lost their competitive position and prospects will worsen once a gradual breakdown of tariff structures with respect to the Common Market countries sets in. Velasco argues that financial institutions should undertake sound planning and should build a new infrastructure in the old industrial centres: communications, roadworks, education, and energy supplies (Velasco 1977: 417-56). CLP has accumulated sufficient experience to enable it to play a role in this respect. Fundamental aspects of the transformation of the provincial economy are now within reach of its activities.

CONCLUSIONS

CLP's economic performance as a credit cooperative has been a powerful one. It has been benefitted from the strength of savings banks among Spanish financial institutions, in that the legal position of credit cooperatives is closely linked to that of savings banks. Also, it has consistently used its annual profits to strengthen its financial structure; apart from the ten per cent allocation to social projects, the entire annual surplus has been added to its own funds.

There is no indication that CLP has come to a standstill in Guipúzcoa; on the contrary, as recently as 1979 its annual deposits increased by 27.5 per cent as compared to 14.5 per cent for all other savings banks in the province. The fact that CLP continues to open new branch offices in other Basque Provinces may be taken as an implication that this trend will gradually emerge there also. As is the case with credit cooperative organisations in several other countries, CLP has become a strong and viable financial institution.

CLP's objectives, however, are rather different to the usual criteria of high profitability and the provision of credit to its members. Its resources are used for the transformation of socio-economic structures. Such an abstract goal has always been part of CLP's long-term strategy, undoubtedly as a result of Arizmendi's influence. This goal has been spelled-out in rather specific objectives, relating to education, research and development, to the need for supporting 'production' of private and public goods, for the creation of employment, and for income policies. A fundamental issue is that of ownership of associated cooperatives. CLP itself has undergone a major change in this respect: individual ownership claims have been reduced over a period of about 15 years from 95 per cent to less than 40 per cent.

CLP's objectives entail a need for thorough planning: long-term plans are required to determine strategic issues, medium-term ones to operationalise these issues in concrete targets, and annual plans to guide the decisions with respect to financial allocations. In 1980 the future was more uncertain than it was in 1960 when opportunities for profitable investments were many. Spain's future membership of the European Economic Community, together with the increased competition of transnational companies, implies that CLP's Management Services Division will have to deal with far more complex tasks than has ever been the case previously.

NOTES

1. For information on cooperatives, see publications by the International Co-operative Alliance; in particular the *Review of International Co-operation*.
2. See Chapter II for details of the Contract of Association, statutes and bylaws.
3. The Law on Credit Cooperatives, revised in 1974 and in 1978, is the most important source which sets the framework for CLP. Other laws on banking, such as the 1954 Law on Agricultural Credit, and rulings by the Central Bank of Madrid are among further constraints that need to be taken into account.
4. Producer cooperatives send one delegate to the General Assembly for each 20 cooperators; consumers' cooperatives one delegate for each 200 members (CLP Statutes, 1979).
5. An important reason to join as an associate member of CLP is the opportunity to obtain credits after pledging the 'entry fee'. It is worth mentioning that a cooperator may temporarily — for a maximum period of four years — transfer part of the capital account. By that time replenishment should have taken place. If a cooperator fails to comply, the transfer — to CLP — becomes permanent; in other words, the amount will be transferred from an individual account to 'social property'.
6. In 1977 the following levels were applicable:

Staff of CLP		115,000 pesetas	
Cooperators of associated cooperatives		minimum 2000	
Associated cooperatives	minimum 300,000; otherwise	20,000 per cooperator	
Consumers' cooperatives	minimum 25,000; otherwise	50 per cooperator	
Education cooperatives	minimum 25,000; otherwise	50 per cooperator	
Housing cooperatives	minimum 50,000; otherwise	1,000 per cooperator	
Other organisations	minimum 50,000.		

7. In 1978 CLP became a 'qualified credit cooperative', meaning that more banking operations were allowed to be undertaken from then on.
8. In addition to sinking fund capital, obligatory capital and voluntary capital, there is thus a fourth category of partnership capital. CLP *Informe* (1976a: 149-155; 1977: 291-308).
9. In the Basque Provinces in 1976 savings banks held about four million accounts of which five per cent were with Caja Laboral Popular. In 1977, the average amount per account in Spain was 72,000 pesetas; in the Basque Provinces 75,000; and in CLP 104,000 pesetas. In the Basque Provinces savings banks account for about 50 per cent of total deposits with financial institutions; in Spain at large these financial institutions hold about one-third of total resources.
10. CLP *Informe* (1977: 291-308). EFMA (1977) provides a useful survey of the measures taken in 1971, 1974 and 1977 to provide institutional support to small and medium-sized industries.

V

ECONOMIC PERFORMANCE
OF THE COOPERATIVE FACTORIES

INTRODUCTION

Any in-depth investigation of the economic performance of a group of cooperative factories encounters considerable problems at both the theoretical and the empirical level. For example, a specification of the objectives and of the operational behaviour of firms first has to be made before it is possible to test whether a real case fits a specific theoretical model. At a high level of abstraction, a self-managed enterprise whose aim is to maximise income per worker may be contrasted with a capitalist enterprise whose goal is the maximisation of profit. Several hypotheses for self-managed firms have been developed at this level; for example, Ward, Domar and Vanek (Ward 1958; Domar 1966; Vanek 1970) have theorised on the behaviour of self-managed enterprises. The first of these hypotheses is that their level of output is lower than that of the 'capitalist-twin' enterprises; at the same time, the level of employment is less than that of capitalist enterprises. Secondly, self-managed firms are more likely to operate on a scale that still shows increasing returns to increments of production factors rather than to expand further, as capitalist firms would do under similar conditions.[1] Thirdly, self-managed firms generally have a lower capital-labour ratio than capitalist enterprises. Various authors (Vanek 1970; Drèze 1976) have shown that a self-managed *economy* — like the capitalist twin economy — is able to reach a Pareto-optimum equilibrium, but the need for entry of new firms and for a high degree of capital mobility creates additional difficulties in the adjustment process of a self-managed economy (Meade 1979).

The objective function of the capitalist firm is more complex in that it is influenced by various forms of ownership and control relationships, by pricing policies, by variations of market strength, by long-term strategies as well as short-term interests (Jacquemin & de Jong 1977: 159-197; Stewart Howe 1978: 11-47; Dunning & Stilwill 1978; Penrose 1980: 27-30).

Notes to this chapter may be found on pp. 128-130.

Self-managed enterprises, in a similar way, have a multi-purpose objective function rather than a simple maximising-income-per-worker objective. Various objectives have been explored, particularly in the context of researching the behaviour of Yugoslav enterprises: maximising income for the collective of workers; maximising income per embodied unit of labour; maximising a range of objectives which include collective consumption and social objectives; or the combination of maximising pure surplus and a target increase of wages, are some of the objectives of a variety of theoretical models, which do greater justice to the actual behaviour of self-managed enterprises (Horvat 1967; Jan Vanek 1972; Vanek 1975: 29-33; Vanek & Miović in Vanek 1977).

Research into the economic performance of the Mondragon enterprises must therefore also focus on the various elements that make up their objective function.

Our investigation of the economic performance should also be seen in the perspective of the debate on the feasibility of collective organisation of production, and of the economic potential of self-managed enterprises.

Some authors, e.g. Alchian & Demsetz (1972) hold the pessimistic view that the growth of collective organisations will be impeded because their managers earn less than their counterparts in capitalist enterprises. The negative opinion held by the Webbs — and more recently by Jensen and Meckling — was based on the fear that collective organisations would lack the adequate level of control which is crucial for modern factory operations (Jensen & Meckling 1979).

Vanek holds an altogether different view of the economic feasibility of labour-managed enterprises. There will be greater identification of workers with the objectives of the enterprises and less alienation, while productivity is bound to compare favourably with that of capitalist enterprises. A similar opinion is held by Cable and Fitzroy who predict 'a positive collusion to maximize joint wealth' (Cable & Fitzroy 1980b).

At the empirical level the situation is characterised by: 'Not much quantitative work has been published in the general area of the economic performance of participatory firms. While there are notable exceptions, such as the studies by Espinosa and Zimbalist (1978) and Barkai (1977), most of the published literature is of a qualitative character' (Jones 1980b: 15).

The work of Espinosa and Zimbalist on Chilean firms covers too short a period to enable an evaluation of their economic performance or for conclusions to be drawn; moreover, the data constraint was considerable. Barkai's economic analysis of communes in production covers half-a-century of community-type work organisation, but the extreme egalitarian ideology makes it impossible to draw general conclusions, while there is hardly any comparison with non-participatory factories. A 'non-feasibility hypothesis' regarding self-managed enterprises can be rejected in these cases. Jones's (1980a) research throws new light on the economic behaviour of producer cooperatives, focussing as it does on the 'survival potential' as a key indicator of performance and showing convincingly how producer cooperatives — small in number and size — are able to survive for several generations under adverse conditions.

Our study of the economic performance of the Mondragon cooperative enterprises is concerned with the theoretical and practical issues introduced above. Comparisons will be made at each stage with private enterprise to the extent that the scarce data permit.

Firstly, we shall examine the record of aggregate growth performance, in terms of sales, value added, exports, and investments. This will permit the 'weak-survival' hypothesis to be tested, and the dynamic behaviour of cooperative enterprises to be evaluated. The comparison with the aggregate performance of the provincial economy is of particular importance because the late 1950s and sixties were years of rapid industrial growth in Spanish industry at large.

Secondly, we shall investigate the productivity and profitability of the enterprises, in order to discover how efficient they have been in using the resources at their disposal, and also in order to be able to evaluate their record from a commercial perspective. The measurement of efficiency, in particular, brings us face to face with major theoretical problems in that the concept of efficiency is related to the objectives of an enterprise. We shall therefore need to elaborate on this aspect when selecting from among the methods — e.g. production function analysis and ratio analysis — that are at the researcher's disposal for such work.

The economic performance of different groups of cooperatives will then be analysed — five main categories being distinguished. Attention will also be given to the spread of performance of individual enterprises: this relates to the functioning of the entire system of cooperative factories, and to the problem of economic risk of specific branches and of individual enterprises. The scale of the cooperatives is also considered — an important field of study in the literature of the theory of the firm and of industrial organisation (Penrose 1980: 215-228). In the case of self-managed enterprises, scale relates directly to the level of workers' participation. In Yugoslavia, for instance, much effort has been devoted to sub-dividing huge industrial conglomerates into so-called 'basic organisations of associated labour' of a size of between 350 and 500 members, in an attempt to reconcile a relatively small size with economies of scale.[2]

The 'age' of the cooperatives will then be focussed upon. Although there is bound to be some overlap with the discussion of size, the situation of the 'youngest' cooperatives, which were established during the years of economic crisis, is of particular interest. Have they faced other problems than those which confronted cooperatives that started in the initial years? If so, what consequences are involved?

The financial situation will be examined. Available resources — through depreciation, and self-financing through retained profits — form the collateral on which bank loans can be secured from the CLP. This aspect concerns the 'dilemma of the collateral' (Vanek 1977: 176). Self-financing also determines the level of capital intensity of production and the scope for further capital accumulation.

ECONOMIC GROWTH

The cooperative group of Mondragon took full advantage of the rapid industrialisation that occurred in Spain in the 1950s and sixties; during the following decade it was found necessary to adjust to new and adverse economic conditions. We have seen in Chapter II how national industry developed behind tariff barriers and also that insufficient attention was given to stimulating indigenous research and development projects in the 1960s. Dependence on foreign technology was an additional problem because any major improvement in national export performance had to depend largely on technological innovations. Surveys among entrepreneurs during the 1970s showed that a weak demand for products was the principal cause of economic difficulty — hardly surprising after a period in which sales had boomed under protective conditions.

All these economic conditions provide a good background against which to assess cooperative performance under varying circumstances. As we have seen, the Mondragon group consists of small to medium-size enterprises, with the exception of Ulgor which has played a crucial role in the group's history, accounting for a large percentage of the sales of consumer durables which, over the years, have formed the nucleus of cooperative sales. Ulgor's huge production capacity — a maximum of about 2000 refrigerators, 1000 cookers and 650 heaters per 24 hours — gives some indication of the impact that it must have within the relatively small group of cooperative factories (70 in 1979) of which it is, directly and indirectly, a part.

The case of Ulgor illustrates the difficulties of comparative analysis.[3] In 1966 and again in 1974 Ulgor attempted to decentralise by hiving-off first Fagor Electronica and then Fagor Industrial. A comparison of its sales record with that of a leading capitalist firm in the same branch — Orbaiceta in Pamplona — which in 1971 occupied second position after Ulgor in electric consumer durables on a national basis, is therefore of only limited value. Orbaiceta has continued to expand, partly through mergers with smaller enterprises, whereas Ulgor has followed an opposite trend. In 1976, as a consequence, Orbaiceta's sales were greater than those of Ulgor, which still kept a close watch over its independent daughter companies.

In Table 1, the first column gives the annual sales of the enterprises which have formed the Ularco group from 1964 onwards.[4] Annual sales (given in current prices) got off to a quick start, well in excess of inflationary trends, amounting to 7.3 million pesetas in 1957, the first full year of production. In 1965 the 1000 million barrier was crossed, to be doubled only two years later. In 1970 a small drop occurred for the first time; since then the upward trend has been strong.

Data on sales of all Mondragon's industrial cooperatives are given in column 2. Aggregate sales have increased even more quickly than sales of the Ularco group, whose share in total sales fell gradually from 58 per cent in the mid-1960s to 44 per cent in 1979.[5] Column 3 gives information on sales of all associated cooperatives from 1972 onwards, including the consumers' cooperative, the service cooperatives, and agricultural activities. In 1979, non-industrial sales represented almost 15 per cent of sales of all associated cooperatives against about three per cent in 1972. This indicates the diversification and expansion into new branches of economic activity (see also Chapter VII on the total picture), but it also shows that 85 per cent of sales, i.e. the core of activities, originate in a relatively narrow production range.

The growth record in real terms can be perceived from the information given in the following columns. The late 1960s showed extremely high – 27, 13, 13 and 57 – growth percentages that have not been achieved again since. Nevertheless, with the exception of 1975, during which a fall in real terms occurred, performance is still impressive, with an average percentage of 8.5 for the years 1970 to 1979.[6]

The relative performance with respect to similar branches of economic activity, i.e. mechanical, engineering and consumer durables, is shown in column 5, from which it appears that the market share has increased from less than one per cent in 1960 to 10.6 per cent in 1976.[7] In only one year, 1973, was there a fall in market share because the growth rate declined from 20 to 10 per cent, which was more rapid than the rate at which similar economic activities dropped in the national branches.

Sensitivity to the national market is illustrated by the figures of production. Ulgor's annual production of refrigerators rose from 50,000 in 1965 to 280,000 in 1974; a decrease then set in, and in 1975 'only' 200,000 refrigerators were made; in 1976 the figure was up again to 300,000. The market share dropped first from 28 to 18 per cent, and then recovered to reach 29 per cent. A similar phenomenon occurred with respect to the production of cookers: the market share fell from 36 per cent in 1973 to 14 per cent in 1975, after which – with an annual production of 224,000 – a share of 20 per cent was noted in 1976. The output of heating appliances dropped from 183,000 in 1973 to 122,000 in 1976 – the market share dropping from 33 to 13 per cent; washing machines increased to 115,000 in 1975, capturing a market share of 15 per cent as against 10 per cent in 1973.

Table 1. *Sales by Cooperatives (1956-79)*

Year	Sales of Ularco (current prices)* (1)	Sales of all Mondragon industrial cooperatives (current prices)* (2)	Sales of all Mondragon cooperatives (after 1971; current prices)* (3)	Sales of all Mondragon industrial cooperatives (constant – 1976 – prices)* (4a)	Index of growth in real terms (annual growth percentages in brackets) (4b)	Cooperative sales as % of sales in similar national branches (5)
1956	.4	.4		1.8	.01	.004
1957	7.3					
1958	27					
1959	66					
1960	120	200		700	5	.7
1961	167					
1962	250					
1963	490					
1964	850					
1965	1100	1900		5200	37	3.5
1966	1600	2900		6600	47 (27)	
1967	2250	3350		7300	53 (13)	
1968	2550	4000		8350	60 (13)	
1969	3850	6300		13000	94 (57)	
1970	3800	7100		13900	100 (6)	8.9
1971	4850	8100		14750	106 (6)	8.9
1972	6100	10400	10700	17600	127 (20)	9.3
1973	6700	12600	13200	19400	140 (10)	9.0
1974	7800	16100	17700	21450	154 (10)	9.9
1975	8300	17900	19700	20600	148 (–1)	10.3
1976	10900	22500	24800	22500	162 (9)	10.6
1977	14100	30000	34100	24200	174 (7)	–
1978	18600	38200	43570	25900	186 (7)	–
1979	22000	50000	57245	28750	207 (11)	–

* million pesetas

Sources: Internal documents of CLP Division Empresarial; Annual reports of CLP from 1968-1979; *Anuario Económico y Social de España, 1977:* Table 3.1.5, 275, Table 3.7.1, 295; *Informe Económico 1976,* 123.

In 1975, dependence on the Spanish domestic market clearly meant that when demand for electric consumer durables experienced a major slump, several cooperatives including Ulgor were compelled to cut back production. This posed a major challenge to the managers of the cooperatives and renewed the awareness that permanent alertness and updating of skills were necessary if the cooperatives were to maintain their leading position in the market. The crisis served to emphasise that continual expansion cannot be guaranteed and that corporate planning calls for new competences.

In spite of their status in several domestic markets, the factories of the Mondragon movement have not become giants in the sense of ranking among Spain's twenty-five biggest enterprises. In 1976, in fact, Ulgor ranked 92nd out of 1500 enterprises; Ederlan numbered 868, Danobat 1205, and Arrasate 1469, in a ranking of these enterprises by sales.

The Provincial Economy

The small province of Guipúzcoa is heavily industrialised; in 1979 its total employment was estimated at 240,000 with the secondary sector accounting for 46 per cent of the total. In terms of per capita income, Guipúzcoa has been among the highest five of Spain's 50 provinces. The recession has seriously affected the provincial economy, however, and this privileged position is slowly being lost. Guipúzcoa's economy depends highly on the consumption of iron and steel by the national Spanish market, on the level of national industrial production, on demand for its capital goods, and on possibilities to find markets abroad, which is why its cyclical behaviour is more pronounced than that of the economy at large.

About 90 per cent of the production of the cooperatives originates in Guipúzcoa, which therefore has to be taken as point of reference for comparative purposes. Table 2 gives figures on Gross Value Added (GVA) from 1964 to 1977, in 1976 prices. During that period GVA as a percentage of provincial production rose from three to just over eight per cent. Given reports on further cutbacks and taking into account the continued growth of the cooperatives, it may be assumed that at the end of 1979 the share in provincial production amounted to about 10 per cent. A CLP internal report has stated that, within a few years, the cooperatives will produce about 20 per cent of provincial GVA, due to the fact that they have continued to invest on a large scale during the years of crisis while elsewhere investments have dropped considerably.

In the mechanical and engineering and consumer durables branches, the percentage of cooperative GVA as of provincial GVA increased by ten per cent in absolute terms between 1972 and 1977, reaching 31 per cent of provincial production in 1977. This shows clearly that the Mondragon group has a highly visible impact in an important segment of industry, and it may be expected that Mondragon's industrial production will soon be a central element of the provincial economy.

Table 2. *GVA in Mondragon cooperatives and Guipuzcoan industry**

Year	Cooperative GVA in constant (1976) prices (million pesetas)	Cooperative GVA as % of provincial industry	Cooperative GVA (mechanical and engineering and consumer durables) as % of provincial production, same branches
	(1)	(2)	(3)
1964	975	3.0	
1967	1950	4.0	
1969	3200	5.0	
1971	4000	6.0	
1972	4750	6.5	21
1973	6150	8.5	25
1974	6950	7.5	25
1975	6750	8.0	24
1976	8000	8.0	30
1977	8550	8.3	31

* Cooperatives not located in Guipúzcoa have been excluded.

Sources: CLP Division Empresarial, internal documents; Banco de Bilbao 1977: 123; Cameras de Comercio 1973: 183-198; *Económia Guipuzcoana* 1971-77.

Exports

Around 1965 the cooperatives began an active exploration of foreign markets; in 1970, as a result, about ten per cent of aggregate sales were sold abroad (see column 2 of Table 3). This percentage has risen steadily to reach 18 per cent in 1979, reflecting a conscious policy of CLP's planning department that 30 per cent of aggregate sales should go to foreign markets by 1985.

From 1970 onwards the share of cooperative exports in total provincial sales abroad has amounted to about 10 per cent and in the engineering and consumer durables branches has averaged 40 per cent from 1971 to 1977.

The impact of the cooperatives is indicated by a brochure on national exports which lists 350 companies of importance for Spain's exports: 95 of these are located in the Basque provinces, and 23 of them belong to the Mondragon group.[8] In 1980, a special cooperative organisation – *Lankide Export* – was established by CLP and by representatives of several groups of cooperatives to specialise in export trading and to design an institutional framework within which risks related to such trading might be curtailed.

Investments

A last and most crucial developmental indicator is the amount of investments made.[9] A frequent but unfounded criticism of self-managed firms is that workers prefer to enjoy a high take-home pay rather than to invest in their own

Table 3. *Exports of cooperatives* and industry located in Guipúzcoa*

Year	Cooperative exports constant (1976) prices (million pesetas)	Cooperative exports as % of cooperative sales	Cooperative exports as % of provincial exports	Cooperative exports as % of provincial exports, similar branches
	(1)	(2)	(3)	(4)
1965	80	1.5	1	–
1969	1020	7.7	7	–
1970	1470	10.6	10	35
1971	1900	12.9	10	40
1972	2300	13.1	11	39
1973	2400	12.4	10	33
1974	2650	12.4	8	42
1975	3100	15.1	12	43
1976	3000	13.3	10	48
1977	3300	13.6	10	
1978	3975	15.4		
1979	5150	11.9		
1980	6500	20.0		

* The very small exports of cooperatives not located in Guipúzcoa are not known separately and are therefore not deducted from the total.

Sources: see Tables 1 and 2.

enterprises. This has been proven invalid in the Yugoslav economy for example, which for many years has sustained a high propensity to invest. The same has happened in the Mondragon case. The percentage of GVA invested by the cooperatives – an average of 36 per cent – between 1971 and 1979, compares very favourably with that of Guipuzcoan industry as a whole which, from 1971 to 1977, invested 8.4 per cent of its GVA.

This investment performance is naturally a major reason for the rapid rate of growth that has been reported on in this section. A comparison of gross investment figures shows that the cooperatives invest on average four times as much as private enterprises.

Columns 1 and 2 of Table 4 give figures in current and constant prices of 1976, both showing that the cooperatives continued to expand investments rapidly up to 1976; thereafter a considerable reduction in real terms occurred, reflecting the worsening economic performance of the preceding years. The development of cooperative and provincial investments from 1970 to 1977 is illustrated in Graph 1. Such a short period does not permit definite conclusions to be drawn, but it seems justified to hypothesise that cooperative investments, representing 62 per cent of total industrial investments in 1977, display a more regular pattern than the cyclical behaviour of private investments. This is even more apparent when a comparison is made between cooperative and provincial investments in the mechanical and engineering and consumer durables branches. In 1973 and 1976, in fact, the cooperatives were the only enterprises to invest in these important industrial branches.

Table 4. *Gross investment of cooperatives and of all industry in Guipúzcoa**

Year	Cooperative invest-ment in current prices*	Cooperative invest-ment in constant (1976) prices*	Cooperative invest-ment as % of pro-vincial investment in industry	Cooperative invest-ment in engineering and consumer dura-bles as % of provin-cial investment similar branches
	(1)	(2)	(3)	(4)
1971	800	1450	16	19
1972	700	1185	11	28
1973	1400	2150	55	98
1974	2400	3200	46	58
1975	2900	3300	52	66
1976	3600	3600	55	95
1977	4000	3200	62	
1978	3700	2950		
1979	3900	2300		

* million pesetas.

Sources: CLP 1976b: 152, 84; CLP internal documents (various years); *Económia Guipuzcoana*, 1971-77.

Graph 1. *Gross investments of cooperatives and of Guizpucoan industry (current prices)*

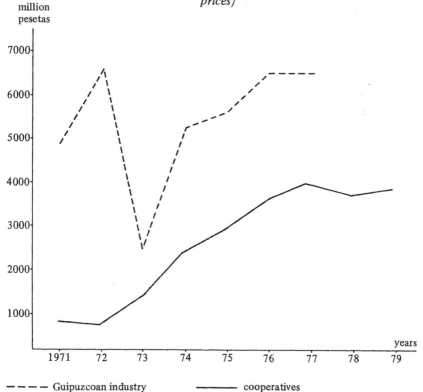

Trends of growth, whether of cooperative sales as compared to national sales in engineering and consumer durables, of GVA as compared to provincial production in industry, of export or of investments, indicate that the Mondragon cooperatives not only have 'survived', but also that their growth record is superior to that of private enterprises. A crucial aspect of that growth record is the strength of their investment programmes, even during years when economic conditions were adverse and when the percentage of unused industrial capacity increased.

Mondragon is thus an example of a new type of organisation which has shown economic feasibility over a relatively long span of time.

COOPERATIVE PRODUCTIVITY

The growth performance of the cooperatives has been strong, but has it also been efficient? The study of efficiency, i.e. the productivity of scarce resources, belongs to the core of economic analysis and has a long history.[10] There is the distinction between technical and price efficiency with given technology on the one hand, and on the other, the structural dynamic efficiency which takes technological change into account. Production function analysis is most commonly used in relating outputs to inputs, but a major weakness of this method is the great sensitivity that the estimation of parameters shows to the manner in which the model is specified (Timmer 1970; Page 1980).

The strongest objection to the use of production function analysis derives. from its assumption that enterprises are primarily interested in maximising their profits. In spite of such problems, however, the method continues to be widely applied in assessing the economic behaviour (efficiency) of enterprises, branches of industry, or even of countries.

There are at least three reasons why we should now proceed with great caution. Firstly, the Mondragon 'behaviour' is Schumpeterian, dynamic and innovative of character rather than static. Secondly, the objectives of self-managing enterprises are somewhat complex and invalidate the use of tools which derive from a simple model. 'The necessity of judging efficiency in relation to purpose' (Nove 1978: 83), or to put it differently, 'Rationality is relative to the institutional environment and needs to be measured on norms endogenous to the group' (Yotopoulos 1978: 264), are statements that underscore the need for careful definition of efficiency. Thirdly, the Mondragon enterprises belong to different economic branches; to impose one model in estimating a single production function for such enterprises would thus obviously be inadequate.

For our purposes, the crucial question is to investigate the relative efficiency of cooperative use of production factors as compared to that of capitalist enterprises. If data would permit, one could design Farrell frontiers for capitalist enterprises and so discover whether cooperative performance is stronger, equal, or weaker in comparison (Timmer 1970). The quality of data on private enterprises is extremely weak, however, whereas that on cooperative performance is excellent. We have therefore chosen the ratio-analysis method which is commonly used with regard to business accounts. In the given circumstances this method allows the best use to be made of cooperative and capitalist data for comparative analysis; it also permits a more general – commercial – evaluation of the economic performance of the cooperatives.[11]

In Table 5, three indicators of productivity are given, each of which permits comparison with private enterprises during particular years. Column 1 shows an approximation of total factor productivity, and columns 2 and 3 indicate partial productivities of labour and capital respectively.

Table 5. *Cooperative productivity (1971-79)**

Year	Value added per factor of production**	Value added per person**	Value added per fixed assets
	(1)	(2)	(3)
1971	160	245	.64
1972	210 (195/150)	320 (230)	.88 (.27/.73)
1973	240	350 (285)	1.00
1974	265	360	.98
1975	245	340 (300)	.76
1976	275	385	.77
1977		350 (330)	
1978		370	
1979		405	

* Figures within parentheses are values calculated for Spanish industry; where two figures are mentioned (columns 1 and 3) the first belongs to the 500 largest companies and the second to the remainder.
** Thousand pesetas, constant (1971) prices.

Value added divided by factors of production (column 1) has been devised by CLP's research department in order to indicate changes in productivity levels,[12] with the use of the following formula:[13]

$$\text{Index of factor productivity} = \frac{S-P}{N + \dfrac{F}{E} + \dfrac{W}{E}}$$

in which:

S = Revenue from sales   F = Cost of fixed assets per annum
P = Purchases from third parties W = Cost of working capital per annum
N = Number of cooperators   E = Average annual earnings of cooperators.

The numerator gives the amount of GVA on an annual base. The denominator is a composite number with three elements: number of workers; annual costs of capital divided by average earnings of cooperators; and the cost of working capital divided by average earnings of cooperators. The contribution of capital to the production of value added in this way is measured in equivalent 'labour units'. The result is an adequate approximation to a production function: i.e. it measures value added as a function of the factors used in production. Apart from the usual difficulties in measuring the costs of fixed and working capital, this formula is both practical and theoretically acceptable, an important point being that the level of earnings is linked to that of similar branches of economic activity (see Chapter VI) so that no bias is introduced by using average annual cooperative earnings. This productivity index has grown from 160,000 pesetas per 'labour unit' in 1971 to 275,000 in 1976, showing that total factor productivity has increased considerably. The dependency on outside markets is marked: in the five years 1971-76 annual changes were 31, 14, 10.4, -7.5 and 12 per cent respectively. A comparison with Spanish industry can only be made for 1972, in which year cooperative efficiency exceeded that of the largest enterprises by 7.5 per cent and of medium and small-sized enterprises by 40 per cent. These figures are important: similar results in later years would be proof that the cooperative movement occupies a strong position among Spanish industries.

Value added per person – column 2 – rose from 245,000 pesetas in 1971 to 405,000 in 1979. In 1972, notwithstanding a downward bias of this ratio due to greater employment creation, the cooperatives performed far better than small and medium-sized capitalist enterprises: cooperative labour productivity stood at 320,000 pesetas per employee versus private sector labour productivity of only 230,000. Again, in 1973, the cooperative enterprises showed higher labour productivity (350,000 pesetas) than the provincial industrial average of 285,000 pesetas; in 1975, cooperative labour productivity of 340,000 compared with a value of 300,000 in Spanish industry, while in 1977 the cooperatives maintained a slight edge over provincial labour productivity, as evidenced by the figures 350,000 and 330,000 respectively.

The strong emphasis on employment creation has negatively influenced cooperative labour productivity. The lead with respect to private enterprises narrowed from 40 per cent in 1972 to six per cent in 1977; if we allow for the fact that cooperative employment has further expanded whereas industrial employment has fallen, then the positive margin of the cooperatives was reduced in 1977 to about 25 per cent.

Value added per fixed assets – Table 5, column 3 – indicates the productivity of capital, a ratio that is commonly used for the analysis of the 'survival potential' of enterprises. This value – an average of .85 – is low by international standards. Value added per total assets during this period averaged .34, which is less than is needed for a 'healthy' enterprise, and indicates the degree of protection from which Spanish industry has long benefitted. It also explains why the penetration of multinational enterprises and Spanish membership of the European Community will pose a major threat. The cooperatives, as we have seen earlier, have anticipated such a development by implementing a strong investment programme; recent levels of sales and particularly of exports indicate that these endeavours are yielding the desired results.

Our analysis of productivity has shown that the cooperatives are more efficient than many private enterprises, though the fluctuations of the indicators used reveal strong sensitivity towards general market conditions.

COOPERATIVE PROFITABILITY

Net profits are of critical importance in any evaluation of business accounts, indicating as they do the potential for capital accumulation and thus for dynamic development. Pure surplus (defined as GVA from which advances for earnings, interest on capital accounts, and depreciation, have been deducted) is the cooperative concept which approximates capitalist net profits. In this study of Mondragon, cooperative pure surplus may be compared directly with capitalist net profits since there is a close linkage between cooperative earnings and average levels of pay in the surrounding labour market.

As regards *pure surplus as a percentage of sales*, Ulgor had very high margins in the early 1960s, i.e. 18 per cent in 1962 and 1963, 12 per cent in 1964 and 10 per cent in 1965.[14] Annual cooperative profitability from 1966 until 1970 averaged 9, 7.5, 6, 9 and 7 per cent. In comparison to those years, this index — see Table 6 column 1 — has since fallen considerably but still compares favourably with the values obtained for other enterprises, which reported an average profit margin of 3.6 per cent as compared to 7.8 per cent for the cooperatives between 1972 and 1976.

Data on net profits as percentages of GVA and of sales from 1967 onwards are presented in Graph 2; for the years 1972 to 1977 data are also given of net profits for Guipuzcoan industry as a whole.

This time series shows clearly that 1971 was a difficult year for the Mondragon cooperatives, while 1978 was even worse, following a peak performance in 1973. A small recovery took place in 1979 but it is obvious that the entire movement is now experiencing the most difficult time since its inception in 1956. Even so, there can be no doubt that the cooperatives have been more profitable than capitalist enterprises.

Pure surplus as of own resources — Table 6 column 2 — is high if judged by Bilderbeek's norm for 'safe conduct'. In each of the seven years the index was greater than the seven per cent which indicates sound profitability. A study by

Table 6. *Cooperative profitability (1971-79)**

Year	Pure surplus per sales (%) (1)		Pure surplus per own resources (%) (2)		Pure surplus per 'cost added'** (%) (3)		Pure surplus per person*** (thousand pesetas) (4)		
1971	4		8	(11)	14/24		35	35	
1972	8	(5)	17	(12)	30/40	(11)	80	75	
1973	10	(4)	21		40/45		120	102	(48)
1974	8	(4)	17	(7)	30/33	(16)	110	80	(58)
1975	6	(3)	11	(4)	17/17	(7.5)	85	53	
1976	7	(2)	14	(1)	21/15	(6)	125	68	(16)
1977	6		12	(-5)			120	53	
1978	2.5						65	24	
1979	4						130	41	

*   The figures within parentheses denote values for the private sector.
**   The first figure refers to all industrial cooperatives; the second figure excludes Ulgor.
*** The first column indicates current prices; figures in the second column (as well as those within parentheses) are given in 1971 prices.

Source: Own calculations; see note 3 and Tables 1 and 2 for sources of data.

Wemelsfelder of Dutch industry, for example, reports that the average yield on own resources for the years 1970, 1974 and 1975 amounted to 4.7, 5.3 and 5.1 per cent respectively.[15] In our own particular study, we are also able to compare results with those achieved by capitalist enterprises in Guipúzcoa. These stand at 11 per cent against a cooperative eight per cent in 1971, at 12 against 17 per cent in 1972, and at an average of 1.75 per cent during the years 1974-1977 against a cooperative average of 13.5 per cent.

The year 1971 was clearly a difficult one for the cooperative movement, its performance being less than the industrial average. In each of the following years, however, cooperative performance was very good, and better than that of capitalist enterprises.

Pure surplus as of cost added − Table 6, column 3 − is another innovative index introduced by CLP's research department, and indicates the ability of the cooperatives to accumulate capital, and to invest in educational and social projects. The formula is as follows:

$$\text{Index of profitability} = \frac{\text{pure surplus (= net profits)}}{\text{earnings + depreciation + interest payments}}$$

The denominator equals GVA minus surplus, which is equal to the rewards for factors used in production; earnings of cooperators are counted as a price for the use of a factor of production. Like value added per factor of production, this indicator is more comprehensive than ratios that focus on profits per worker only or profits per capital only. The ratio shows considerable fluctuations: a value of 14 in 1971 is followed by high values − 30, 40, 30 − in the next three

Graph 2. *Cooperative and Guipuzcoan industrial profitability (1967-79)*

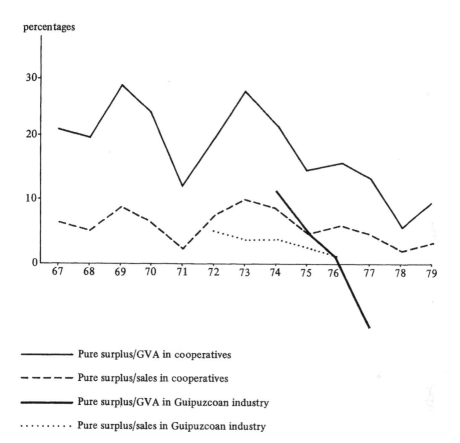

_____ Pure surplus/GVA in cooperatives

– – – – – Pure surplus/sales in cooperatives

▬▬▬▬▬▬ Pure surplus/GVA in Guipuzcoan industry

· · · · · · · · · · Pure surplus/sales in Guipuzcoan industry

Source: Calculated from data sources mentioned in Note 3 and Tables 1 and 2; the data on provincial profitability are derived from two sources, which explains why these two lines are not entirely compatible.

years, and by a drop to 17 in 1975, recovering somewhat to 21 in 1976. The second set of figures in this column indicate the profitability of the cooperative movement, excluding Ulgor. From 1971 until 1974, the group's performance was hampered by the difficulties that Ulgor faced, but the picture changed in 1975 when Ulgor's performance became identical with the aggregate performance. In 1976, Ulgor's performance was quite high, as a result of which the aggregate profitability amounted to 21 per cent instead of 15 per cent. A comparative study with a large number of capitalist enterprises during the years 1972 and 1974-76, yields the following values for non-cooperative enterprises: 11, 16, 7.5, 6. We thus obtain ten per cent as the average value of net profits with respect to cost added in capitalist enterprises, and almost 3½ times that figure as the profitability for cooperative enterprises.

Pure surplus per person − Table 6 column 4 − which indicates the possibilities for cooperators to accumulate their individual capital accounts, also shows sizeable fluctuations. In current prices, the 1979 value was only slightly in excess of that of 1973; in real terms, the 1979 surplus per person was almost equal to that of 1971. An analysis of the cooperators' stake in the enterprises is given in Chapter VI.

We have now analysed profitability from four perspectives:
(1) Profitability with respect to aggregate sales permits a comparison with private enterprises; as has been the case with the other indicators, i.e. trends of growth and of productivity, cooperative performance is favourable.
(2) Profitability with respect to own resources is a commonly-used yardstick in business analysis, in which a yield of 10 to 15 per cent is usually taken as a target level.
(3) Profitability with respect to 'cost added' is the best ratio with which to illustrate the potential to accumulate and to invest in capital goods as well as in social projects.
(4) Lastly, profitability per person is of importance from a distribution perspective. As with the level of profitability in the first three dimensions, the cooperatives indicate a strong comparative performance. The fluctuations of nominal and real yields imply that cooperators are made to realise that the wellbeing of the factory is greatly dependent on general business conditions.

COOPERATIVES AND BRANCHES OF ECONOMIC ACTIVITY

'The lack of good studies from the output side means that we are far from even knowing how productivity differences in the individual industries vary around the national mean differences, and still further from an ability to explain the reasons for these differences' (Kravis 1976: 39). Available evidence suggests, however, that economic performance varies widely from industry to industry and that it is almost impossible to discern any systematic pattern (Holland & Myers 1980: 329) — an indication of the difficulties frequently encountered in productivity studies. Nevertheless, an understanding of the economic structure of the Mondragon group of cooperative factories, which cover a number of economic branches, necessitates dis-aggregate analysis.

Firstly, there is the problem of allocative efficiency which could perhaps be improved if there were a wide dispersion of performance between branches and between individual cooperatives. Next, the important issue of the risk that is involved for separate branches and for individual cooperative factories. How sensitive are the composite sub-groups, in particular, to cyclical changes in performance of the economic sectors at large?

Cooperative production focusses mainly on household goods, but the strategy has always been to include other production processes such as the foundry which was set up in the 1950s. Although each cooperative maintains its independence, the policy of 'linking' their products is still a strategic element of Mondragon's cooperative policy.

Trends

In Table 7, attention shifts away from aggregate performance towards the main industrial branches,[16] relative weights in terms of sales, employment and surplus being given for five categories. Cooperatives that produce consumer durable goods are the most important in terms of percentage of aggregate sales and aggregate employment. The picture varies with respect to the creation of surplus. Heavy machinery-producing factories had a difficult time around 1968, but moved to the fore in 1971 in terms of contribution to total surplus, while losing out again somewhat from 1976 onwards. Tools and engineering products started poorly, reached a relatively strong position in 1975, but losses were barely prevented in 1978. Intermediate goods make a relatively high share of total surplus, except in 1975 and 1976 when they accounted for only nine and three per cent. Consumer durables were very weak in the early 1970s, when the other cooperatives did well, but were strong in years when the capital-intensive cooperatives faced difficulties. Finally, construction followed its own cycle, making between 10 and 20 per cent, except in 1977.

With regard to sales and employment, gradual changes in relative weight took place during this 13-year period. Pure surplus in heavy machinery, intermediate goods and construction during the same period was greater than its proportionate position with respect to sales; the opposite occurred with respect to tools and engineering products and consumer durables.

In each of the five categories considerable fluctuations around the trend values have been observed.

Table 7. Sales, employment and pure surplus over five categories of cooperatives (percentages) (1967-79)

Year	Sales					Employment					Pure Surplus (= net profits)				
	Heavy machinery	Tools and engineering products	Intermediate goods	Consumer durables	Construction	Heavy machinery	Tools and engineering products	Intermediate goods	Consumer durables	Construction	Heavy machinery	Tools and engineering products	Intermediate goods	Consumer durables*	Construction
1967	19	12	13	47	9	24	19	27	20	10	16	5	21	45	13
1968	15	14	17	44	10	21	17	25	26	11	0	9	33	39	19
1969	12	12	15	52	9	17	16	24	34	9	12	9	21	48	10
1970	13	15	16	47	9	15	17	24	35	9	29	10	25	23	13
1971	13	14	15	50	8	14	17	22	38	9	41	10	23	7 (-3)	19
1972	11	14	16	51	8	14	16	22	39	9	20	18	18	34 (23)	10
1973	12	19	16	43	10	14	19	23	35	9	16	20	20	31 (22)	13
1974	14	20	17	38	11	13	20	24	34	9	26	23	16	25 (18)	10
1975	13	22	16	37	11	14	20	24	32	10	25	26	9	21 (24)	20
1976	14	21	17	37	11	14	20	23	32	11	12	19	3	50 (48)	16
1977	-	-	-	-	-	-	-	-	-	-	8	17	24	48	4
1978	14	19	19	39	9	14	21	25	31	9	21	1	18	43 (32)	17
1979	14	20	19	38	9	13	21	26	31	9	18	14	24	34	10
Number of cooperatives: (1979)	7	22	25	11	5										
Average profitability: (1967-79)											19	14	20	34	13

* Figures within parentheses indicate the position of Ulgor.

Productivity

Table 8 gives information on value added per factor of production in the five categories of cooperatives during the years 1971-76. The narrow spread of efficiency is striking, indicating as it does that the cooperative group has been successful in allocating its resources. The only exception is the intermediate goods category which fell behind considerably in 1975; this may have been due to the fact that this category, more than the others, sells its products to other cooperatives and thus enjoys some greater degree of protection.

Table 8. *Value added per factor of production* (1971-76)*

Year	All industrial cooperatives	Heavy machinery	Tools and engineering products	Intermediate goods	Consumer durables	Construction
	(1)	(2)	(3)	(4)	(5)	(6)
1971	160	200	165	155	130	185
1972	225	245	235	205	210	230
1973	280	305	300	260	265	325
1974	365	440	405	325	335	360
1975	390	450	425	325	380	435
1976	505	500	535	415	500	545

* thousand pesetas (current prices)

Profitability

For an analysis of profitability of each of the five categories we take the ratio of pure surplus per sales from 1967 until 1979. Table 9 shows that the position of each category fluctuates sometimes strongly with respect to the group's average values, which 'peaked' in 1969, 1973 and 1976, but showed trough values in 1968, 1971, 1975 and 1978.

Heavy machinery showed a relatively weak performance during 1967 and 1968, followed by a major improvement which lasted till 1974, after which a downward slide occurred to a low of four per cent in 1978. Tools and engineering followed the average figure closely except in 1978 when profitability dropped to a very low figure. As for intermediate goods, profitability in 1975 and 1976 fell far below the average, but there was some recovery in 1978. Consumer durables performed weakly during 1970, 1971, 1974 and 1975, but relatively well in 1976 and 1978, thus contributing greatly to total profits of the movement during those years. Construction in most years did better than the average, with the exception of 1974.

We have now analysed the average behaviour of cooperative enterprises in each of the five branches, but it goes without saying that *individual* performance may

Table 9. *Cooperative pure surplus as percentage of sales by branches (1967-79)**

Year	All industrial cooperatives	Heavy machinery	Tools and engineering products	Intermediate goods	Consumer durables	Construction
	(1)	(2)	(3)	(4)	(5)	(6)
1967	7.5	4	6	12	7	11
1968	6	- 2	6	12	6	13
1969	9	6	10	12	8	11
1970	7	9	10	12	3	10
1971	4	12 (3)	2 (2)	5	.5 (4)	9
1972	8	13 (4)	9 (6)	9	6 (3)	9
1973	10	13 (4)	10 (3)	13	8 (3)	13 (4)
1974	8	16 (4)	10 (3)	7	5 (4)	7 (1)
1975	6	10 (2)	6 (3)	3	4 (2)	10 (6)
1976	7	6 (2)	7 (2)	1	8 (1)	10 (2)
1977	6	-	-	-	-	-
1978	2.5	4	.1	2.5	2.5	5
1979	4.0	4.5	2.5	4.0	3.0	3.5

* Figures within parentheses indicate averages calculated for national branches; sources are indicated in Note 3 and Tables 1 and 2.

Source: Calculated from CLP data.

differ widely from average group achievement. It has always been quite usual for one cooperative factory or even more temporarily to experience a loss due to problems of adjustment. This has changed in recent years: in 1977, for instance, 70 per cent of all cooperatives made a positive pure surplus, 20 per cent reported a loss, and 10 per cent just broke even; in 1978 these percentages were 60, 35 and 5 respectively. The speedy reaction of the entire cooperative system to reported losses is indicated by the fact that almost all cooperatives which had reported a loss in 1975 greatly improved their results in 1976. The manner in which CLP's Management Services Division monitors economic performance has been discussed above in Chapters II and IV.

Sector analysis has shown that, with the exception of the construction group, each category of cooperatives made extremely low yields during one or more years. The strong sensitivity to general conditions in the sectors concerned makes for a policy of evening-out fluctuations in order to safeguard an adequate cash flow each year. This applies in particular to individual cooperatives which sometimes made heavy losses for several years in a row. The monitoring and assistance provided by CLP's Management Services Divison has undoubtedly been the main reason why failures have so far been prevented. With the unfortunate exception of the fishing cooperative Copesca (discussed in Chapter II), a solution, in the sense that bankruptcy has been prevented, has always been found, even when problems seemed insurmountable.

SCALE OF OPERATIONS

We have seen earlier that self-managed firms may remain comparatively small, perhaps not even reaching the optimum size indicated by the borderline between increasing and decreasing returns to scale, a factor which in itself would justify research into the relationship between economic performance and the scale of cooperatives. Although in our case data on industry in general with respect to problems of scale are not available, it is worthwhile investigating the economic performance of different size-categories of the Mondragon cooperatives.

Dis-economies may differ between enterprises.[17] The greater such dis-economies, the smaller will be the optimum scale. Elements of control, of supervision, of managerial error, generally weigh heavily as factors that cause dis-economies of scale, factors which, albeit in a different context, also play a central role in participatory self-managed work relations.

Concern has sometimes been expressed in the cooperative group about the magnitude of some of the cooperatives, of which Ulgor provides the best-known case. The Mondragon planners would like to see cooperatives of at most 350 to 500 members since, in their opinion, the participatory process will otherwise be hindered.

Over the years, the cooperative enterprises have increased considerably in size (see Chapter III). In 1965 the average size of 22 enterprises — excluding Ulgor — was 110 cooperators; by 1978 — again excluding Ulgor — that average had increased to 304 per cooperative. Eight more had expanded from 27 to 98 over the same period.

Table 10 shows that the Mondragon industrial structure deviates considerably from the provincial pattern. The share of small enterprises (1-99 cooperators) is also low by international standards.

Table 10. *Distribution of work places (percentages)*

Employment:	1-99	100-500	>500
Mondragon cooperatives (1976)	12.5	40.5	47.0
Mondragon cooperatives (excluding Ulgor, 1976)	16	53	31
Industry in province of Guipúzcoa (1978)	37	36	27

Source: Censo Industrial 1978.

Productivity

For an analysis of productivity we refer to Graph 3, showing the trends of total

Graph 3. *Productivity by scale of cooperatives (1971-75)*

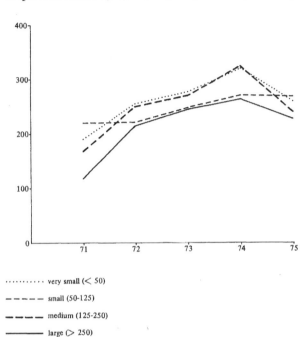

.... very small (< 50)

– – – – – small (50-125)

— — — — medium (125-250)

———— large (> 250)

factor productivity for five consecutive years, during which the largest enterprises showed the lowest results.[18]

General conclusions cannot be drawn from these data because they cover too
short a span of time. They do suggest, however, that value added per person does
not rise in relationship to increased size, as is generally found in other situations
(Lydall 1979: 307). This finding could well reflect the attention that CLP gives
to the smaller cooperatives by providing credit and managerial services, a channel
of support to which small industrial enterprises usually have little access.

Profitability

Table 11 gives data on profitability, i.e. pure surplus as a percentage of sales over
a period of seven years. The very small and small categories take first position
with an average of eight per cent, followed by the middle category and large-
scale enterprises, with average percentages of 7.5 and 6 per cent respectively.

This result brings us to a tentative conclusion similar to that in the case of the
productivity figures: the relatively small enterprises appear to have the edge in
terms of productivity and profitability. In 1976 and in 1978, however, the larger
cooperatives showed the strongest performance in terms of profitability, and it

Table 11. *Profitability by scale of cooperatives (1971-78) (percentages)**

Year	(<125)	Pure surplus per sales (125-250)	(>250)
1971	9	2	3
1972	11	9	7
1973	12	11	9
1974	11	13	7
1975	5	13	4
1976	6	4	8
1978	2.6	1.5	3.3
Average percentages (1971-78)			
	8.08	7.64	5.90

* Applies only to cooperatives that existed in December 1971. Figures for 1977 are not available.

may well be that these enterprises are better equipped than their small counterparts to sustain a worsening economic climate.

There is thus no evidence that the Mondragon cooperatives operate inefficiently due to their small size. It could perhaps be hypothesised that the strict terms laid down in the Contract of Association (see Chapter II) create the conditions under which these enterprises can operate on a scale that is commensurate with optimum efficiency. CLP's supporting activities thus may have provided the circumstances under which such an operational target can be achieved. It seems, moreover, that the cooperatives have managed to reach a minimum scale. that is greater than the 'minimum efficient size of plant – MESP' (Lyons 1980: 19).[19] The fact that there is no evidence of a positive correlationship between profitability and size may represent a strong barrier to further expansion, e.g. beyond 500 workers per cooperative.

ECONOMIC PERFORMANCE AND THE 'AGE' OF COOPERATIVES

Three phases may be distinguished in the history of the industrial cooperatives. The years 1956-60 represented the formative period for the entire cooperative structure, Ulgor having started in 1956. Rapid expansion then took place, and the first cooperative *group* (Ularco) was established in 1964. Since 1971 active promotion of new cooperatives by CLP has characterised a phase of consolidation. Could it be that enterprises which associated with CLP under widely differing circumstances have also performed differently?

It might be hypothesised that the pioneers, inspired by the person of Arizmendi, behaved more dynamically than later members who joined because of their own lack of financial means or the absence of marketing prospects. To test this hypothesis we have divided the cooperatives into four categories: the 'old' ones that associated between 1956 and 1964; the 'middle-aged' which started between 1965 and 1971; the 'young' firms set up between 1971 and 1976; and the 'very young', established since 1976.

The quantitative position of the four categories is summarised in Table 12, which gives information for each on sales, employment and pure surplus in 1978.

Table 12. *Sales, employment and pure surplus per 'age'-category of cooperatives in 1978* (percentages)*

	A	B	C	D
Sales	77	16	5	2
Employment	72	20	5.5	2.5
Pure surplus	100	9	-4	-5
Cooperatives (number)	27	15	11	13

A : 'old'   — established before 1965
B : 'middle-aged' — established between 1965-71
C : 'young'   — established between 1972-76
D : 'very young' — established in 1977 and 1978

The cooperatives that existed in 1964, i.e. 27 in total, accounted for more than 70 per cent of total sales and employment in 1978; in terms of surplus creation their record is even more dominant. The cooperatives that have joined since 1971 accounted only for a small percentage of sales and employment in 1978, and for an aggregate loss equal to the surplus created by the 'middle-aged' factories.

The Mondragon movement has preserved its momentum under adverse economic conditions, as evidenced by the association since 1971 of 24 new small firms which in 1978 employed 1200 cooperators. CLP has played a central role in this process of expansion, but could not have done so if the other big cooperatives, through their seats on CLP's Supervisory Board and their votes in its General Assembly, had not supported such a policy of growth, even to the extent of being prepared to support loss-making new cooperatives for a considerable length of time.

This strategy is clearly visible in the cooperative investment strategy. In 1979 investments per person were 297,000, 150,000, 394,000 and 810,000 pesetas respectively for the old, middle-aged, young and very young cooperatives. Irrespective of the dismal cash flow position during the start-up years, the young and very young cooperatives have been given strong support in their investment programmes.

All this, of course, does not provide any insight into the internal conditions

Table 13. *Productivity and profitability by 'age' of cooperatives (1971-78)*

	Value added per 'factor'*			Pure surplus per sales**				Pure surplus per person*			
	A	B	C	A	B	C	D	A	B	C	D
	(1)	(2)	(3)	(4)	(5)	(6)	(7)	(8)	(9)	(10)	(11)
1971	164	157	–	3	4	–	–	32	26	–	–
1972	227	203	–	8	6	–	–	83	48	–	–
1973	228	259	–	10	11	–	–	122	98	–	–
1974	369	347	329	8	9	3	–	120	100	40	–
1975	408	345	329	6	5	0	–	92	51	-4	–
1976	–			8	4	.6	–	150	47	-85	–
1978			–	3	1.5	-2	-7	90	30	-50	-125
Average performance:				6.6	5.8	.4	-7				

* thousand pesetas, current prices
** percentages

A: 'old'　　　　　　 – established before 1965
B: 'middle-aged'　 – established between 1965-71
C: 'young'　　　　 – established between 1972-76
D: 'very young'　　 – established in 1977-78

of the various categories of cooperatives: external market conditions caused by the serious economic recession have simply prevented sufficient demand from being created, and thus explain the weak performance of some members of the group.

Productivity and profitability

Total factor productivity, shown in Table 13, columns 1, 2 and 3, is highest in the oldest enterprises, except in 1973.

Pure surplus as a percentage of sales – columns 4, 5, 6 and 7 – has averaged 6.6 per cent in the 'old' category, 5.8 in the 'middle-aged' and .4 in the 'young', while a loss of seven per cent was incurred by the 'youngest' category.

Pure surplus per person – columns 8, 9, 10 and 11 – clearly confirms the general picture. In 1978 net profits in the 'old' cooperatives amounted to 90,000 pesetas per person and in the 'middle' category to 30,000; in the 'young' net losses occur to the extent of 50,000 pesetas per person, and in the 'very young' of 125,000 pesetas. It is clear that most of the latter two categories, with a total employment of 1200 cooperators, would have been bankrupted within the shortest span of time due to insufficient cash flow if Caja Laboral Popular had not provided the necessary support, in anticipation of positive results once the initial difficulties had been overcome.

The Mondragon group is still relatively young in that the 'old' factories are hardly one generation old. Yet some factories, best illustrated by the difficulties of Ulgor in the early 1970s, have already experienced a phase during which organisation and activities had to be completely overhauled. The finding that the 'old' category averages the best performance is an indication that 'ageing'-problems can be handled adequately.

Nowadays, new firms start under conditions that are entirely different to the favourable economic climate experienced during the early years, but in spite of these difficulties the cooperative group has decided to expand further by the association of new members. We have seen in Chapter IV that expansion provides CLP with outlets for its financial resources; without the support of the cooperative factories, however, such a policy could not have been implemented.

The recovery of the group in 1979, the continued emphasis on investments, and the strengthening of CLP's Management Services Division, show that this policy has a positive yield. It will be of interest to continue to monitor the economic performance of the young and the very young cooperatives in order to ascertain whether the new 'entry' of firms is indeed feasible under such adverse conditions.

Lastly, 'age' should not be confounded with size: it has been seen above that the small and medium-sized firms performed better than the larger ones. Formal-

Graph 4. *Hypothetical long-run average cost curves of cooperatives*

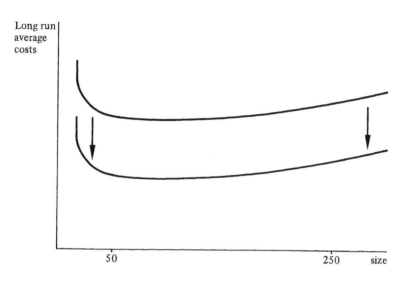

ised conclusions about the relationships between 'scale' and 'age' and economic performance are shown in Graph 4. The 'very young' cooperatives face a cost-situation which does not permit positive yields. CLP's support and monitoring, as well as its experience that has been gradually acquired, enable the cost curve to be brought down to a stable position, its shape being characterised by a low MESP point.[20] Available data suggest a long-run average cost curve of the shape indicated in Graph 4.

FINANCIAL STRUCTURE

Two aspects of the economic structure of the Mondragon group will now be investigated: the financial position and, closely related, the capital intensity of production.

The financial position derives from amounts that are set aside for depreciation, and from profitability. Information on depreciation as a percentage of annually adjusted values of fixed assets is given in Table 14. During 1970, 1971 and 1972 Spain's 500 largest enterprises set aside about 4.5 per cent of fixed asset value. Cooperatives can replace their equipment after a period of about 10 years, whereas elsewhere fixed assets are written off after 20 years.[21] Contrary to the popular notion that cooperatives tend to put short-term interest over

Table 14. *Financial position 1970-79 (percentages)* *

	Depreciation per fixed assets	Salary expenditure per GVA	Cash flow per GVA	
1970		55	42	
1971	11	64	30	
1972	13	57	39	(23)
1973	13	55	42	(21)
1974	11	61	34	(25)
1975	9	67	26	(20)
1976		66	27	(14)
1977		65	28	
1978		64	30	
1979		60	35	

* Statistics for the private sector within parentheses.

long-run perspectives, the Mondragon group thus follows a very strict regime with respect to depreciation.

The healthy financial position of the cooperatives is indicated by the data on cash flow, i.e. depreciation and pure surplus taken together, per GVA (Table 14, column 3). A rapid increase in take-home pay during the 1970s considerably weakened the cash flow position, which reached a bottom of 26 per cent in 1975. Since then, much effort has gone into improving productivity and into designing new systems of payment (see Chapter VI). As a result, the position had much improved by 1979. Again, and this cannot be a surprise after our earlier analysis of profitability, the cooperative situation is far better than that of private enterprises: 33.5 per cent as against 20.5 per cent between 1972 and 1976.

The strong financial position of the industrial cooperatives is shown in Table 15.[22] The ratio of own resources to fixed assets slightly exceeds one, indicating a safe and strong position: there is no danger at any time that outside interests (including CLP) could pressure the associated cooperatives and force them to part with fixed assets in order to meet financial demands.

Immediately important to any company is the relative position of its own resources (the second column of Table 15) and any claims that creditors may have. This ratio dropped slightly in Mondragon to .46 in 1976. Taking general economic conditions into account, and also the fact that many newly joined cooperatives were in need of considerable loans, this indicates a strong financial position. In Belgian industry, for example, this ratio dropped from about .50 in 1964 to .29 in 1977; in Italy between 1968 and 1977 the average ratio for enterprises fell from .21 to .15.[23] Union Cerrajera, the major non-cooperative employer in Mondragon, reported in 1977 that its own resources made up about one-third of total assets, while the whole of Basque industry showed a ratio of .28. Furthermore, it makes a considerable difference whether the main creditor is Caja Laboral Popular, or 'foreign capital' which has penetrated into a large number of industries and supplies a reported 25 per cent of their medium to long-term capital needs.[24]

Table 15. *Financial position of industrial cooperatives (1968-76)*

Years	Own resources/fixed assets (1)	Own resources/total assets (2)
1968	1.15	.55
1969	1.18	.51
1970	1.12	.50
1971	1.11	.50
1972	1.24	.48
1973	1.38	.51
1974	1.27	.47
1975	1.11	.48
1976	.99	.46

CAPITAL-INTENSITY OF PRODUCTION

On average the cooperatives are characterised by medium capital-intensity, on which profitability exercises a direct influence. If capital goods are to be replaced after ten years, then sufficient resources will have to be secured during that period of time. More specifically, the costs of each new workplace can be related to the required pure surplus per person, if financial resources are to be secured through self-financing. The two objectives, self-financing and employment creation, are closely linked. Given a specific level of profitability and a target increase of employment, it is possible to derive the permitted capital-intensity; or, given a target capital-intensity and a certain level of profitability, the feasible employment expansion can be derived directly.

The data do not allow for exhaustive comparative analysis. In 1972 fixed assets per cooperator amounted to 390,000 pesetas (current prices) as compared to 280,000 in small and medium-sized national industry; Spain's 500 largest companies reported a capital-intensity of 1520,000 pesetas per worker. The costs of a new workplace in the mechanical and engineering branches in the province of Guipúzcoa in 1976 amounted to 1½ million pesetas, whereas in the same year the cooperatives invested on average 2½ million pesetas in each new workplace. To the extent that non-cooperative data can be relied upon, it appears that the gap is widening between cooperative and capitalist capital-intensity, with the exception of the very large industries. This agrees with our earlier finding that cooperative policy gives considerable emphasis to investment plans. It is reported that 52,000 million pesetas have been earmarked for investment during the coming five years and that 5000 new jobs will be created.

The greater part of that enormous amount is naturally needed for replacement investments.[25]

This indicates once again the difference in economic performance between the cooperatives and capitalist enterprises. Elsewhere, investments continue but capital-intensity is relatively low, and many jobs are lost due to company failures. The cooperatives adopt a higher capital-intensity and simultaneously expand the number of workplaces. This is only possible, of course, if capital-intensity is closely guarded.

The problems involved can be understood from the fact that a new job investment of 2.5 million pesetas would demand an annual pure surplus per person of 250,000 pesetas in order to raise the necessary funds. The 'young' and 'very young' cooperatives which reported losses of respectively 50,000 and 125,000 pesetas per person in 1978 (see Table 13, columns 10 and 11), thus clearly have a long and difficult road before them.

A relatively low capital-intensity is a generally accepted characteristic of cooperative enterprises. The analysis and data given above, however, show that in Mondragon such has not been the case, capital-intensity there being even higher than that of average enterprises in the mechanical and engineering industries.

CONCLUSIONS

This chapter has dealt with the practice of self-managed firms. It would obviously have been impossible to deal comprehensively with all relevant facets of such firms, while also giving adequate attention to the industrial organisation of the corresponding branches of economic activity. The analysis has therefore focussed mainly on key aspects of the theory and of past experience of self-managed enterprises.

Different models of self-managed firms have been developed elsewhere. In a survey of these theories, Jacquemin and de Jong conclude that 'The main interest of this recent research is to establish that such a socially appealing form of industrial organization is compatible with economic efficiency' (Jacquemin & de Jong 1977: 196). At the theoretical level this has been proven conclusively. In our research it is elaborated upon with the use of empirical data; other aspects, such as size, financial structure and capital-intensity, which have drawn much attention in studies of workers' self-management, have also been investigated.

Various indicators have been used to explore the economic efficiency of the Mondragon group of cooperatives. During more than two decades a considerable number of cooperative factories have functioned at a level equal or superior in efficiency to that of capitalist enterprises. The compatibility question in this case has been solved without doubt. Efficiency in terms of the use made of scarce resources has been higher in the cooperatives; their growth record of sales, exports and employment, under both favourable and adverse economic conditions, has been superior to that of capitalist enterprises.

It is tempting to conclude that we have identified a case in which X-efficiency figures prominently: the 'non-price' efficiency that derives from a better-motivated labour force (Leibenstein 1978 and 1979; Frantz 1980: 524). Yet caution is warranted since the concept of X-efficiency typically is developed for American enterprises which have gone only a few steps along the road towards workers' self-management.

It has been hypothesised also that owner-controlled enterprises are more efficient than manager-controlled firms (Leibenstein 1978; Thonet & Poensgen 1979; Frantz 1980). Is Mondragon such a case?

We have found that dependency on external markets plays a strong role in the analysis of economic performance. Great risks are involved in exports; products change almost from year to year;[26] considerable research and development is needed to survive in national and international markets. These are key factors in explaining differences in efficiency between enterprises, and in the same enterprise through time. In our view, the principal conclusion to be reached is that industrial cooperatives are capable of dynamic and efficient performance despite a high degree of dependence on a market economy. Perhaps this factor has not been given sufficient attention in analysis of self-managed enterprises such as those undertaken by Cable and Fitzroy in West Germany and by Jones in Great Britain and the United States (Cable & Fitzroy 1980a, 1980b; Jones 1977b, 1980b).

Efficiency has been defined in terms of growth performance and of use made of scarce resources. In Chapter VII we shall elaborate further on the maximand – the objective function – of the cooperative group and evaluate efficiency in a broader context. To agree once again with Nove: 'Efficiency criteria, it must again be emphasised, depend very greatly on the circumstances of the case, and generalisations can be dangerously misleading' (Nove 1978: 103); yet, for the economic survival of a group of cooperatives in a mixed economy, efficiency in the narrow sense, as used by us, is of critical importance.

Economic performance varies considerably between enterprises but relatively little as between groups of cooperatives belonging to different branches. This is well in line with international investigations that generally pay little attention to the branch of economic activity in assessing the economic performance of specific enterprises (Bilderbeek 1977: 28). In the case of Mondragon all cooperatives have identical organisational structures, thus eliminating degree of participation as a variable which could explain variations in economic performance. The variables size and age have been taken up in two separate sections.

Given the stability of organisational structures and the strength of inter-cooperative linkages, one tends to conclude that external factors such as prices on input and output markets and the marketability of products, are the main factors causing differences in economic performance between individual cooperatives. It is somewhat puzzling, therefore, to find a low degree of inter-branch variations in efficiency, while there is a considerable spread of efficiency between individual enterprises; also, the same enterprise may show considerable fluctuations from year to year.

The static theory of self-management underscores the risk of under-investment, but in other cases, such as Yugoslavia and the Kibbutzim in Israel, one in reality finds a high preference to invest. Undoubtedly, the pressure of external markets compels a strong investment programme. Adequate measures have been taken to secure a strong financial structure, which provides the collateral on which further credits can be obtained from CLP. As for the size of enterprises, evidence suggests that the cooperatives aim at operating on the horizontal part of their long-run average cost curve, stretching from about 50 to 250 work places. CLP assistance makes it possible for small cooperatives to overcome barriers to entry; the cooperatives themselves aim at size limitation, since there is a consensus that large size jeopardises meaningful participation.

As for financial resources, we have seen in Chapter IV that the Mondragon group has overcome the credit bottleneck. We have now also found that sufficient pure surplus is secured to lay the foundation for a strong internal financial base. The system of distribution, discussed in Chapter VI, determines to what extent yields are available for ploughing-back into cooperative investments.

In analysing efficiency under different political systems, Brus at one point writes: 'The difficulty of finding hard evidence that democracy is positively correlated with economic efficiency could, at least in part, be overcome by extensive field studies in the course of which not only new data but also appropriate new methodologies might be discovered' (Brus 1980: 45). Mondragon's performance does not offer new evidence for nation-wide transformation, but its history does meet Brus's challenge in an affirmative sense at an intermediate level: as a self-managed sector within a mixed economy.

NOTES

1. Vanek (1970, and 1977: Chapter 9) gives a comprehensive and in-depth analysis of the problems that occur when the assumptions of theory are not valid; the charging of a scarcity price for the use of capital is a fundamental issue in this respect.

2. According to Sacks (1980), the measurement of concentration in Yugoslav industry is entirely dependent on the data source that is used; he argues convincingly for the use of BOAL criteria rather than aggregate data for conglomerates.

3. Data on the Guipuzcoan economy are weak in quality, and therefore cannot be used for precise analysis, such as an investigation of the role of the industrial cooperatives with

the aid of provincial input-output analysis. The main sources for a study of economic conditions in the Basque Provinces are published by the Chambers of Commerce at San Sebastian and Bilbao, by the Bank of Bilbao, and by CLP's research department at Mondragon. The best source available at the time of this research was an input-output table for 1972 produced by the Bank of Bilbao (Banco de Bilbao 1977). CLP 1976a and 1977 and IKEI 1979 are important sources about the Basque economy. Fomento de la Producción 1973 and 1977 have been used as sources of data on private enterprises. Various other publications are mentioned as references for Tables 1 and 2 of this chapter. As for definitions, Gross Value Added (GVA) equals sales revenue minus purchases. It consists of earnings and related costs, interest on own capital, depreciation and pure surplus. Cash flow is the sum of pure surplus and depreciation. In accounting financial results, cooperative practice follows established practice: earnings are booked as costs, interest on own capital is then deducted, and the end result is called 'the remaining surplus', which is identical to the net profits of capitalist enterprises.

4. See Chapter II for a brief history of Ularco; and for a discussion of the importance of cooperative groups.

5. Ulgor's sales still play a vital role in the annual total; over the years they have accounted for at least 50 per cent of the sales turnover of the Ularco group, and recently their share in annual sales of the movement has stabilised at 25 to 30 per cent.

6. Another indicator of expansion is the amount of land owned and built upon. In 1956, out of about 9000 m², this amounted to less than 2000 m². In 1974 more than 200,000 m² of 546,000 m² owned – a hundred-fold increase – had been 'developed'.

7. See Note 3; according to Fomento de la Producción (1975), the Mondragon cooperatives accounted for five per cent of the national sales of consumer durables, about three per cent in the mechanical and engineering sector, and just over one per cent of reported national sales of heavy machinery.

8. Document available at the Chamber of Commerce, San Sebastian.

9. With regard to data on investments in the province of Guipúzcoa, the problem of choosing a specific series of data is almost insurmountable. Among the many sources available, which yielded a wide range of values for any year investigated, our final choice fell on a series that had been constructed by CLP's research department (CLP 1976b).

10. For literature on this problem see Griliches & Ringstad (1971); Johansen (1972); Zellner & Revanker (1969); Kravis (1976); Barkai (1977); Jacquemin & de Jong (1977).

11. An excellent survey of the literature on all possible ratios and of their respective merits, as well as a thorough analysis of these ratios, is given by Bilderbeek (1977), who deals with the works of Beaver, Tamari, and Altman.

12. To our knowledge this is an innovative monitoring instrument; a shortcoming of this index is that it does not take into account the skill composition of categories of labour. In any case this creates a downward bias for the cooperatives that have invested huge amounts in educational programmes.

13. It is regrettable that data which permit the calculation of the same ratio for Spanish industry are only available for 1972; Caja Laboral Popular's department of research kindly made available the calculations made for that year.

14. Ballasteros (1968: 214-215).

15. Wemelsfelder (1978) and Bilderbeek (1977: 102-103).

16. Gorroño (1975: 145-151) has included some financial ratios in his work. He gives four ratios which refer to each of the years 1967 until 1973. The ratios used for the analysis of branches in our study give slightly different results from those obtained by Gorroño because some cooperatives have changed 'status' in terms of branch of activity; e.g. some have shifted from producing intermediate goods to producing tools. Adjustments have therefore had to be introduced to permit the construction of a series which would refer to the same set of enterprises.

17. Sutherland describes the problems that are met with in real cases; he argues for a range of 'optimal scales', dependent on organisational complexity, and discusses the risk of running losses if scale economies are not realised. He makes the distinction between 'procedural' and 'allocative' dis-economies (Sutherland 1980).

18. Cooperatives that have been established since 1971 have not been included in the research on scale aspects, since the process of learning would interfere with the scale. The categories chosen are commonly used in research that investigates the various problems related to the scale of enterprises; see e.g. Petrin (1978).

19. Lyons defines MESP as 'the lower bound of the smallest size class that is relatively successful' (Lyons 1980: 20). This concept marks the beginning of the horizontal part of the long-run average cost curve; it is of crucial importance to identify the point at which these costs come down.

20. The data of our research indicate a MESP point of around 50, which is markedly lower than the values calculated by Lyons for British industry in 1968; these fall mostly in the range from 150 to 200 work places (Ibidem: 28-30).

21. Depreciation percentages are taken of fixed assets that are revalued annually according to fluctuations in the general price level.

22. The average figures conceal huge variations; e.g. the young cooperatives have a self-financing percentage of about 20 per cent.

23. Medio-Banca (n.d.: 34, 35); Bilderbeek (1977) and Slot & Vecht (1975: 52, 53).

24. CLP Informe (1977).

25. It is remarkable that in 1981 the national daily *El Pais* devotes much attention in its columns to the plans of the Mondragon group.

26. CLP's Management Services Division has estimated that, in less than 10 years, 50 per cent of all products have either disappeared from the market or have changed to such a degree as to be better characterised as new products.

VI

DISTRIBUTION OF EARNINGS AND SURPLUS

INTRODUCTION

The distribution of earnings and of surplus is another focal point in the evaluation of any group of cooperatives. Could it be that a high degree of efficiency is reached at the price of considerable inequalities in earnings and other incomes? Does the Mondragon group face such a dilemma? Can efficiency and equity be peaceably combined? Each of the cooperative principles of distribution deals with an aspect of equitable earnings policies (see Chapter II).

The linkage of cooperative earnings levels to results attained by trade unions through collective bargaining in the metal and engineering branches, for example, denotes a micro-incomes policy. In general, an incomes policy as an economic instrument is a subject of some controversy. In the socialist countries of Eastern Europe it is an integral ingredient of socio-economic planning; in capitalist countries it has frequently been adopted in an effort to combat inflation, but rarely with any noticeable degree of success.

The aim of the Mondragon group to achieve an average level of earnings that is identical for all cooperatives, whether in construction, engineering, capital goods, banking or education, implies that inter-industry earnings differentials are not envisaged. This eliminates an important cause of earnings differentials which in Yugoslavia, for instance, has contributed considerably to the existing earnings inequality, which nevertheless is still relatively low in comparison to other countries (Estrin 1979).

The three-to-one principle, which sets limits for intra-cooperative earnings differentials, is another interesting instrument with which to narrow those differentials. In this respect we are able to draw definite conclusions about the performance of the Mondragon group, since it includes a wide variety of enterprises in terms of product, size and organisational complexity.

Finally, there is the complex phenomenon of distribution of incomes from wealth which, under conditions of private ownership of capital, is usually wider than that of earnings differentials, and often increases incomes inequality. Under

---

Notes to this chapter may be found on pp. 161-163.

conditions of state ownership the phenomenon obviously does not play such a role. Does the form of mixed ownership that has been adopted in Mondragon lead to 'capitalism' or to 'socialism'? Or is it more comparable to the 'social ownership' found in Yugoslavia?

Mondragon evinces many fundamental problems of the theory and practice of distribution of earnings and incomes. Any evaluation of its achievements should be seen against the background of its modest role in the provincial economy.

Earnings differentials will be investigated in two phases. First, the annual planning of earnings distribution, including a discussion of the annual debates held in this respect from 1968 up to 1979. Next, a report on a typical monthly pay-statement. The objective is to discover the manner in which decisions about earnings differences are taken, and the extent to which the outcomes are conform to the results of participatory procedures. A short section will then be devoted to the manner in which social security arrangements are made. In other countries, cooperators, being self-employed, have to face many problems in this respect.

The last major issue refers to the distribution of ownership of resources, and the manner in which pure surplus is distributed. Mondragon has adopted a form of mixed ownership in which total capital is divided between collective reserves and individual accounts which cannot be traded in the same way as shares. Another feature is that an individual account gives entitlement to financial rights, but in no way implies control of the cooperative enterprise. We shall therefore analyse the financial stake that each cooperator has in the own enterprise, and the manner by which profits and losses are shared.

The concluding section of this chapter will focus on wider policy implications and will give particular attention to 'incentives'. Earnings differentials – both inter-cooperative and intra-cooperative – are very narrow, which could have a negative impact on the incentive structure. Our earlier study of economic performance, however, has shown that Mondragon has a highly favourable efficiency record, and careful investigation of this problem is thus in order.

PLANNING OF EARNINGS

We have been able to trace the main elements of the annual consultations which are held with respect to the distribution of earnings, from 1968 onwards.[1] In that year, routine procedures had already been established, such as the publication of an annual work norms brochure.[2] More important was that from the late 1950s onward, basic guidelines had been decided upon. These guidelines – a three-to-one earnings differential, a common average earnings level for all associated cooperatives and, finally, a linkage with local private enterprises – have time and again had to be invoked in order to prevent a widening of earnings differentials.[3] Considerable attention was also given to the ways in which a co-operative social security system could be adopted, which in itself created many difficulties.

A 48-hour working week was introduced in 1968, making the total hours to be worked per year 2376 (down from 2769 in 1960); moreover, index 1 earnings were set at such an hourly rate that the annual wage equalled 84,600 pesetas, with 135 hours paid as holiday time (compared to 105 hours in 1960).

In 1969 the norm for the workweek remained at 48 hours; index 1, following considerable wage increases paid by the two competing capitalist firms, was increased to 90,170 pesetas per year. Much time was spent on determining the exact working hours, which were set from Monday till Friday at 09.00 to 13.40 and from 15.00 to 19.00, leaving Saturday as a half-day. It was also agreed that social security deductions would not be made from overtime pay, which would be at most 10 per cent higher than the normal rates, thus permitting a considerable increase in net earnings for overtime.

In that same year a remarkable decision was made regarding social security deductions. All members, irrespective of rank, would be charged a flat rate, set at 2130 pesetas. The result, of course, was an immediate widening of differentials in consumption since net amounts received were affected. Differentials actually increased from three-to-one in gross terms to almost four-to-one in terms of take-home pay. Cooperators of higher rank were then encouraged to increase their deductions, particularly the premium for temporary inability to work, in order to secure higher payments during illness or other such absences — higher, namely, than the minimal amount of 6630 pesetas which would be paid per month, irrespective of the index assigned in the three-to-one range.

In 1969, too, an interesting study was made of the need to introduce criteria that would permit a more 'balanced' comparison of the enterprises of the Mondragon movement. Ulgor's situation had changed dramatically since 1956, and some of the other cooperatives had become quite large in their market while others were in the initial stage of establishing themselves. The proposal was made that enterprises should be distinguished by a weighted system of four criteria: number of jobs offered; size of sales; amount of fixed assets; and degree of technological advance. The result would have been to establish three major categories of enterprises, each with other differentials: five-to-one in the highest category (only Ulgor would qualify for this class); four-to-one in the next category (six cooperatives would have qualified); all others would fall in the usual three-to-one range of permitted differentials. This proposal was not adopted for implementation, since it would violate the solidarity among associated cooperatives.

In 1970 CLP's Workers Council rejected a proposal by its Supervisory Board that the working week should be reduced to 45 hours, placing strong emphasis on solidarity with non-cooperative workers, who would continue to work 48 hours. Another objection was that adoption of this proposal would imply forfeiting growth potential. The policy document published in that year decided that an extra month's pay would be part of the 'income contract', and that in special circumstances a 4.5-to-1 differential rule might apply. Under a system whereby flat rate social security deductions are made, this could have resulted in a six-to-one net earnings (take-home pay) differential. Take, for example, gross amounts of 293,000 to 96,000 in 1970; the former might then increase maximally to 439,500; after a fixed deduction of about 25,000 pesetas, this would leave a difference ranging from 412,500 to 71,000 pesetas, reaching almost a six-to-one range. This shows clearly how two reasonable policy changes − a bonus for exceptional cases, and an adjustment in social security deductions − might have doubled the earnings differential that had universally been agreed upon.

In 1971 the working week was kept at 48 hours, or 2376 paid hours per year. Discussions were held about the considerable increases in payroll costs, leading ultimately to a discussion in Ularco's General Assembly as to whether the basis of comparison with the two local capitalist enterprises was sound according to economic principles. The Assembly formally adopted a specific set of formulae to be used from that time on. It also discussed whether, as a general guideline, the average level of earnings should be linked closely to those of Union Cerrajera and Elma, adding a small percentage to anticipate dynamic developments during the current year, or whether they should be linked to the cost of living index, to which one per cent would be added by way of standard practice. Preference was given to the first alternative.

In 1972 the annual number of hours to be worked was reduced from 2376 to 2218, while it was also decided to add an extra one-third month to the holiday pay, making a 15 per cent increase over the previous year in annual wages and salaries. This increase was more than would have resulted from application of the second alternative − cost of living plus one per cent − which would have resulted in a 8.3 per cent addition to the total payroll.

In 1973 discussions were held at Caja Laboral Popular as to whether the level of earnings of Ularco − the core of the cooperative factories − could continue to be the norm for all associated cooperatives. The outcome was positive, thereby adhering to one of the principles of cooperative solidarity. Firstly, there was a lot to be said for one standard method of calculating hourly earnings and social security contributions − in short, all the distributive details that had to be discussed each year. Secondly, Ularco employed approximately 50 per cent of all cooperators. Thirdly, Ularco's performance was the best of all the associated cooperatives, and thus should set a standard for the entire movement. Finally, a better system had not yet been devised which could incorporate the various principles of the group with respect to earnings policies.

In 1973 the annual wage increase was set at 15.4 per cent, slightly in excess of the cost of living increase during that year. Social security deductions were fixed at a flat 3238 pesetas per month. Voluntary additional deductions were encouraged, however, in order to guarantee that everyone would be paid 80 per cent of the usual wage in case of temporary inability to work.

In 1974, after much trial and error, particularly with regard to social security deductions, a standard system was elaborated for determining deductions from gross income, and to cover the full range of differentials. This included the possibility of a 50 per cent increase above the three-to-one rule for individual earnings in exceptional cases, and 10 per cent extra pay for overtime. A new procedure for social security deductions was decided upon, doing away with the flat rate deductions which had been in force since 1968.[4] A fixed amount was set for part of the social security coverage, and a percentage to cover temporary absence from work, disablement and retirement pension. The effect was to reduce, in one decision, the net earnings ratio to 3.5-to-1 (see Table 4).

In 1974, also, a study was made of labour market conditions for higher positions. Top salaries in the Mondragon movement had an annual maximum of about 558,000 pesetas, while levels in Spain as a whole were at least 100 per cent higher. The managing director of a small company elsewhere, for example, would earn over a million pesetas, while his equivalent in a company whose sales approximated Ulgor's 5000 million pesetas per annum would have a yearly salary in excess of 1½ million pesetas.

There was some anxiety in Mondragon that the narrow earnings differentials would be a barrier to securing the best quality managers for the cooperative groups. Nevertheless, the three-to-one principle continued to be the guideline for the entire system.

By 1975 considerable concern was being expressed about the fact that insufficient new workplaces had been created. Furthermore, there were misgivings about whether sufficient amounts were being set aside for technological innovation: 'We live in a market economy and that situation dictates what needs to be done.' The rate of innovation had apparently slowed down as compared with earlier years. The increase in consumption levels tended to become excessive, apparently as the result of a *mini-inflationary spiral*: good future prospects in the cooperatives and the higher level of consumption possibilities, caused by high internal mobility due to training and education, exercised upward pressure in the local market. The two major capitalist enterprises in Mondragon were now being forced to raise their salary levels in order to attract workers in competition with the cooperatives. The result was a vicious circle: the cooperative movement's payroll followed that of the enterprises because of the solidarity principle; 'The fish is eating its tail', said an economist.

The 'brakes' were applied in 1976 when strong emphasis was laid on increasing productivity, more efficient purchasing, increasing the prices of final products 'even at the risk of damaging the competitive position somewhat and adding to new inflationary pressures'. The cooperatives had now gained absolute dominance over a wide area, and new tensions had arisen in the cooperative group due to differences in levels of development.

CLP again discussed whether it was appropriate that the level of earnings of Ularco should be imposed on all other associated cooperatives. It was argued that independent studies could determine an earnings pattern for CLP and the new associated enterprises, and for those with heavy financial obligations to CLP. This matter was of such significance and there is such unique information available on the actual pattern of wage setting in a cooperative system which operates within a capitalist environment, that the 1976 situation will now be discussed in some detail.

In Table 1, on earnings in 1976, the first column gives the occupational structure in terms of indices that are equivalent to job descriptions used in the two capitalist enterprises, Union Cerrajera and Elma. Columns 2 and 4 indicate the percentages of total members (5128) of Ularco, and of employees (2600) in the other two firms. In column 3 Ularco's gross earnings are reported. Gross earnings of each of the five categories in the two competing enterprises are given in column 5, and column 6 shows how, on average, gross earnings in Ularco are about eight per cent lower than those of the competing enterprises. The difference is small for less skilled workers, skilled workers and supervisors, but from then on the gap widens to 39 per cent for managing directors; 15 per cent of cooperators are found in the higher ranks (2.05 and above) as against six per cent elsewhere.

The picture changes as we move to the right-hand side of Table 1, which shows net earnings after deductions for state social security in the two enterprises and for cooperative social security in Ularco. Average earnings elsewhere are slightly below the average salary bill in Ularco, but there are considerable differences per job category. The great majority of Ularco members enjoy a slightly higher take-home pay than workers in Union Cerrajera and Elma, whereas the top managerial levels earn considerably less, namely 39.5 per cent. Deductions for social security are reported in columns 7 and 9. Ularco's own provisions prove more efficient than the state system: not only do they cost less, but the burden is distributed more equally. In the capitalist enterprises 94 per cent of the workers pay out at least 29 per cent of gross earnings for social security; in the Mondragon group no-one pays over 23 per cent, while percentages are about equal at the top levels, i.e. about 16 per cent.[5]

Ularco's decision to adhere to this method of wage determination, i.e. of taking equivalent amounts of net earnings, has important implications. By keeping some approximate parity with levels of take-home pay in local engineering firms for the majority of workers, 'wage drift' has been avoided; as a result, a greater pure surplus can be allocated to other purposes. The prospects for increasing employment through investment and expansion, a primary aim of the founders, are thus guaranteed.

Table 1. Earnings in self-managed and capitalist enterprises (1976)

| | Ularco | Ularco | Union Cerrajera and Elma | Union Cerrajera and Elma | Ularco | Ularco | Ularco | Union Cerrajera and Elma | Union Cerrajera and Elma | Ularco |
| Index* | Percentage of cooperative members | Annual gross earnings thousand pesetas | Percentage of employment | Annual gross earnings thousand pesetas | with respect to capitalist firms** | Percentages deducted for social security | Annual net earnings thousand pesetas | Percentage deducted for social security | Annual net earnings thousand pesetas | with respect to capitalist firms*** |
(1)	(2)	(3)	(4)	(5)	(6)	(7)	(8)	(9)	(10)	(11)
1.53	65	444	73	476	– 6.7	22.5	344	30.0	333	+ 3.3
1.79	20	520	21	522	– 0.4	20.5	413	29.1	370	+ 11.6
2.05	9	596	4.5	677	– 12.0	19.3	481	26.0	501	– 4.0
2.49	5	722	1.4	897	– 19.5	17.6	595	22.3	697	– 14.6
2.98	1	866	0.1	1425	– 39.3	16.4	724	16.0	1197	– 39.5
	100%		100%							
	(5128 cooperators)		(2600 employees)							

* Average index of Ularco equivalent to job categories of Union Cerrajera and Elma
  1.53 workmen and assistants
  1.79 professional and supervisory jobs
  2.05 technical positions at intermediate level
  2.49 senior executive and technical positions
  2.98 most senior executive and technical positions
** average amount of gross earnings in Ularco 8% below competitors
*** average amount of net earnings in Ularco 3% above competitors

Source: Normas Laborales (1976), and internal document of CLP (1976).

In 1976 it was reported that 95 per cent of the cooperatives followed Ular-co's proposal in determining the average level of gross earnings as well as of differentials. Less than one-half per cent set a slightly higher average scale, and 4.5 per cent operated at slightly below average. On the whole, therefore, inter-cooperative solidarity was still practiced.

In 1977 the issue of rapidly increasing levels of earnings was again taken very seriously by CLP's economic department, which felt that the specific nature of banking as an occupation was very different to that of the engineering sector. In the department's opinion, an alternative productivity norm should be considered for bank employment, against which the trend in earnings over the past years would be compared. Consideration was given to the rising trend in the number of bank creditors (net deposits), which affects the bank's lending power, to-gether with the increase in pure surplus over sales of the entire cooperative movement. This exercise in finding an alternative approach to the settlement of wage levels is illustrated in Table 2.

Many outcomes are feasible, but the important point is that the productivity supplement (column 4 in Table 2), to be added to the cost of living index, should reflect an underlying trend in bank productivity. This formula therefore indicates the imputed productivity of bank-workers to the two principal facets of CLP's activity as a supporting cooperative: the channelling of savings to asso-ciated producer cooperatives, and the provision of managerial and auditing ser-vices to these cooperatives in the interest of increasing their productivity. Hence, the use of a value that reflects pure surplus as a ratio of the cooperative sales revenue, to which the bank and its workers could claim to have contributed. The exercise ended with the suggestion that, on this postulated productivity basis, the ideal wage trend would lead to a basic hourly wage (index 1) in CLP of 114.86 pesetas in 1977, whereas the real trend led to 23.8 per cent in excess of this rate.

The attention which CLP's Economic and Management Services Division paid to the level of earnings can be characterised as a search for an internal 'incomes policy', and is best understood when viewed from this perspective.

At the same time, the issue of a national earnings policy demanded much attention in the national government's attempts to reduce inflation, to restore the balance-of-payments position, and to prevent worsening of the employment situation. The so-called Pact of Moncloa, dated November 1977, contained details of a wage settlement for the public sector and for those private enter-prises that wished to benefit from available subsidies and supporting policies, such as tax concessions and credit facilities. The 1978 work norms stated ex-plicitly that the Mondragon cooperatives would adhere to such guidelines on the grounds of 'our principle of solidarity with other workers'.

Changes in the national tax system were introduced by decree on 1 Septem-ber and 1 December 1978, resulting in the introduction of a personal income tax of moderately progressive nature.

Table 2. *Postulated alternative basis for computing CLP's earnings levels**

Year	Cost of living increase (A) (%)	CLP's productivity (B)**	50% of pure surplus/sales of all industrial cooperative enterprises (C)	Supplement in earnings (%) over cost of living (D)	Index 1 'ideal' trend in earnings (E) (pesetas per hour)***	Index 1 real trend in earnings (E) (pesetas per hour)
	(1)	(2)	(3)	(4)	(5)	(6)
1970	–	–	3.5	–	–	–
1971	9.7	5.0	2.0	–	42.60	42.60
1972	7.3	5.0	4.0	4.25	48.54	51.00
1973	14.2	5.0	5.0	3.50	53.78	59.10
1974	17.9	5.0	4.0	4.50	63.73	72.92
1975	14.1	4.7	3.0	5.00	78.33	92.80
1976	19.8	5.0	–	4.35	92.78	110.20
1977	–	–	–	4.00	114.86	142.20

* Per hour, including holiday payment.

** The method of calculating a value for the productivity of CLP (Column 2) is to divide the increment in net deposits by 6, with a cut-off or maximum value of 5, i.e. $\dfrac{\Delta \text{net deposits}}{6} \leqslant 5$. D can be calculated in various ways, depending on the lags introduced.

E.g. $\Delta D_t = \dfrac{B_{(t-1)} + C_{(t-2)}}{2}$ to fall in between specific narrow limits, e.g. between 2 and 5. Here t is the current year, t – 1 the previous year, and so on; A, B, C, D and E refer to the columns of this table.

*** $E_t = E_{t-1}(1 + A_{t-1} + D_t)$.

Source: Internal document of CLP (1977).

The work norms document for 1979 took both these fiscal changes and the national guidelines on earnings into account; the earnings levels of Union Cerrajera and Elma are now no longer deemed representative of the 'environment'. The inclusion of the new policy variables signals yet another phase in the annual debates on earnings which will concentrate less on equivalence with local enterprises in take-home pay and more on the regional and even national scene.

1979 marks the end of the period under study. Both the deepening economic crisis and the emergence of other groups similar to Ularco may result in some loosening of ties with respect to inter-cooperative earnings differentials. Linkages with local firms have been substituted by adherence to provincial and national earnings levels. The three-to-one differential, however, may be maintained as a guideline for earnings differentials within the cooperatives.

Finally, Table 3 shows the pay structure for each level within Ularco in 1979, being representative of the broader picture within the associated cooperatives. Column 1 gives the indices of five job description levels, from which all intermediate index values may easily be calculated. The second column gives earnings per hour, i.e. the base of the entire earnings system. In column 3 monthly gross earnings at each of the five levels are given, showing that the 'three-to-one' rule is strictly applied. Next we have two columns, 4a and 4b, for social security deductions: the first for the flat rate applicable to all; the other for a fixed percentage that yields different absolute amounts necessary to meet the requirements of the variable elements in the social security system, i.e. widows and orphans pensions, and 80 per cent of salary during temporary absence from work.

Column 5 of Table 3 shows net earnings (take-home pay), indicating a ratio of 3.4 to 1 between highest and lowest ranks. Since 1979, tax deductions have been included in the work norms document, and the monthly take-home pay after tax deduction is given in column 6. The last column, 7, gives annual take-home pay after tax deduction, further reducing the inequality ratio to 3.14 to 1.

TRENDS

The trend in real earnings from 1963 onwards is presented in Graph 1 which shows that, during what might be called the expansionary period (1961-70) of the Mondragon group, real wages (take-home pay) increased slowly, if at all. Purchasing power rose by 1.5 per cent over the same period, while net deposits of savings with CLP and number of jobs created both showed rapid growth. Wages were therefore not being paid at rates which would handicap the movement's aim of accelerating investment for the creation of new jobs. The net asset value of each capital account held by a worker also rose during the period, and the

Table 3. *The structure of earnings in the Mondragon cooperatives (1979)**

Index	Gross earnings per hour	Gross earnings per month	Social security flat rate	Social security variable amount	Net earnings per month before tax deduction	Net earnings per month after tax deduction	Annual net earnings after tax deduction (pesetas)
(1)	(2)	(3)	(4a)	(4b)	(5)	(6)	(7) (= (5) x 14)
1	225.50	41,750	7,000	4,000	30,750	28,600	400,400
1.5	338.25	62,650	7,000	6,500	49,150	43,750	612,500
2	451.00	83,500	7,000	9,000	67,500	59,500	833,000
2.5	563.75	104,400	7,000	11,500	85,900	74,800	1047,200
3	676.50	125,250	7,000	13,900	104,350	89,800	1257,200

* In previous years the deduction for tax is not included in the work norms document. In 1979 for the first time a moderately progressive income tax was officially introduced and it thus may be expected that from 1979 onwards, tables of earnings will have the format shown above. CLP follows the Ularco tables exactly.

Source: Internal Document CLP 1979; *Work Norms* (1979).

Graph 1. *Net annual earnings in real terms* (1963 = 100)

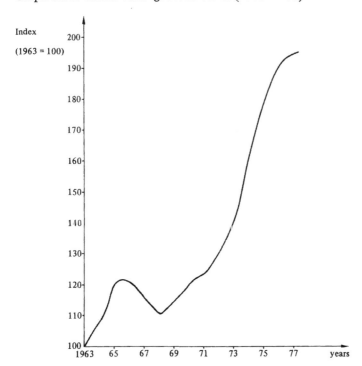

monetary threshold of entry for newcomers to the movement was increased. In spite of high inflation, the real wage rose by 50 per cent in the six years between 1971 and 1977, a far greater increase than had been the case in earlier years.

Table 4 gives a comprehensive overview of annual amounts of gross and net earnings for indices one and three from 1964 to 1979. The differential of three-to-one was maintained with mathematical precision for gross earnings but fluctuated for net earnings, dependent upon the social security premium system. A disequalising trend was shown in 1964-69, but this narrowed again in later years.

We have seen that the implementation of guidelines with respect to earnings is a complex matter for which new solutions repeatedly need to be found. If intense consultations did not take place each year, the pressures of the market would undoubtedly cause the basic principles to become nothing more than slogans. Earnings differentials would by far exceed the three-to-one rate; inter-cooperative solidarity would wither away; and take-home pay levels would by far exceed the average level of earnings in Mondragon and its environment, leading to the phenomenon of privileged cooperators.

These pressures will become greater with the passing of time. It may safely be

Table 4. *Annual gross and net earnings for index levels 1 and 3 (1964-79)*

Year	Index 1		Index 3		(4)/(2)
	Gross earnings (thousand pesetas)	Net earnings (thousand pesetas)	Gross earnings (thousand pesetas)	Net earnings (thousand pesetas)	
	(1)	(2)	(3)	(4)	(5)
1964	54.8	42.9	164.5	128.8	3.0
1969	90.2	64.6	274.8	249.2	3.86
1974	182.7	137.3	558.0	481.9	3.51
1979*	584.5	430.5	1753.5	1460.9	3.39

* The figures of columns 2 and 4 amount to 400.4 and 1257.2 after tax deduction, reducing the ratio of inequality to 3.14.

Source: Internal document CLP (1977).

assumed that earnings differentials in private enterprises will exceed a ten-to-one ratio, indicating the pressures that provincial and national labour markets will exert on the Mondragon group.[6]

PAY DIFFERENTIALS

Empirical analysis of earnings differentials can focus on a variety of aspects: occupation, branch of economic activity, region, or distribution within the work organisation. Given the principles of the Mondragon group, it seems logical to concentrate on differences in intra-factory earnings. The largest and oldest cooperative factory, Ulgor, where the greatest inequalities may be found, will be studied for illustrative purposes, making it possible to see whether the principles are 'violated' in actual practice.

Inspection of a normal monthly earnings statement, in which earnings of all ranks including apprentices and senior managers are recorded, has shown that, out of about 2500 cooperators, only 25 per cent worked the number of hours, 181.33, that had been agreed upon for that month.[7] Many workers work less hours for various reasons — illness, training, military service, etc. — while others work overtime. To gain a good idea of earnings differentials, therefore, we have chosen a subset (640 workers) of those who had worked exactly 181.33 hours during the month selected (May 1977) for investigation. Graph 2 shows a concentration of net monthly earnings between 22,000 and 29,000 pesetas; all earnings below 17,700 pesetas were compensated for by social security payments. The picture differs slightly for the total sample of cooperators (2500) whose earnings profile is also shown in Graph 2, a profile which spreads out markedly to the right, obviously as the result of overtime. 37 per cent of workers earn between 22,000 pesetas and 29,000 pesetas monthly, 39 per cent

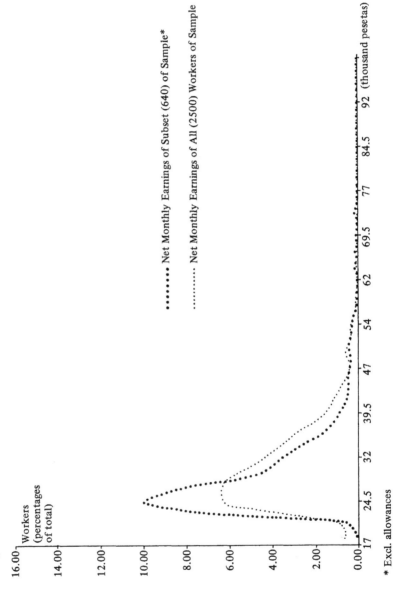

Graph 2. *Net Monthly Earnings (May 1977)**

•••••••• Net Monthly Earnings of Subset (640) of Sample*

·········· Net Monthly Earnings of All (2500) Workers of Sample

* Excl. allowances

Source: Ularco data

between 29,000 and 39,000; whereas among the smaller subset 27 per cent were found in the higher bracket and 58 per cent between 22,000 and 29,000.

For greater insight into the differences between the top incomes and that at the bottom in Graph 2, Table 5 gives *precise* values of the highest and lowest paid members, thus obviating the need to 'estimate' the highest salaries. Values for the subset are given in 5a. The very highest cooperators earning 89,229 pesetas per month relate to four junior cooperators with monthly earnings of only 17,725 pesetas at five-to-one. The top one per cent relates to the bottom one per cent at 4.1-to-one; the top five per cent to the bottom five per cent makes for 2.8-to-one; while for the highest and lowest deciles the ratio is 2.2-to-one.

In considering the entire work force (Table 5b), little difference is found with respect to top incomes. In other words, top salaries already compensate for extra hours worked and no further compensation is granted. This reinforces the impression gained from the subset. Lowest earnings are far below 17,725 pesetas in cases of absence, illness, training, etc., and this figure is thus taken as the lower limit of individual earnings.

Table 5 illustrates that various allowances, such as extra payments, social security benefits, and so on, do not increase differences in earnings.

Actual practice yields no surprises in the sense of violation of the norms, the outcomes being largely in accordance with the analysis of the earnings system given earlier in this chapter. Earnings differentials in absolute terms are small, and only in a few cases is the ratio of four-to-one for net monthly earnings surpassed. Differentials are obviously much smaller when comparisons are made for the same age categories: above, we have compared the most senior positions with the most junior. The differences found are modest by any standard, and there is little need for comparisons with other companies in Spain, firstly because such precise data are not available for private enterprises, and secondly, because the outcome of such a comparison can be anticipated.

A final comment concerns inequalities in Mondragon as compared to 'participatory situations' elsewhere. As far as we know, data of the same excellent quality are not available for producer cooperatives in other countries, and we have thus not been able to compare their differences in earnings with those of the Mondragon group. This makes it necessary to turn to another situation, such as the social sector in Yugoslavia which comprises the greater part of the country's economy. Earnings differentials in Yugoslavia compare favourably — in the sense of being smaller — with differentials in 'capitalist countries'. In 1969, for example, the top one, five and ten per cent of Yugoslav earnings proved to relate to median values as 2.9, 2.5 and 2.3. The situation in Mondragon in this respect shows that its principles of solidarity have been translated successfully into real practice: the ratios of the top one, five and ten per cent relate to median values as 2.7, 2.1 and 1.8 in the subset of 640 members, and as 2.1, 1.8, and 1.6 in the sample of 2500 members.[8]

Table 5. *Earnings differentials* (May 1977)*

(a) *Net annual earnings of 640 members (excl. allowances)*

		Highest 1%	Highest 5%	Highest 10%
A	Maximum individual earnings	73.5	55.5	48.3
	89.2			
		Lowest 1%	Lowest 5%	Lowest 10%
B	Minimum individual earnings	18.0	20.0	22.0
	17.7			
A/B	5.0	4.1	2.8	2.2

(b) *Net annual earnings of 2500 members (excl. allowances)*

		Highest 1%	Highest 5%	Highest 10%
A	Maximum individual earnings	63.6	54.1	48.6
	89.2			
		Lowest 1%	Lowest 5%	Lowest 10%
B	Minimum individual earnings	18.0	21.0	22.5
	17.7			
A/B	5.0	3.5	2.6	2.2

(c) *Net annual earnings before tax of 640 members (incl. allowances)*

		Highest 1%	Highest 5%	Highest 10%
A	Maximum individual earnings	73.4	52.9	49.0
	92.2			
		Lowest 1%	Lowest 5%	Lowest 10%
B	Minimum individual earnings	18.0	20.0	22.0
	17.7			
A/B	5.2	4.1	2.6	2.2

* In thousand pesetas.

Source: Own calculations

The evidence presented here justifies the conclusion that in the Mondragon group the high standards set with respect to equal distribution of earnings have largely been met. Those standards compare favourably with the norms of private enterprises and with participatory conditions in other countries.

SOCIAL SECURITY

The social security system necessarily plays an important part in any study of distributional aspects.

Cooperators in Spain and in many other countries face particular difficulties in this respect, since they do not have access to national social security arrangements. As self-employed workers, they have to find their own solution to social security, and this obviously forms an important aspect of their work conditions: health and family assistance are involved, as well as compensation for temporary absence from work, and pensions. CLP has from the start given special attention to these problems. As long ago as 1966, the cooperative Lagun-Aro was set up to take responsibility for problems of social security, and all other cooperatives now have their individual associations with it. When stronger legal status was granted to Lagun-Aro in 1973, it was seen as a considerable achievement.

Our examination of work norms has shown that much attention is given to the social security deductions from the monthly pay check. Percentages of premiums for social security have changed gradually, with a modest drop for the lowest index and a considerable increase for the higher ranks.[9] In 1979 the fixed monthly premium amounted to 7000 pesetas plus a variable 14.75 per cent of earnings per month. Although the aggregate percentage is still lower than that paid in firms under the state social security scheme, the trend is likely to continue its upward direction until, over a period of some years, the premium will equal that of the state social security system. Annual allocations have risen to a huge amount, i.e. 1705 million pesetas, of which 990 million fall into three major programmes: family assistance, health programmes, and compensation for temporary absence.[10]

There is also a solidarity aspect to the social security system which is of great interest. Quota are uniform for all cooperative enterprises, including the CLP and other cooperatives of second degree. These are divided into 13 communities of cooperatives, the largest two of which are the Ularco group and a community consisting of CLP, Alecoop, and a few others. At the end of 1978 only a few retired people were drawing pensions, thus forming a separate category. Each of the 13 communities has to keep a record of total receipts and payments for all members registered in the community of cooperatives, specified according to: medical assistance, family assistance, earnings compensation; and these receipts and payments must balance. If there is a surplus under any of the headings, then 50 per cent of it is refunded to the members.

In 1978, for example, 11 communities received a bonus for medical assistance while two exactly matched their payments and receipts. The picture with respect to compensatory earnings is quite different: five communities received a refund, while six were fined in that extra payments had to be made.[11] The solidarity aspect thus influences the structure of the social security system as follows. Firstly, payments and receipts are shared with members of other enterprises in one of the 13 'communities'. Next, each community receives a refund or has to pay a further amount which partly compensates either for the total excess payments made to Lagun-Aro or the excess amounts received from the collective social security system.

Most expenses closely follow the annual income for each specific item, such as expenditure on health and family assistance. Major difficulties, however, are faced in the area of pension funds. The age composition of the cooperators is such that as yet very few cooperators have retired. The implication is that huge resources need to be accumulated in order that, towards 1990 and beyond, monthly pensions can be paid. Rapid inflation such as occurred during the 1970s poses major problems for this relatively small pension fund, which is not backed by government guarantees and which is very strictly regulated as far as investments in assets are concerned. This explains why, in 1976, it became necessary to decide on a considerable reduction in pension rights. Until that year, a member with 30 years service was entitled, at age 65, to a yearly pension equal to the full amount of average earnings enjoyed over the last ten years of work. For the first ten years one would be entitled to 60 per cent of that amount, with each additional year of service adding two per cent. Thus, a member who had been associated with a cooperative enterprise for 30 years would have received the full equivalent of the average of the last ten years as pension. The new regulations stipulate a maximum of 60 per cent of the average of the last ten years. Ten years of work entitle a worker to only 36 per cent, with each additional year adding another 1.2 per cent, thus making the said 60 per cent after 30 years of work in a cooperative enterprise.

Lagun-Aro has slowly widened the scope of its activities beyond responsibility for the social welfare problems of associated cooperators. It has been involved in studies on absenteeism, and on environmental and health hazards. Discussions have started about the establishment of a local hospital with better facilities than those at present available, and Lagun-Aro also cooperates with regional health authorities in a new Mondragon Plan for cardio-vascular research and programmes of preventive care for schools.

The running of a micro-social security system implies high calibre expertise: it is necessary to plan for the lifetime of a rapidly increasing number of cooperators. The Mondragon group has found its own solution to the problem. For the time being, monthly deductions are less than those in other private companies, but the gap will gradually be reduced. When that time comes, the advantages of Lagun-Aro, which provides equal or better services than the state social system, will disappear and the risks with respect to the level of pensions will increase: an element that may have a considerable and as yet unpredictable impact on the functioning of the Mondragon group.

DISTRIBUTION OF SURPLUS

A worker becomes a cooperator by signing a contract and opening a cooperative capital account. The first item on that account consists of two amounts: 15 per cent of the total entry fee is nowadays allocated to the cooperative's reserves; the remaining 85 per cent is entered under the name of the person concerned, and may be increased by a third category of voluntary contributions. This entry fee, generally consisting of the first two components, forms the basis for self-financing the costs involved in one's job. The rapidly increasing level of necessary investments, however, is endangering this objective. In 1958 the total entry fee was equivalent to twice the average level of annual earnings; in 1977 the fee — in spite of having increased from 50,000 to 175,000 pesetas — covered about five to six months of annual average earnings. By 1977 also, the new investments in a job already exceeded two million pesetas of capital investment. The entry fee has to be paid within two years of joining a cooperative. Apart from a down payment of at most 25 per cent of the total, this is normally done by monthly deductions spread over two years. The entry fee paid by new members of Ulgor, for instance, increased from 3350 pesetas per month in 1974, to 4750 pesetas in 1975, to 5450 pesetas in 1976, and to 6900 pesetas per month in 1977.

These threshold payments are adjusted each year according to the following formula:

$$C_n = C_{n-1} \cdot \frac{Res._n / Cap._n}{Res._{n-1} / Cap._{n-1}} \cdot \frac{Price_n}{Price_{n-1}}$$

in which C_n is the new capital contribution; C_{n-1} is the contribution of the previous year; $Res._n$ and $Res._{n-1}$ stand for the collectively-owned reserves of a cooperative in the current and the past year; $Cap._n$ and $Cap._{n-1}$ stand for the total amount of individually held capital accounts; while the last term indicates the percentages of inflation or deflation in the current year as compared to the previous one. The adjustment thus consists of two parts:

(a) a factor which reflects changes in the weight of collectively-owned reserves versus individually-owned capital accounts;

(b) a factor which reflects changes in price levels during the current year.

Each individual account is annually re-valued and is also credited with the amount allocated from the pure surplus in that year, if such has been made.

Three Funds

Before investigating the allocation of pure surplus to the accounts of individual cooperators, we first have to know how they are distributed among three funds: a social fund, the collective reserve, and the fund from which allocations to individual capital accounts are made. The pure surplus is distributed according to the following formula.[12]

$$\alpha = \frac{Y}{Y + Z} \times 100$$

α = the percentage of pure surplus to be allocated to collective reserves and social fund (called 'the alpha-coefficient'); Y = pure surplus; Z = the sum total of payroll costs, and interest payments on own resources (called the 'computable base'). In practice, the distribution of pure surplus is subject to further constraints. Firstly, 60 per cent of the sum total of the computable base (Z) is the maximum that may be paid out to individual members' accounts; secondly, at least 30 per cent must be made available for allocation to the social fund and collective reserves. The social fund is usually allotted a flat 10 per cent of the pure surplus.[13] As pure surplus increases in absolute terms, the proportion allocated to reserves thus rises from a minimum of 20 per cent to a high proportion of the total available.

The resultant allocation for a wide range of theoretical values of pure surplus is shown in Table 6, which gives a realistic idea of the workings of the mechanism. The formula is seen to apply to a range of values where pure surplus is high in relation to payroll costs. In the majority of producer cooperatives, the pure surplus has been less than 43 per cent of payroll costs from 1975 onwards: the allocation has therefore been 10 per cent to the social fund, 20 per cent to the reserves for job creation and contingencies, and 70 per cent for distribution to members' capital accounts. In 1976, for instance, 70 per cent of the aggregate pure surplus – the result of adding the positive and negative net profits of 62 cooperatives, excluding Ulgor – was allocated to individual capital accounts, 10 per cent to social funds, and 20 per cent to reserves for various purposes. Individual differences, however, were considerable. Some enterprises had experienced losses that were debited to individual capital accounts and reserves; the losses of others were shared by a collective fund of the entire group of cooperatives, set up for this purpose. Yet others with negative results debited part to individual capital accounts and also received a refund from this fund. Many of

Table 6. *Distribution of pure surplus according to Mondragon formula: an hypothetical example*

Payroll costs and interest payments on own resources Z (1) Pesetas	Pure surplus Y (2) Pesetas	Social and reserve fund allocation* $\alpha = \dfrac{Y}{Y+Z}$ (3) (3a) %		Distributed to members* $(1-\alpha)$ (4) (4a) %		Unconstrained distribution (5) Pesetas	Constrained distribution (6) Pesetas
100	0	0		0			
100	10	9	(30)	91	(70)	9	7
100	20	17	(30)	83	(70)	17	14
100	30	23	(30)	77	(70)	23	21
100	43	30	(30)	70	(70)	30	30
100	50	33	(33)	67	(67)	33.3	33.3
100	75	43	(43)	57	(57)	42.9	42.9
100	150	60	(60)	40	(40)	60	60
100	200	67	(70)	33	(30)	67.9	60
100	300	75	(80)	25	(20)	75	60

* The 'constrained' percentages are given within parentheses (columns 3a and 4a).

Source: Own calculations.

Diagram 1. *Distribution of pure surplus (net profit), given a computable base of 100 (pesetas)*

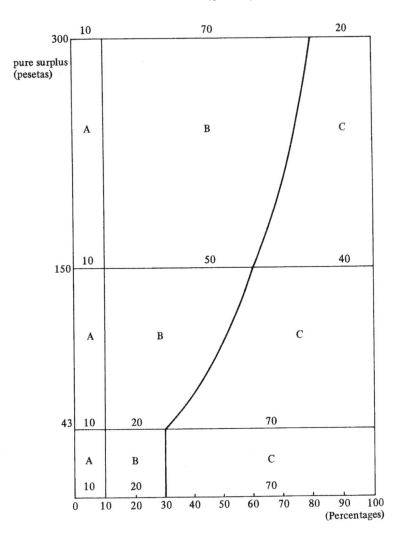

Source: see text

the cooperatives that made a surplus allocated 70 per cent to individual accounts; those that made high yields in relation to the computable base (Z) were able to allocate higher absolute amounts – but smaller percentages – to individual members. In 1976, for example, seven cooperatives allocated less than 55 per cent to individual accounts.

In Diagram 1 the y-axis gives the pure surplus in pesetas, while the x-axis indicates the percentages of the hypothetical example given in Table 6. The allocative decisions can be read off at each level of pure surplus: A for the social fund, B for the reserve fund, and C for individual capital accounts. The effect of this system of distributing part of the surplus to the collective of cooperators is shown in Graph 3. In Zone I they receive up to 30 pesetas of each additional 100 pesetas of pure surplus. In Zone II this amount rises more slowly from 30 to 60 pesetas, and in Zone III no further additions are given (assuming a 'computable base' of 100 pesetas). The distance between 00' and 00'' (the 45 degree line) indicates amounts that are not distributed to individually-held accounts.

Graph 3. *Pure surplus capitalised in individual accounts, given a computable base of 100*

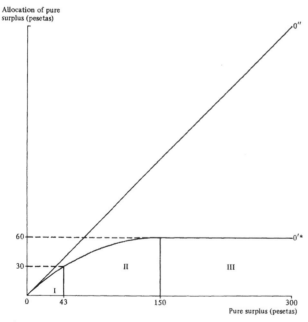

* 00' = pure surplus allocated to individual accounts

Source: see text

Rigorous adherence to this practice of capital accumulation through what can be termed 'forced savings', ensures job security, the financial viability of enterprises, and long-run growth and profitability. Should losses occur, the formula's constraints are reversed: not more than 30 per cent of the losses may then be written-off from collective reserves, the difference being made up from the capital accounts of members.

Individual Accounts

The collective cooperators' fund is then distributed according to total earnings of each member and interest received, a remarkable characteristic of the Mondragon movement. Rather than distributing pure surplus according to the capital stake of each member, as would be the case under capitalist practice, the cooperators allocate the pure surplus principally on the basis of each member's labour contribution. If, for example, a surplus of 100 pesetas were to be distributed *equally* between two members, one of whom was on index 1 and the other on index 3, then each would receive 50 pesetas; if a *weighted* system were to be applied according to index, the first would receive 25, the second 75 pesetas. Assuming, *furthermore*, that the first had received a salary of 150 and 20 interest, whereas the latter had 450 and 150 interest, then the distribution would be 22 against 78 pesetas.

In algebraic terms:

$$(1 - \alpha) \cdot Y = \alpha \cdot Z = \frac{\Sigma_j (E_j + I_j)}{E + I} \cdot \alpha \cdot Z$$

in which α = alpha-coefficient
Y = pure surplus
Z = computable base
E = total payroll costs
I = total interest paid out
j = 1, ..., k number of cooperators.

As a general rule, wealth is distributed far more unevenly than earnings; in the Mondragon cooperatives, the system that has been adopted enables it to be allocated on a much more equitable level.

The full significance of this method of distributing wealth can be gathered from Tables 7a and b, which record the accounts of two members who joined the movement in 1956. One of these, a 'typical average' cooperator, began with a gross wage of 1.25 times the basic rate; in 1976 he earned 1.6 times the basic rate. His more upwardly mobile colleague, an 'above average' cooperator, started work in the same year at index 1.6 and by early 1977 had been promoted to index 2.9; in other words, to senior executive level. The mobility of both men over the 20-year period is shown in column 1 of their respective record which shows the earnings index as compared to the basic rate of one for each year.

Column 3 in Tables 7a and 7b shows the amounts contributed by the two members as threshold payments. In the late 1960s the 'above average' cooperator, probably on seeing the excellent yields, voluntarily contributed additional amounts to his capital account. The average worker had accumulated almost two million pesetas while his fellow cooperative member on a higher salary held almost 3.5 million pesetas, or 1.75 times more, in his account. This is an extraordinary achievement if we consider the gross salary differential and the fact that the above average worker had made voluntary contributions. The outstanding feature is not that the highly mobile worker has accumulated a considerable amount of capital, but that the 'typical average' cooperator has accumulated such a huge amount through forced savings. The percentages shown in column 4 indicate that revaluation is almost identical for both our examples: the percentages of distributed 'dividend' are higher for the top positions because 'dividend' is calculated on the basis of annual earnings and interest received. Over the entire period, however, the gap between these 'dividends' gradually decreases; column 8, in particular, shows clearly that from 1970 onwards the total gains expressed as percentage of total accumulated amounts have become very close to each other.[14]

These facts show that the earnings and wealth position of cooperative members is definitely more favourable than that of employees in capitalist enterprises. Their position is more secure because of the high priority given to employment in the cooperative movement. Their receipts of interest on capital – six per cent on considerable amounts accumulated – are influenced positively by the very favourable percentages accumulated by the accounts, while, after 40 years of cooperative membership, the amassed 'forced savings', which themselves add to pension rights under Lagun-Aro's social security arrangements, put a huge fund at the disposal of the respective cooperator.

It needs to be realised, however, that cooperators simultaneously have a heavy financial stake in the own cooperative which diminishes in value if losses are incurred. In that case the same rules work in the reverse direction. Firstly, interest on own resources will not be monetised but credited as deferred payments. Next, at most 30 per cent will be written-off against reserves, whereas the remainder of the loss will be deducted from individual capital accounts. Then there is an obligation to restore the reserves when more favourable times return. Each cooperator thus contributes part of the entry fee to the reserves, agrees to the reservation of part of the annual surplus to those reserves, and runs an additional risk with respect to the own accumulated capital stake.

The capital stake differs from cooperative to cooperative. Although some

Table 7a. *Capital accumulation by the 'typical average' cooperator**

Year	Rank (index)	'Threshold' payments (thousand pesetas)	Revaluations** (thousand pesetas)	Pure surplus** allocations (thousand pesetas)	Capital account (thousand pesetas)	'Yield' on capital account (4)+(5) %	Average yield for 5-year periods from 1958 %
(1)	(2)	(3)	(4)	(5)	(6)	(7)	(8)
1956	1.25	99.0	(0)	0 (0)	99.0	0.0	
1957	1.25	50.0	(0)	0 (0)	149.0	0.0	
1958	1.25		8.2 (5.5)	0 (0)	157.2	5.5	
1959	1.25		5.0 (3.2)	32.0 (20.4)	194.2	23.6	
1960	1.25	2.1	.3 (0)	36.5 (18.8)	233.1	18.8	14.9
1961	1.25	10.0	2.1 (0.9)	30.0 (12.9)	275.2	13.8	
1962	1.25		6.1 (2.2)	28.6 (10.4)	310.0	12.6	
1963	1.25	-14.0	13.8 (4.4)	33.5 (10.8)	343.3	15.2	
1964	1.25		13.0 (3.4)	33.1 (9.7)	389.4	13.1	
1965	1.40		10.3 (2.6)	47.3 (12.2)	447.0	14.8	14.7
1966	1.40	10.0	22.4 (5.0)	53.1 (11.9)	532.5	16.9	
1967	1.50	4.3	9.2 (1.8)	63.0 (11.8)	600.4	13.6	
1968	1.50	2.0	13.3 (2.2)	65.9 (11.0)	681.6	13.2	
1969	1.50		24.9 (3.7)	79.1 (11.6)	785.6	15.3	
1970	1.50		45.5 (5.8)	47.8 (6.1)	878.9	11.9	11.4
1971	1.50		4.3 (.5)	19.4 (2.2)	902.6	2.7	
1972	1.50		47.8 (5.3)	79.1 (8.8)	1029.5	14.1	
1973	1.50		62.7 (6.1)	94.0 (9.1)	1186.5	15.2	
1974	1.50		175.6 (14.8)	71.8 (6.1)	1433.6	20.9	
1975	1.60		161.8 (11.3)	55.7 (3.9)	1651.1	15.2	17.0
1976	1.60		196.5 (11.9)	81.0 (4.9)	1928.6	16.8	

* In this table no reference is made to interest payments (6% per annum) to cooperators (see text for explanation).

** Percentage increase with respect to capital account of previous year is given within parentheses.

Table 7b. Capital accumulation by the 'above average' cooperator*

Year	Rank (index)	'Threshold' payments (thousand pesetas)	Revaluations** (thousand pesetas)	Pure surplus** allocations (thousand pesetas)	Capital account (thousand pesetas)	'Yield' on capital account (4)+(5) %	Average yield for 5-year periods from 1958 %
(1)	(2)	(3)	(4)	(5)	(6)	(7)	(8)
1956	1.60	82.3	0 (0)	0 (0)	82.3	0	
1957	1.60	16.7	0 (0)	0 (0)	99.0	0	
1958	1.60		9.3 (9.4)	0 (0)	108.3	9.4	
1959	1.70	1.5	3.4 (3.1)	41.7 (38.5)	154.9	41.6	
1960	1.80		.2 (.1)	50.5 (32.6)	205.6	32.7	24.8
1961	2.00	26.3	1.7 (.8)	41.9 (20.4)	275.5	21.2	
1962	2.00		5.4 (2.0)	47.7 (17.3)	328.9	19.3	
1963	2.00	-20.0	13.8 (4.2)	66.7 (20.3)	389.4	24.5	
1964	2.30		13.8 (3.5)	53.4 (13.7)	456.6	17.2	
1965	2.50		11.6 (2.5)	86.0 (18.9)	554.2	21.4	20.0
1966	2.50	40.8	26.3 (4.7)	90.3 (16.3)	711.6	21.0	
1967	2.70	91.0	2.4 (.3)	111.8 (15.7)	916.8	16.0	
1968	2.70	76.4	19.4 (2.1)	115.8 (12.6)	1128.4	14.7	
1969	2.90		40.0 (3.5)	153.8 (13.6)	1322.2	17.1	
1970	2.90		76.6 (5.8)	88.7 (6.7)	1487.5	12.5	12.4
1971	2.90		7.3 (.5)	36.4 (2.4)	1531.2	2.9	
1972	2.90		81.0 (5.3)	145.4 (9.5)	1757.6	14.8	
1973	2.90		107.1 (6.1)	180.7 (10.3)	2045.4	16.4	
1974	2.90		302.8 (14.8)	131.7 (6.4)	2479.9	21.2	
1975	2.90		280.1 (11.3)	106.1 (4.3)	2866.1	15.6	17.9
1976	2.90		341.2 (11.9)	187.8 (6.6)	3395.0	18.5	

* In this table no reference is made to interest payments (6% per annum) to cooperators, which are paid in cash (see text for explanation).

** Percentage increase with respect to capital account of previous year is given within parentheses.

Source: The primary data consist of a record of all amounts entered into the account under a specific heading. Tables 7a and b have been constructed on this base.

balancing is done between cooperatives, members of the very successful enterprises accumulate a greater stake over the long run as compared to their counterparts in enterprises that yearly show a less effective performance. The Mondragon group has therefore tried to combine several elements into its distribution formula. Each cooperator has an own capital stake which, however, cannot be monetised until the day of retirement. There is thus a great difference between these capital stakes and shares that can be traded on the market. As in the case of the social security system, however, some balancing-off of annual profits and losses is made in order to ensure that excessive inequalities will not occur.

CONCLUSIONS

The scale of the Mondragon group determines the extent to which general issues of earnings and income differentials can be raised. Problems of national policy making, such as foreign trade control, market regulations and price policies, are beyond the Mondragon experience.[15] To the extent, however, that a small group of cooperatives has had to find practical solutions to the distribution of earnings and surplus, interesting results have been accumulated.

France, England and the Netherlands, all have their examples of cooperatives which have linked their average level of earnings to that applied in industry at large (SWOV 1979: 25-116, 249). The Mondragon group, which could have created a privileged earnings situation, has not experienced any difficulty in adhering to a self-imposed norm to limit the earnings level to that of industry at large.

During the 1970s there was concern that real wages elsewhere were rising too rapidly; this would erode the financial health of enterprises as it did of provincial industry. Mondragon's experience, however, shows that it is not all that difficult to reach consensus on earnings levels which will safeguard the adequate level of cash flow necessary for new investment programmes to be put in force. It may well be that the combination of general guidelines and of annual participatory discussions provides a climate in which cooperators are willing to accept a policy of earnings restraint; on a larger scale, this could be a significant instrument in attempts to bring down inflation rates.[16]

An hypothesis put forward by Vanek and Horvat relates to the size of 'collective consumption', which supposedly will be higher in self-managed as compared to capitalist enterprises (Vanek 1975: 33-36; Horvat 1976a: 24-42, 1976b: 179-187). In a narrow sense, Mondragon shows no support for this expectation: in line with Spanish law, the cooperatives earmark annually exactly ten per cent of the surplus to a fund for social projects. In a wider sense, projects in the fields of education, health, environmental studies, and urban planning, imply involvement in the production of 'public goods'.

It is remarkable that Mondragon's overall structure of earnings has remained stable for so many years. It might have been expected that inequalities would increase, as so often happens on a large scale when per capita income rises in an underdeveloped country. No such evidence has been found. On the contrary, during the 1970s in particular, attempts were made to maintain one level of average earnings, irrespective of the branch of economic activity, for all cooperatives.

The earnings structure is very similar to that found almost universally in the world, irrespective of the kind of economic order. It is directly linked to the division of work, which is the outcome of job evaluation. In Mondragon as elsewhere, such factors as education, experience, responsibility and sex are the main explanatory variables for differences in individual earnings.[17] If, at a certain moment in time, it seems preferable to narrow these differences, then the focus of activity needs to be a modification of the work organisation. Forces 'inside the market' such as on-the-job training, and 'outside the market' such as programmes of education, then need to be steered in such a manner that the required skills will become available (Thurow 1975).

In this respect the annual debates on earnings provide strong support for an hypothesis, put forward by Thurow, that enterprises generally have considerable freedom to change their wage structures quite suddenly; at the same time, there is considerable interest in keeping those structures stable. Flexible wages, in fact, have a negative impact on the readiness of more experienced people to teach their younger colleagues. The cooperatives have occasionally taken measures that were of immediate consequence for the pay structures, indicating that rapid adjustments are feasible. On the other hand, such adjustments have rarely occurred. This was perhaps due to the necessity to stimulate on-the-job training as much as possible.

Forces are in operation which may cause a widening of earnings differentials. Firstly, the three-to-one differential may provide such a dis-incentive that insufficient staff will be available for senior positions (although this has not yet happened on a noticeable scale). Elsewhere, ten-to-one ratios between highest and lowest earnings are found. Another problem regards the monthly deductions for social security: if flat amounts are deducted from gross salaries, the earnings margin widens considerably. A third factor is the difference in size of factories; larger size could lead to greater inequality.

Another very important finding is the narrow spread of wealth distribution. Except, of course, under conditions of state ownership, it is normal practice that the distribution of ownership far exceeds the inequalities deriving from earnings; in Mondragon, however, the reverse is found. The distribution of wealth among cooperators who enter a cooperative in the same year is remarkably equal, and narrower than that of earnings. This will probably continue to be the case if the entry fee remains identical for all new cooperators, irrespective of whether they start at index 1 or at the higher rank close to index 2, for instance.

Final evaluation of the distribution formula cannot yet be undertaken as the cooperatives are only one generation old. Research into the performance of cooperatives has shown that, in both England and the United States, cooperatives have 'disappeared' during the 19th and 20th centuries, partly due to mergers and to selling-out when the original founders reached retirement. It is unlikely that this will happen in Mondragon because the group has expanded rapidly, thereby maintaining a low average age of members. The founders have no excessive power, and the 'entry fee' gives all new cooperators equal rights in the General Assembly. This makes it unlikely that a relatively small group would be able to exercise an influence that might jeopardise the continuation of the cooperatives. Furthermore, the Mondragon group has a strong institutional stability which prevents any sudden action by a small group; for example, the rotating and interlocking membership of CLP's Supervisory Board, and the Contract of Association between CLP and each cooperative.

Nevertheless, cooperators are entitled to withdraw their entire individual capital account on retirement, entailing the risk of considerable decapitalisation towards the end of the 20th century. This problem has been recognised, and it may be expected that measures will be taken to encourage recapitalisation of the monetised accounts.[18]

This interim evaluation reveals some important aspects of the ownership problem. Firstly, each cooperative has a strong financial base due to a high degree of profit re-cycling. The so-called 'dilemma of the collateral' does not exist in Mondragon: i.e. a situation in which a cooperative, due to lack of own resources, is unable to go to a bank to obtain necessary credits. Secondly, each cooperator has a strong stake in the own cooperative. As one young woman said in an interview about the machine she was working on: 'I feel that this machine in part is mine.' A third aspect is the absence of 'second-class citizenship'. The motivation of all cooperators to contribute to 'planning from below' may be heightened because, at the end of each quarter, the state of their individual accounts is a vivid illustration of the results achieved in the previous three months.

A fourth point concerns the differences in net worth between cooperatives. The fact that monthly average earnings are almost the same for all cooperatives causes differences in reserves and individual accounts, since profitability differs between cooperatives. At retirement age, therefore, cooperators who have worked continually in a more than averagely successful cooperative, will have a larger account to draw upon than their colleagues in less successful cooperatives. The exact impact of this phenomenon will be seen only when larger numbers of cooperators reach retirement age.

Reviewing the available evidence, we have to conclude that the cooperators of the Mondragon group have maintained a narrow range of differences of earnings, and of incomes from ownership of resources for a considerable period of time.

The Mondragon system deviates considerably from the behaviour that is thought to be optimal under conditions of workers' self-management. Vanek, for instance, lists income-sharing in a work organisation as a main feature of self-management — obviously after a scarcity price for the use of capital resources has been set aside. Horvat, in a similar approach, favours the taxing-away of all rents, after which the labour income is at the disposal of the work organisation (Horvat 1976a). In Mondragon the reverse is the case. First, patterns for earnings are set; the remainder is then distributed in such a manner that about 90 per cent is available for new investments. Some rents in this way may be included in the amounts that accumulate in individual accounts. The Mondragon solution seems to be a practical one. For instance, it avoids the prisoner's dilemma which may jeopardise the fair distribution of payment 'according to the quantity and quality of the work' performed.[19]

This leads us to a final aspect: the incentive structure. The Mondragon distribution can perhaps best be characterised by its narrow individual differences and its collective incentives. The combination of participation in decision making with respect to the organisation of work and the distribution of earnings; of narrow differences and fixed wages; of an extensive programme of education and on-the-job training; of a high degree of security of employment; and of a financial stake in the ownership of the own cooperative factory, adds up to a system of collective incentives which is not found in private enterprise, and which partly explains why performance in the cooperatives has achieved such a high degree of efficiency. With regard to many aspects of distribution, therefore, the Mondragon experience provides a good model for a collective and participatory approach to problems of distribution.

NOTES

1. The main source used for this section is *Work Norms*, a document which is produced each year after the details of work conditions and remuneration have been agreed upon. Twelve such documents have been analysed, from 1968 onwards.
2. The analysis of problems related to organisation, such as the system of job structuring according to indices, has been dealt with in Chapter IV.
3. See also Chapter II, where the principles of 'solidarity' have been introduced.
4. The formula applied is the following:

$$A_c = \frac{A_t - k}{1 + c}$$

in which A_c is advance for consumption
              A_t is total advance
              k   is the flat rate for social security
              c   is the percentage deducted for social security.

The percentages deducted for purposes of social security are expressed in terms of gross earnings, A_t, see Table 1.
5. From Table 1 it is not possible to draw conclusions about the ratio of extreme earnings in Union Cerrajera and Elma since the five categories report average earnings of the classes

concerned. Gutierrez-Johnson (1978: 274-275) has interesting figures for 1973, 1974 and 1975, which indicate that the difference at the levels of management has become less, while at the lower levels a further small rise is noticed with respect to similar ranks in the two capitalist enterprises.

6. J. Jané Solá (1969: 124-125); for information on the contracts of collective bargaining see e.g. *Texto del convenio colectivo sindical para las industrias siderometalurgicas de la provincia de la Coruna* (enero 1974). Facts on wages and salaries in Spain are published, e.g., in *Anuario Económico y Social de España* (1977: 429-431).

7. The analysis is based on a study of a payroll statement of 2500 cooperators during May 1977. This 'sample' includes only 'internal' cooperators; 'external' members — on assignment elsewhere, e.g. for marketing, servicing, etc. — are not included.

8. See Lydall (1968) for a comparative study of earnings differentials. Thomas (1973) gives comprehensive information on the distribution of earnings in a 'self-managed economy'; the cases compared are so different that exact conclusions cannot be drawn. The differentials would be still less if life-time earnings could be measured by way of net present value of the discounted earnings stream.

9. *Social security provisions (in percentages of gross earnings)*:

year:	1968	1969	1970	1971	1972	1973	1974	1975	1976	1977	1978	1979
Index 1	28.3	28.3	26.9	28.4	27.4	27.3	24.8	24.5	25.1	26.9	28.8	26.3
Index 3	9.5	9.3	7.9	9.3	9.3	0.9	13.6	12.9	14.9	16.3	18.0	16.7

10. *Distribution of social security premiums (percentages)*

	1972	1973	1974	1975	1976	1977	1978	1979
Family Assistance	25.5	21	25	25	20	14	13	12
Medical Assistance	21	21	21	24.5	22	18	17	17
Temporary Compensation for loss of earnings, due to various reasons	8.5	7.5	7.5	5	9	11	11	11
Pensions	21	22	19	19.5	22	23	25	25
Obligatory Reserves	21	23.5	23.5	23	22	30	30	30
Other	3	5	4	3	5	4	4	5
	100.0	100.0	100.0	100.0	100.0	100.0	100.0	100.0

Source: Lagun-Aro: *Annual Reports* (1975, 1976, 1977, 1978).

11. The precise formula is:
In case of a bonus: .50 (A - B);
In case of a fine   :   (B - 1.10 A),
in which A is total payments for social security and
        B is total receipts from the social security system.

12. The so-called alpha coefficient is derived from the following equation:
$Y = \alpha.Y + \alpha.Z.$
The idea is that α is chosen in such a manner as to exhaust the pure surplus when a percentage $-\alpha-$ allocated of surplus to *collective* purposes is equal to that percentage of Z — the computable base — which is allocated to *individual* accounts.

13. While it is true that if 30 per cent of pure surplus is allocated to social funds, the distribution has generally been 10-20, a ratio of 15-15 has been adopted in certain years, and sometimes even of 8-22. Another complicating factor is the possibility of running losses that are temporarily compensated by other cooperatives. If the situation improves after some years, the rules of distribution are changed somewhat in order to redress the negative balance in the Fund for Losses of the Community of Cooperatives.

14. Tables 7a and 7b show that the formulae have been applied correctly: e.g. in 1976,
$$\frac{\text{Index } 2.90}{\text{Index } 1.60} = 1.8125 \text{ and } \frac{\text{Pure Surplus: } 187.8}{\text{Pure Surplus: } 81.0} = 2.3185,$$
which is slightly higher due to the inequality in receipts of interest.

15. Lydall (1979: 183-204) provides a good introduction to aspects of a national income policy.
16. For the common viewpoint see, for example, Wood (1978: 222-223).
17. Phelps Brown (1977: 322-332) is an excellent reference for comprehensive analysis of pay structures.
18. Several studies have been undertaken by CLP's research department to analyse this problem.
19. On the relevance of games theory – in this case the Prisoner's Dilemma – and for an analysis of collective solutions to problems of distribution see Sen (1973: 96-99); also van den Doel (1978: 77-105).

VII

A SELF-MANAGED SECTOR

INTRODUCTION

The Mondragon experience, which has been analysed in previous chapters from an equity and efficiency perspective, will now be studied from that of its potential for further transition towards a new system of social relations of production. In general, self-managed enterprises have aimed at transforming the existing capital-controlled production system, but only meagre results have been achieved. This is why we have been able to make reference to only a few cases, e.g. some producer cooperatives in industrialised countries, some communes of production in Israel, a social property sector in Peru, and the Yugoslav system of self-management.

Cooperatives of various kinds have attempted to strengthen their position by forming national associations, even an international cooperative alliance. In European countries, e.g. France, Italy and Poland, and in developing countries, e.g. India, Peru and Colombia, regional and/or national associations meet more or less frequently, gather information, publish periodicals, and organise educational activities; in short, they attempt to bring greater cohesion among the various cooperators and to defend their interests. An important example of their work can be seen in their efforts to improve the social security position of cooperators.

These supporting supra-cooperative structures have not obtained any major success in the sense that cooperatives have acquired an accepted 'domain' in the national economy, whether in developed or developing countries. And the experience of producer cooperatives, even though their efficiency record has been slightly better than is generally believed, is only a small part of the global cooperative phenomenon.

The Kibbutz movement of production organisation was established in Israel in the 1920s; by the 1970s there were more than 100,000 members in some 250 communities with a strong aggregate record in terms of equity and efficiency. This experience is a valuable one in that it contributes to the debate on the

---

Notes to this chapter may be found on pp. 192-193.

feasibility of a socialist strategy of allocating scarce factors of production without direct linkage to the mechanism by which the fruits of work are distributed: 'to each according to his need' (Barkai 1977, 1978).

The concept 'movement', however, refers to a strong nationalist, communitarian and highly egalitarian ideology rather than to a strong suprastructure, with linkages between communes of production creating a micro-system of economic relationships with further transitional processes in perspective. This naturally makes the Kibbutz system less relevant as a lesson for other situations.

Considerable attention has been attracted by the Social Property Sector which was established in Peru in 1974; by 1979 this included 60 self-managed factories with 9000 workers, a national council, eight regional councils, and a funding agency.[1] In this case, the attention of analysts is attracted by the way in which the suprastructure was built rather than by the socio-economic performance that has been achieved. To what extent can such a sector co-exist with a capitalist and a state sector? If a Social Property Sector is to expand, ultimately to become the dominant sector of the economy as envisaged by the late President Velasco, how long will this take? Is it feasible, given national and international constraints? The concept of a social property or cooperative domain within a mixed economy has been given new meaning. In spite of a change in Peru's government, these new impulses have not been stifled but in fact have become part of the new government's strategy, albeit in a considerably modified and less ambitious form.

Yugoslavia is the exceptional case in which strong economic performance as well as a unique structure — a national constitution based on principles of self-management in all spheres of life — has been in force for several decades. For almost 30 years Yugoslavia has displayed a strong growth of Gross Domestic Product; during the 1960s it ranked next to Japan in terms of growth percentage. In the space of one generation, Yugoslavia's predominantly rural economy has been transformed into a modern industrial one. In terms of income and wealth distribution, an unusual degree of equality has been maintained; in terms of employment creation and regional development, major difficulties have been experienced from which much may be learned.[2] A process of transition towards self-management has occurred which includes the democratisation of production processes, of the distribution and spending of incomes, and of the socio-economic system of coordinating economic decisions. In each of these dimensions achievements have been considerable. Economic performance over the years has been sufficiently pronounced to allow lessons to be drawn on the basis of which feasibility problems in a decentralised socialist economy might be solved. The country is also prepared to introduce changes in its institutional aspects, even including the national constitution.

The Mondragon experience is presented in the perspective of these cases. We have seen that 'Mondragon' in the first place is a group of factories that have performed impressively in terms of equity and efficiency. Its complex structure displays many new features from which those who study the measures that might be taken in support of the cooperative phenomenon may learn a great deal, and which cause the unusual external dynamics of this cooperative phenomenon. Below we shall first review the economics of Mondragon, integrating some key aspects of the economic performance of the associated cooperatives and of the bank.[3]

The objectives of the entire group will be studied, since the aggregate is not identical to the sum of the individual parts. Will the simultaneous pursuit of efficiency and of equity cause tension and create new problems? Does the strong role played by internal financing pose problems? Is it possible to extend the cooperative sector towards a wider range of capital intensity? All these questions will be examined below.

Emphasis then falls on the economic structure of the cooperatives as compared to that of the Basque Provinces, and on the geographical expansion of the former. Linkages between cooperatives, i.e. the 'constitutional arrangements', and the opposing of bureaucratic tendencies are key elements which characterise 'Mondragon' as a self-managed sector.

At each stage reference will be made to the international examples mentioned above in order that the Mondragon system may be evaluated in a wider context of self-managed forms of production.

In the concluding section of this chapter we shall evaluate Mondragon in terms of the criteria (mostly economic) mentioned in the introductory chapter, and shall also discuss some of the cooperators' own opinions about Mondragon.

THE ECONOMICS OF MONDRAGON

This last overview will focus on the performance of the entire Mondragon group in order to deepen our insight into the equity and efficiency aspects of this case of self-management. Equity concerns those who already work in the cooperatives and others who wish to join them. It concerns a range of phenomena — distribution of earnings, of wealth, of education, and of employment — which indicate the extent to which the distribution of incomes and the opportunities to earn these have been democratised. With a few precautionary remarks, we hope to put Mondragon's impressive record into realistic perspective for the future.

Firstly, differences in earnings between cooperators within one enterprise, between different cooperatives, and between cooperatives and capitalist firms are narrow and are apparently compensated by other than monetary incentives.

This raises the issue of labour mobility, which in the Mondragon case is reported to be quite low. If labour mobility needs to increase for some reason, instruments other than earnings differences have to be used.[4]

Secondly, cooperators have a strong financial stake in their own cooperatives and there is little inequality of accumulated wealth in individual accounts, to the extent that annual surplus is allocated to these accounts. It is frequently said that a cooperator's financial stake is a powerful incentive for him to work hard in the own factory. But this is an aspect which also reduces labour mobility unless a way can be found by which ownership becomes readily transferable. Thirdly, considerable efforts are made to spread education widely and to distribute 'human capital' evenly, a necessary condition for productive participation, e.g. by cooperators who are elected to Social Councils. Wider distribution of information, however, and of knowledge with which that information can be understood, does not guarantee access to 'better' jobs: the hierarchical structure restricts upward mobility, and in the long run may cause frustration, higher absenteeism, and even a reduction in productivity.

Fourthly, employment creation is perhaps the most important equity aspect in that it prevents the emergence of a cooperative elite. If this had not been adopted as a basic principle by all cooperators and translated into operational guidelines by management, either the levels of earnings would have risen beyond the average take-home pay of the province, or the financial stakes would have increased excessively. There is no guarantee that at a future date the distinction between 'rich' and 'poor' cooperative enterprises may not lead to dis-integrating tendencies.[5]

Lastly, will it indeed be feasible to maintain an identical level of average earnings between a bank, industrial cooperatives and education cooperatives if the group should become geographically more widespread? The bank might easily become a 'rich' organisation that will not be able to withstand the temptation to increase the average level of earnings beyond that which is generally accepted.

Efficiency analysis has proven that a group of cooperative factories, provided it has access to credit sources and management services, can develop strongly during times of economic boom and also during a recession. The cooperatives have made excellent use of available production factors; however, their dependency on markets for purchases of inputs and for sales of their products causes considerable vulnerability. It is an interesting fact that, when the recession of the 1970s started, the cooperatives needed time to adjust to the new circumstances. A few years passed before effective policies could be adequately implemented which enabled strong investment and export promotion to be continued. The results achieved in 1979 and the forecasts for the period 1981-85 indicate that the group will play a stronger outward-oriented role in the provincial economy, and ultimately in the entire Basque economic structure, if plans work out as envisaged. It remains to be seen whether the good efficiency record can then be maintained. Firstly, there is some uncertainty as to whether the many cooperatives established during the seventies will be able to attain a stable cashflow and healthy financial situation. Secondly, will CLP have sufficient instruments at its disposal to enable it to play such a strong role in the larger economy? It must be remembered that its present position is conditioned by the prevailing law on credit cooperatives.

The records show that CLP has become the fastest growing financial institution in the Basque Provinces; its yields have been adequate but there is no guarantee that it would be able to secure sufficient financial outlets for much greater resources and maintain its high level of profitability. These remarks are in no way intended to modify the interpretation of past evidence, but rather to emphasise that new problems will need to be solved at each new stage of development, as occurred in the past.

A general assessment of Mondragon confirms that self-managed organisations can combine 'equity and efficiency'. Similar results have been found in production cooperatives elsewhere. Mondragon also reveals the complexity of *an economic system*, showing on a small scale the same phenomena for which the Yugoslav self-managed system needs to find solutions: how can the emergence of 'rich' versus 'poor' enterprises be prevented? How can an incomes policy be designed simultaneously with mechanisms with which to coordinate economic decision making? How can employment creation be safeguarded and a fair distribution and provision of education and training be assured?

A Mondragon Model

We now have sufficient evidence at our disposal to formulate a Mondragon model, its objectives, as well as its methods of operation.

The primary aim of the associated cooperatives is to earn at least the target level of earnings, which has been determined by extensive studies. Their next objective is to maximise surplus with respect to the own resources; this surplus should be minimally equal to eight per cent of own funds, and preferably of about 15 per cent. A further crucial guideline is the 'open door' principle. If the yield on own funds exceeds eight to 15 per cent, there will be an urge to expand employment. If the yield falls below eight per cent, employment needs to be reduced in order to restore an adequate long-term capital intensity. From a macro-economic perspective, such a policy is preconditional to allocative efficiency.

During boom years the cooperatives have indeed shown expansionary tendencies. In fact, they implemented the 'open door' principle to such an extent that CLP became concerned that the profitability of some associated cooperatives might be in jeopardy. A useful rule-of-thumb method which CLP introduced at that time was to advise cooperatives not to increase employment by more than 12 to 15 per cent in a given year; only under exceptional circumstances would profitability be sufficiently strong to sustain an expansion of employment of more than 15 per cent per annum.

This was the reason why CLP's Management Services Division introduced an index with which to analyse and monitor the economic performance of the factories: a comparison of profitability and employment expansion over five-year periods. All enterprises are ranked in these respects. Enterprises that score high on profitability (whether in terms of 'cost added' or of persons employed) are expected to increase employment at a greater-than-average rate; the opposite holds for less-than-average performance.

If all firms adhere to this goal, subtraction of the profitability ranking from that according to employment expansion, gives a value of zero for each enterprise. If there is then a clustering of values around zero, this will indicate that employment expansion is taking place in accordance with CLP's guideline. In reality many enterprises score higher than ten, indicating that rates of employment expansion have been greater than can be sustained in the long run given the level of profitability; others score less than -10, indicating that employment expansion has been insufficient.

The lessons of the recession have been learnt rapidly and pragmatically. Mondragon was already familiar with the custom of exchanging work, of helping factories out in peak seasons, or of assisting factories in temporary difficulties. An active programme has recently been introduced under which 'man months' are transferred from cooperatives in difficulties to other companies. The result is a considerable slowing-down of the overall expansion of jobs. If such a system is effective, one of its advantages is obviously speed of adjustment; capital, on the other hand, is invested in machinery, the life horizon of which determines the possibilities for adapting to new circumstances.

Mondragon's behaviour is therefore in line with the theory of a self-managed economy, in which adjustments in the capital labour ratio and the entry of new firms are of critical significance.

This model is similar to that first postulated by Horvat for Yugoslav enterprises and later analysed in depth by Miović and Vanek (Horvat 1967; Vanek & Miović in Vanek 1977: 104-134; Miović 1975). The latter have shown that such enterprise behaviour is consistent with an optimally functioning economy. On theoretical grounds there is therefore no reason why the Mondragon model could not apply equally well to a provincial or a national economy.

A credit cooperative that is linked to a system of cooperative factories has to cope with some interesting problems. It will be CLP's own efficiency as a bank which will determine whether or not the benchmark yield of 3.25 per cent, for example, will be met. Such a yield is necessary in order to maintain the required level of eight per cent of own funds with respect to total deposits. It has been pointed out that in many countries credit cooperatives have done well, and this has also been the case in Mondragon.

The principal operational pressure will usually be to attract new resources and to maintain growth. As long as the associated cooperatives develop dynamically and efficiently, they will have no difficulty in meeting their amortisation and other obligations to the credit cooperative, and therefore profitability can be maintained.

The situation changes, however, if a bank becomes 'too successful' while aiming explicitly at assisting only associated cooperatives, particularly at a time when cooperatives are heading towards economic recession. Some cooperatives require special assistance to enable them to head off bankruptcy; others may be more cautious about engaging in new investment projects. There thus is a need, to which CLP has responded by associating many new cooperatives, to search for new growth points, since otherwise the existence of the bank would be put into jeopardy. The matter is urgent because in a market economy, as we have seen, the results of a group of factories that is active in only a few branches become very sensitive to general market conditions.

Meso-economics

During the 1970s in particular, Mondragon has transcended the primitive form of being merely a successful group of cooperatives. During those years it began to function as an integrated system in a market economy that was undergoing a major structural recession.

In Table 1 key data are presented for the associated cooperatives and for CLP for three selected years: 1971, before the onset of the economic recession, which began around 1973-74; 1976, when the impact of the recession came to be felt strongly; and 1979 as the year when adjustments to the downswing in the business cycle began to be introduced.

Cooperative employment expansion, shown in column 1, reflects the policies of job expansion described previously; CLP's employment growth, in column 2, is a direct response to the fast increase of its financial operations during the 1970s. Cooperative pure surplus (column 3) serves to strengthen the own financial position (column 5); own funds, in turn, are related to the level of fixed assets aimed at, shown in column 7; the target is to obtain sufficient own resources to equalise fixed assets. CLP's pure surplus and own resources (columns 4 and 6) are linked primarily to total resources (column 9) and need to be equal to at least eight per cent of that amount; fixed assets (column 8) thus could be further increased, i.e. new branches could be opened, but would in turn accelerate the supply of total resources. Columns 10 and 11 indicate CLP's short and

Table 1. *The Economics of Mondragon*

	Employment		Pure Surplus		Own Resources		Fixed Assets		Total Resources	Short-Term loans	Long-Term loans
	A	B	A	B	A	B	A	B	B	B	B
	(1)	(2)	(3)	(4)	(5)	(6)	(7)	(8)	(9)	(10)	(11)
1971	9900	284	575	210	7350	750	6650	675	9700	1890	3100
1976	14450	641	1580	457	12350	1982	12525	1598	22490	5814	6880
1979	17170	892	1300	660	16000	2900	17000	2100	26750	8575	7500

	Sales	GVA	Earnings	Interest	Depreciation	Cash flow	Investments
	A	A	A	A	A	A	A
	(12)	(13)	(14)	(15)	(16)	(17)	(18)
1971	14750	4425	2850	300	700	1325	1450
1976	24800	9920	6550	550	1240	2820	3600
1979	33200	13250	7950	715	3285	4585	2300

Columns 1 and 2 show employment in actual numbers of jobs; columns 3-18 are in millions of pesetas (constant, 1976, prices; 70 pesetas ∿ 1 US dollar). A = Associated cooperatives, excluding education, social security and social services cooperatives; B = Caja Laboral Popular.

Source: Tables given in previous chapters, and internal documents of CLP.

medium-term outstanding loans, i.e. its sources of earnings: namely, the discounting of commercial bills for associated cooperatives, and the financing of their investment plans.

The financial position of the associated cooperatives with respect to fixed assets has weakened with the passing of time; CLP's best year as regards own resources in relation to fixed assets and total resources, was 1979. Changes in relative economic strength of the associated cooperatives and of CLP can be seen by examining pure surplus per person: a major fall occurred in the cooperatives, from 58,000 pesetas per person in 1971 to 760 in 1979 (in 1976 prices), whereas CLP maintained a level of 740,000 pesetas (in 1976 prices) per person.

A further point is the difference in ownership which may create a large scope for inequality of individual financial stakes: the average financial stake in the cooperatives rose from 742,000 pesetas per person in 1971 to 873,000 in 1979; and in CLP from 2,641,000 in 1971 to 3,250,000 per person in 1979.[6] In this calculation allowance has been made for the fact that the collectivisation process has gone considerably further in CLP than in the cooperatives.

Columns 12 to 18 of Table 1 focus on all associated cooperatives which contribute to aggregate pure surplus; in other words, the education, social security, and research and development cooperatives are not included. The significance of the aggregate sales level has been explained in Chapter IV, where we have seen that it is a main source of income for CLP. GVA, see column 13, as a percentage of aggregate sales has increased from 30 to 40 per cent, an indication of the attempts to increase the level of technological advance. Salaries (column 14) and interest payments (column 15) relate to aggregate employment and to yield on the individualised part of own resources. Until 1976, depreciation (column 16) averaged 10 per cent of fixed asset value; however, an extremely high percentage of depreciation is seen for 1979, possibly due to the poor situation in the preceding two years. The recovery that took place in 1979 was thus in first instance used to compensate for the earlier shortfall in depreciation. The improvement in that year is shown clearly in the aggregate cash-flow figures; in 1971 and 1976 these were less than the needs for the investment programme (column 18), but in 1979 they greatly exceeded the reduced level of investments.

The interactions between the cooperatives and the CLP are complex. Successful and dynamic performance on the part of the associated cooperatives exercises considerable pressure on CLP through the demand for credits — pressure which the cooperatives are able to exercise directly through their representatives in the General Assembly of their *own* bank.[7] Strong performance on the part of CLP, on the other hand, entails that it engages in an active search for new and high-yielding projects: the monitoring of cooperatives and the promoting of new entrants are then logical consequences.

The interaction between CLP and the associated cooperatives as regards the provision of short-term credits has been very effective: CLP's short-term loans as a percentage of aggregate sales have been in the benchmark range (see Chapter IV, p. 88). The investment programme is an entirely different matter, however. Even with a strong recovery on the part of cooperative investments, there is an absolute need for CLP to find new outlets; this explains its heavy investment expenditure in the field of education, its promotion of housing cooperatives, and its recently announced readiness to earmark 25 per cent of its loan programme to other than cooperative projects. If all this did not take place, the Management Services Division would have to expand too quickly, with an undesirable effect on the quality of its planning and monitoring.

Stagnation or even worse misfortune of the associated cooperatives would confront CLP with huge problems, all the more so if it has abundant resources at its disposal. Poor performance on the part of CLP would cause the dynamic development of the entire group to slow down and ultimately to come to a halt.

This overview shows that the system has functioned well during difficult times. Doubling of employment was accompanied by a considerable increase in real earnings. If the cooperators had had complete control of earnings policies, they might even have decided to take a smaller increase in real earnings, which would have enhanced the pure surplus for future accumulation. A definite evaluation of their behaviour during an economic crisis should preferably be postponed for another five years. Yet the facts indicate that the first major structural challenge of the mid-1970s has been met in a manner that safeguards further expansion of this self-managed sector. It is tempting to speculate that the data of Table 1 reflect the same phenomena that are found in a macro-economic self-managed context. Crises are characterised, as Vanek has argued, by a slowing-down of growth rates, not by downswings which result in the firing of workers and closing of factories, as occurred on a large scale in the Basque Provinces during the 1970s (Vanek 1970).

Self-financing

Fundamental problems may arise in job creation. For a number of reasons, the capital intensity of production may increase, whether due to successful economic performance or to the need to modernise in order not to lose markets. As a result, it will become increasingly difficult to determine an entry fee for new cooperators which will stand in any realistic relationship to the cost of the workplace. Between 1971 and 1976 average capital intensity in the cooperatives rose in real terms by about 40 per cent — an absolute necessity since much of the machinery had become outdated. Again, from 1976 until 1979 a modest increase of about five per cent was booked. The marginal increase for new jobs has obviously risen far more.

Cooperators need to earn sufficient pure surplus to finance the investment of their own workplace in some ten years by accumulating an equivalent amount on *individual* capital accounts, as indeed has happened in the past (see Chapter VI). Worsening economic results and the rapidly increasing costs of investments, however, together with a relative fall in the entry fee, make it less and less possible to follow such a policy. The result may be seriously to undermine the cooperators' stake in the own enterprise, while the financial collateral simultaneously weakens. In recent General Assembly meetings, cooperators have devoted much time to discussing the financial bases of their own enterprises. Decisions to enlarge the capital base through temporary salary reductions, i.e. forced savings, may be taken in order to cope with this problem, thus reflecting recessionary conditions.[8]

Despite the increments made, the capital intensity of the cooperative group is low: estimates of total assets, capital assets and stocks, or other measures with respect to GVA, indicate values of between two and three for the capital-output ratio.[9] Any major increase in capital intensity, however, would disturb the financial base of the cooperatives in that it would reduce the significance of the financial stake of cooperators, with unpredictable and perhaps undesirable consequences.

A careful balancing of own resources versus other resources, and of individual accounts versus collective accounts, provides a set of policy instruments by which the group may continue to expand even under adverse economic conditions.

In the concluding section of this chapter we shall return to this problem, which is directly connected with the ownership structure. At this point it can be concluded that the Mondragon cooperatives have found an effective solution to the financial problems that in general have plagued producer cooperatives during their first generation of existence.

LIMITS OF TRANSITION?

The Mondragon model may continue to hold for a small segment of industry, but is it realistic to posit that it is also applicable to the entire economic structure in a primary, secondary or tertiary sector? Following from this, is there any scope for further transformation of an economy beyond a rather limited geographical area?

If these questions could be answered affirmatively, the Mondragon case would ultimately become the second case after Yugoslavia, in which self-management is the major characteristic of an entire socio-economic system.

Diversification

Over the last few years, the cooperatives have diversified their activities to some extent, and it is anticipated that the cooperative economic structure (see Table 2) may be identical to that of the entire Mondragon area in a few years' time, and, at a much later stage, to that of the Basque Provinces. CLP's Management Services Division has done research into primary sector activities and has undertaken new projects in the tertiary sector, such as the promotion of housing cooperatives.

Table 2. *Economic Structure (employment, percentages)*

	Basque provinces (1975)	Mondragon area (1975)	Cooperative group (1978)
Primary Sector	10.7	5	1.2
Secondary Sector	44.2	75	83.6
Tertiary Sector	45.1	20	15.2
	100	100	100

Sources: IKEI 1979: Cuadro 1; Chapter III *supra*; CLP and League for Education and Culture (internal documents).

In the *primary sector*, the Mondragon group has to confront the problem of low agricultural productivity: due to fragmented landownership and a weakening rather than improvement of the infrastructure, productivity in the primary sector – i.e. value added per person – is only 40 per cent of that in the secondary sector. The Mondragon group aims explicitly at activities which can guarantee that the average level of take-home pay will be secured by all cooperators. Its agricultural activities, such as cattle farming, dairy products, forestry, animal feeds and fruit conserves, are therefore carefully selected. In this respect, a combination of 'traditional' and 'Mondragon' types of cooperative has been introduced: the members are individual farmers (*socios productores*) and workers of the factory (*socios transformadores*) who form two categories of cooperators. Any future activity in the primary sector will most likely take place in other, more thinly populated, Basque Provinces.

In Yugoslavia the agricultural sector is also very complex, and it cannot be hypothesised that pure self-management is an adequate perspective from which to obtain the best insight into functioning of that sector (Allcock n.d.). Given the importance of agriculture in most developing countries, it would be of great significance if the Mondragon planners were to undertake a major effort to integrate agricultural activities into their meso-economics.

In 1978 15 per cent of all cooperators were active in the *tertiary sector*. This includes such activities as banking, research and development, and a consumers' retail cooperative, all of which are normally found in a market economy, as well as activities that belong typically to the public sector, such as education and social security.

It is interesting to note that, in the Mondragon case, the *consumers' cooperative* started to develop at a later stage. This cooperative phenomenon goes back to the origins of cooperative history, i.e. the cooperative society established in 1844 in Rochdale in the north-west of England. A modern example of the great potential of consumers' cooperatives may be seen in Sweden, where two out of every three households are members of one or more cooperatives (Swedish Institute 1978).

A special type of consumers' cooperative is the cooperative *housing* organisation, which is also found in other countries. In Mondragon the first housing cooperative was set up in the mid-1970s; by 1980 there were a dozen such organisations in the major towns of the Basque Provinces, with some 1200 apartments.

Tertiary activities also include two *service cooperatives*, organisations that are not very common. One of them, with more than a hundred members, is part of the Ularco group, and provides expertise to the other six cooperatives that constitute this group. Rather than forming an integral part of the larger group, it is an independent organisation, set up to secure economies of scale in marketing, purchasing and bookkeeping, in the monitoring of social and economic indicators, and in personnel policies. It is anticipated that each group of cooperatives will gradually develop its own service cooperative in line with the Ularco model.

The other service cooperative, Auzo-Lagun, is for *part-time work* (see Chapter II), employing about 450 women[10] and with the same organisational characteristics as the others. Through their General Assembly the women cooperators are able to exert considerable pressure to secure orders for work from other cooperatives. The distinction between secondary and tertiary sector activities then loses much of its meaning. The part-time work carried out by Auzo-Lagun would normally be included in the secondary sector, i.e. cleaning, laundry, cantine activities. Its independent organisation, which gives the people involved considerably more scope to articulate their opinions, makes it a tertiary sector activity.

It seems likely that CLP's objectives will be reached in the primary and tertiary sectors. Whether or not it will also be feasible and desirable gradually to include a wider range of production processes in industry — including highly capital-intensive activities — is a question which cannot be answered at this stage.

DISPERSION

Diversification of activities is now accompanied by some regional *dispersion*. At first, the activities of the cooperatives were concentrated mainly in Mondragon, although already during the 1960s some associated factories were located at some distance from the town. Greater visibility has now been acquired, particularly since CLP opened branch offices throughout the Basque Provinces. After only one decade, cooperative activities are now to be found in 203 locations (see Table 3). Expansion has been strong in the three dimensions which have characterised Mondragon from the beginning: industry, education and banking. A fourth dimension, still included under 'other' activities, will gradually need to be given greater attention, i.e. the consumers' cooperatives. By the time another decade has passed, if present trends continue, even quite small towns will have a branch of CLP to capture deposit accounts, one or more factories to provide employment, and a consumers' cooperative selling a variety of goods with which to meet household needs.

Table 3. *Regional disperson of cooperatives* (numbers)*

	1968					1978				
	Indus-try	Edu-cation	Bank	Other	Total	Indus-try	Edu-cation	Bank	Other	Total
Guipúzcoa	27	–	26	5	58	38	11	41	13	103
Vizcaya	9	–	12	7	28	17	17	28	5	67
Alava	2	–	1	–	3	5	1	8	1	15
Navarra	–	–	2	–	2	6	1	7	4	18
Total	38	–	41	12	91	66	30	84	23	203

* Emphasis is on cooperative locations; CLP branches are therefore included as independent units. Data on the dispersion of retail outlets by province are not yet available.

Sources: CLP Annual Reports; League for Education and Culture, internal documents.

The economics of Mondragon are not determined by specific territory and should therefore not be identified with regional economics which focus on economic phenomena from the perspective of geographical area.[11] Only after complete transformation of a provincial economy, for example, could there be any convergence of meso- and regional economics.

In a general sense, the geographical restriction has been determined by the decision to focus solely on the Basque Provinces. The main characteristics of the dispersion are clearly functional: of banking, of some production, of education, of consumers' activities. In this context it is important that external dynamics should be tested by monitoring export performance. It has been necessary, for instance, to search for export markets on which to sell products. Will this new network of contacts be used to 'export the model' itself in a second stage? Turn-key plants have been sold to several countries and, theoretically, the monitoring of their operations could also include the provision of knowhow about the ways in which they should be operated.

This aspect has caused considerable problems in Yugoslavia where joint ventures, for example between foreign companies and local enterprises, have necessitated particular legislation which would combine the chance of gaining access to foreign technology with the assurance of maintaining the own model of work organisation. Foreign contacts also have to allow major scope for the implementation of self-management; otherwise it would be necessary to compromise by combining pure self-management at home with market relationships through subsidiaries in other countries (Svejnar & Smith 1980, 1981).

Could it be argued that a wider community − of CLP account holders − has subsidised the 'Mondragon economy' by permitting the bank to collect large financial resources? Strictly speaking, the answer has to be in the affirmative, but the interesting question is whether this forms a barrier to further processes of transition. The critical point is the use that CLP makes of such resources and of its favourable financial results. The bank's actions have been analysed above in considerable detail and we have found that it is bound to use such resources for further transformation of the economy. Its account holders will presumably not raise objections as long as CLP fulfils its obligations under the law, similarly to the other commercial banks. It is not to be expected, therefore, that CLP's financial structure will prevent further geographical expansion of the cooperatives.

DECENTRALISATION

If the Mondragon cooperators had not adopted guiding principles and organisational structures which aimed at achieving decentralisation, a small oligarchy of CLP and of people belonging to the largest cooperatives might have formed a centralised power nucleus. This threat could become more actual if the group's activities are to be further diversified and spread over a wider territory. Analysis of the institutional aspects is therefore essential before the possibilities for further transformation of the provincial economy can be evaluated.

The relationships between cooperatives and between the cooperatives and the wider economy are illustrated in Diagram 1, in which the financial and educational cooperatives are placed in a separate box.[12] In the foregoing chapters it has been clearly shown that the dependency of the industrial cooperatives on outside markets gives rise to considerable fluctuations in their economic performance. The policy instruments used by the support bloc − such as investment and manpower planning — are more within control of the cooperators and enable a higher degree of planning, providing some degree of stability to the entire group.

Formal linkages between the cooperatives are of various kinds. In the first place, the Contract of Association creates a solid relationship between CLP and the associated cooperatives, and also contains the basic economic and organisational guidelines to which each cooperative is bound to adhere. Then there is the fact that individual cooperatives are members of Lagun-Aro, the collective social security system. In the area of education, the League for Education and Culture provides a nucleus which enables the coordination and planning of manpower aspects. The R&D cooperative Ikerlan provides a technological impetus to those cooperatives which are members of its General Assembly. The consumers' cooperative Eroski coordinates activities of the retail branches. It is linked with CLP through its Contract of Association, but its primary contacts are with the tens of thousands of families who, in this way, are able to learn about the role of consumers in their own society. Eroski does not purchase many goods from the cooperatives, but it is likely that it will become more integrated with production activities. Lastly, and of strategic importance in a mixed and open economy, there are the linkages between cooperatives belonging to a particular group. It seems likely that each cooperative will eventually be part either of a functional or of a social group: the former derives its identity from the products that are made; the other from the area in which the member cooperatives are located.

This system of linkages is a principal element that distinguishes Mondragon from other cases, and can only be compared with the complexity of Peru's social property sector. Mondragon is more flexible, however, and more prone to new elements. A key question in the future will be whether or not the democratised relationships can be maintained and perhaps strengthened. The challenges will become all the greater as the group gains success in transforming some part of the provincial and wider economy. A stage will then soon be reached at which the same fundamental problems will have to be solved as those with which the Yugoslavs have struggled for many years. The Yugoslav solution has been to introduce social agreements and social contracts between the various socioeconomic institutions at all levels, from the local one of the communes to the federal level of the state, in order that adequate instruments might be designed with which socio-economic decisions, taken on a self-management basis, might be coordinated.

Bureaucratisation?

'Centralisation leads to more centralisation' — a statement by a senior executive of Ularco — well expresses the dilemma faced by a rapidly expanding cooper-

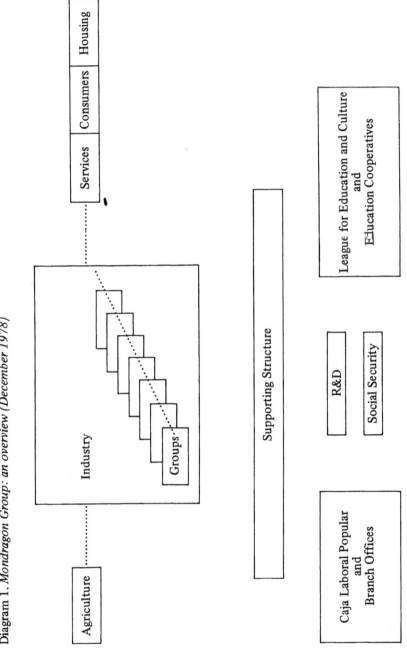

Diagram 1. *Mondragon Group: an overview (December 1978)*

ative movement, whose successful performance depends to a considerable extent on the supporting mechanisms that have been developed. One way by which bureaucratisation has been prevented and self-management has been safeguarded has been the policy of creating new institutions rather than enlarging existing ones.[13] The hiving-off of Fagor Electronics from Ulgor in 1966 and of Fagor Industrial in 1974, of Ikerlan, the R&D cooperative, from the Technical Training School in 1977, and of Lagun-Aro from CLP in 1970, are examples of the decentralisation strategy that has been adopted.

On the other hand, new institutions need to be established, if only to counter the huge concentrations of power in national and international markets: the forming of groups — 'archipelagos' of cooperatives[14] — and the setting-up of a specialised institution to care for export-related problems, are examples of such a trend.

Perhaps the most important way by which a balance is maintained between centralisation and decentralisation is the system of monitoring and planning. Each of the coordinating institutions, CLP, League for Education and Culture, or groups like Ularco, devotes some of its resources to medium-term and annual plans. Each individual cooperative, irrespective of its field of activity, engages in similar planning exercises. The draft plans are submitted to the other organisations for discussion and comment and several iterative rounds of such 'planning from below' take place before some degree of consistency is achieved with respect to finance, manpower planning, marketing, or other important aspects. CLP, in particular, provides for the external dynamics in Mondragon and carries the main responsibility for the decentralisation of power.

A final point of interest in this section is the role played by Spanish cooperative law. Whether in banking, production or education, statutes and by-laws have to be drawn up within the framework of existing legal terms. Spanish cooperative legal provisions are such that the Mondragon system has been able to develop in these three dimensions without encountering insurmountable barriers. At times — with regard to social security problems, for example — considerable attention has had to be devoted to solution of the legal aspects; at others — when setting up CLP, for example — the existing law has provided adequate scope for the design of a structure that was suited to the own cooperative requirements.[15]

Accommodation within the existing legal system needs to be found at each new stage of development. The cooperative law therefore plays a limiting role, in this case and in general. In two self-managed cases which have been particularly considered, on the other hand, the law has played an active and supportive role without which so much could not have been achieved. In the Peruvian case, to begin with, there were only a number of laws with which it was intended to design a new sector of the economy. This may have been a major weakness since the support that could be mobilised for such an initiative from 'above' was insufficient. Yugoslavia has introduced numerous new laws and even major changes to the national constitution, both to consolidate the achievements of the past and to lay the foundations for further steps towards democratisation of the entire economy.

In the case of Mondragon, it is conceivable that the cooperative group will be able to establish suitable relations with the legislative powers in the Basque Provinces.

CONCLUSIONS

An evaluation of a case such as that of Mondragon is bound to give rise to controversy; it is still too early, for example, to evaluate the facts of the late 1970s. In this work, Mondragon has been viewed from the perspective of self-management economics; others may argue that Mondragon 'proves' that a market economy can work efficiently, that the cooperatives illustrate how efficient production can be under competitive conditions.[16]

In this final analysis of equity and efficiency it has been useful to proceed in two directions: by comparison with other cases, and by comparison with the objectives that had been formulated by the cooperators themselves. In both respects it has been possible to draw definite conclusions.

In a comparative sense the record of equity and efficiency constitutes another case in which the two concepts reinforce one another. And in terms of the own objectives, whether with respect to employment creation, earnings levels, training, accumulation, or yield on own resources, the cooperators have done remarkably well. The potential for further transformation towards self-management has also been examined and the conclusion reached that, from an economic perspective, the Mondragon model offers scope for expansion of the cooperative self-managed domain within a market economy. In order to take the analysis of this politically and strategically important question a step further, we now return to the criteria raised in Chapter I: the conditions that need to be fulfilled for a pure, labour-managed, model of self-management, such as have been developed by Vanek in particular.

Control and Participation

The first element by which we can distinguish whether an actual case is to be characterised as 'self-managed' is that of control, which should be considered in a straightforward and formal sense: does 'labour' control, i.e. hire 'capital', or vice versa?[17] The fact that Mondragon's cooperators do not sign a wage contract but become members of the cooperative with a vote in the General Assembly, clearly puts the group into the category of self-managed systems. This implies access, whether direct or indirect, to all facts about the enterprise. For example, data on the distribution of earnings are published annually after having been debated and approved in the General Assembly. It is also obvious that the Mondragon cooperators bear high risks, including those that in other situations are borne by the capital-owners (Jonsson 1978).

An important dimension of this formal definition of control is that in Mondragon no 'degeneration' has occurred with the passing of time. Control is vested exclusively in those who work; and all who work — with the exception of a few highly specialised people on short-term contract — obtain their rights, irrespective of age, experience, sex, or place of origin.

This 'constitutional' arrangement may involve a minimum of participation, or it may imply genuine self-management with a high degree of personal involvement in the organisation of work.[18]

Bradley and Gelb have found in Mondragon an unusual degree of coherence and of trust between all cooperators, and from shop floor to management (Bradley & Gelb 1981a; 1981b). It would be interesting to monitor these aspects over a longer period of time: it seems likely that further democratisation will take place in line with what has been called 'internal dynamics' (Bernstein 1976), or the 'social objectification' of participatory values and procedures (Kester 1980). It would also have been of interest if such studies had been undertaken in the 1960s and early seventies. Since then an entirely new political situation has emerged, in which the trade union movement in particular is of significance to the entire group. Previously, the cooperative's General Assembly — even though highly formalised — was one of the few mobilising instruments that were available to workers.[19] It remains to be seen whether a transition towards more democratic work relationships will have the support of the existing trade unions in the cooperative branches, or whether new tensions will arise. A determining factor in this respect will probably be whether the cooperators can maintain 'open door' policies and do not become a cooperative elite. It will be another five to ten years, however, before such issues crystallise. In the meantime, if the cooperatives should spread more widely into the big urban concentrations, the impact of urbanisation will also need to be reckoned with.

A last point is the rapid development of new technology. Up to the mid-1970s labour exercised considerable control over technology in Mondragon where coordination with their own educational system was particularly successful. If new technologies should need to be introduced rapidly and on a huge scale, as is now occurring with developments in micro-processing, it is by no means certain that that harmony will be maintained. Attempts to further involve workers at all levels of the organisation, including management, may become frustrated. Participation — self-management — as a system of control is strongly embedded in the Mondragon structures; participation as a system of *management-sharing* still poses great problems. 'One of the greatest dangers for self-management is the formation of small oligarchic groups made up of managers, heads of administration, and political functionaries ... which tend to assume full control over the workers' council', according to Marković in his study of Yugoslav self-management (Marković 1970). On a much smaller scale, this may be the major challenge that Mondragon will have to face in the 1980s.

Ownership

The second major criterion is that of ownership, of which Meade says that it is 'still the most crucial issue';[20] Vanek gives it second priority, after control relationships. The Mondragon case knows a variety of ownership forms. All cooperatives have a mixture of individual accounts and collective reserves, but the balance between the two categories is not everywhere the same. In the industrial cooperatives more than 50 per cent of own resources are individually allocated, whereas in the credit cooperative less than 40 per cent can be claimed individually.

It seems that the cooperators are adopting a fairly flexible attitude in this respect. In Alecoop, for instance, a very high percentage of annual surplus is allocated to reserves; in another cooperative − Dormicoop − all members have decided in assembly that, at the time of retirement, individual accounts will become part of the reserves rather than be paid out to individual members.

It is recognised, on the one hand, that individual accounts represent evidence to members that they are stakeholders; individual distribution of ownership on a large scale also prevents 'capital' owners from exercising that sort of control that normally is linked to the size of capital property. From the theoretical and operational perspective, on the other hand, it would be desirable to introduce a form of social ownership which is neither individualised nor liable to play into the hands of controlling groups, e.g. of bureaucrats. From the operational point of view, in fact, social ownership would have the advantage of avoiding the difficult problem of transferring ownership claims from one cooperative to another.

The distinction between individual accounts and collective reserves creates an additional difficulty. We have seen in Chapter VI that own resources − as far as individual accounts are concerned − command a scarcity price which is quite high. This is far less the case for collective reserves, since earnings policies of cooperatives are determined independently. A strong profitability record, combined with the policy of non-distribution of pure surplus, automatically places a scarcity price of capital on collective accounts. If profitability is squeezed and average earnings levels are set 'too high', then the amount available as an equivalent to the scarcity price of capital would be inadequate. In other words, the system would gradually change from labour-managed to worker-managed, with undesirable allocative consequences.

This problem will probably be one of the most difficult to solve when numerous cooperators begin to retire in the mid-1990s and Mondragon has to cope with the consequent meso-economic aspects. In all likelihood, individual accounts will be largely paid out, but CLP has no control over the capital market at large. If money withdrawals were to be re-cycled into the own credit cooperative, this would provide an intermediate solution. The only conclusion that can be reached at present is that Mondragon is a case in which, for a period of about half a century, ownership problems will not interfere with the identity of the model. This in itself is an important aspect in that such a period may see the start of many processes of transition, including political ones. In the long run, Meade may be correct in calling ownership 'still the most crucial issue'. In the meantime, however, control relationships will determine the kind of ownership patterns that will ultimately persist.

Horvat and Vanek both argue for a new concept of ownership which is compatible with self-management (Horvat 1977, Vanek 1977). It remains to be seen whether the path of change selected by the Mondragon cooperators will lead to such a situation. If so, they will have overcome one of the main barriers towards a democratised socio-economic system.

Ownership is an essential element of the collective shares held by workers and trade unions, a problem which is now under discussion in several countries. The Meidner Fund plan, subject of intense debate in Sweden, is perhaps the best known: a plan to introduce profit sharing with workers on a collective basis is seen as a major step towards socialisation of the economy (Meidner 1978).

Capital Accumulation

A third criterion for a self-managed economy is the presence of an institution which safeguards the accumulation of capital and is involved in its allocation. In this respect Mondragon and its CLP are almost flawless, as illustrated by the high cash flow percentage of Gross Value Added, and by the system of distribution of pure surplus. A unique cooperative case, thus, of development in which the provision of capital has not been a bottleneck. Capital is available to enable the associated cooperatives to meet their external financial needs; the resultant loans, of varying maturity, are repaid according to agreed contracts. The provision of financial resources should thus not be confused with ownership aspects.

It has been argued that the natural inclination of the Basques to save money is an important explanatory factor of the rich flow of resources, but the preceding analysis has shown that this is unlikely. The flow of funds is due primarily to two factors: firstly, the rules of distribution embodied in the Contract of Association, the text of which has hardly changed since the late 1950s; and secondly, the various activities of the Caja Laboral Popular, such as monitoring the profitability of associated cooperatives, and providing loan capital. In Yugoslavia too, gross national savings as a percentage of Gross National Product have been high by international standards, ranging from 25 to 35 per cent per annum. In that case, institutional arrangements have safeguarded considerable flows of financial resources. Mondragon's record in this respect reflects the insight of cooperators in their own long-term interests rather than the Basque propensity to save.

Accumulation of capital, and control over its allocation, are fundamental aspects by which one socio-economic system may be distinguished from another. In the Mondragon case capital resources are allocated with two objectives: to gradually increase the capital-intensity of production in order to integrate new technological developments, and to create the highest possible number of new jobs. The fact that both the flow of financial resources and the institutional aspects meet the criteria associated with a self-managed economy could imply considerable scope for further dynamic development. The fast evolution of the past decades, examined from various perspectives in preceding chapters, is closely linked to the manner in which this third condition has been met.

Plan and Market

The fourth criterion refers to the coordinating roles of shelter institutions in the field of economics and of education, and even on the political scene. We have distinguished between cooperatives belonging to the support bloc and those that are more directly dependent on market relationships. The former have greater scope in planning their own activities. In the first two dimensions in particular, i.e. coordination of decision making in the economic dimension through the Management Services Division and in the educational dimension through the League for Education and Culture, the instruments designed are adequate. It is interesting that the cooperators have also adopted a pragmatic position in this respect. The support bloc has expressed a preference for long-term planning; the associated cooperatives recognise the stimulating impact that is caused by market relationships. For instance, a policy by which stronger cooperatives might subsidise their weaker colleagues by purchasing their products at lower than market prices, has never been introduced. On the contrary, there is strong determination to reach the efficiency standards determined by market pricing. One reason for this is undoubtedly the awareness of the difficulties involved in the planning process, particularly if undertaken in an innovative and self-managed manner.

At this stage of the analysis it is hardly necessary to repeat that self-managed planning is quite different from planning under systems of centralised control (Kardelj 1980; Ardalan 1980). The former entails 'planning from below', i.e. involvement of the institutions and people affected, optimal flows of information, and a system of monitoring that is democratically controlled. Plans are a necessary instrument in the efficient allocation of resources and for the generation of information that otherwise may not be available. Given the smallness of Mondragon it is not realistic to carry the analysis further; plans and markets typically belong to socio-economic decision making at the national level. Once Mondragon's impact becomes clearly identifiable in the input-output tables of the Basque economy, however, it will be a key strategic issue.

At the meso- and macro-levels, a strong planning agency is essential as otherwise a self-managed economy could not function. Phenomena such as the entry and exit of firms, and the adjustment processes of capital intensity, can only be realised by careful planning and institutional support (Meade 1979). Mondragon's further development of, and investment in, research and development will also depend on careful planning.

It will perhaps be necessary that the Mondragon cooperators engage in the political dimension. This will raise the issue of links between economic and political democracy, for which innovative patterns still have to be developed in other situations, including the West European political democracies. When systems of democratic control begin to touch upon such issues as income distribution and infrastructural investments, the wider political context needs to be taken into account as a determining factor. The recent changes in Spanish national politics and in regional power structures may give 'Mondragon' an historic opportunity. It is not inconceivable that in a future decade a transition towards self-management in organisations of production and towards self-government in the political field will be mutually reinforcing.[21] Mondragon's further expansion beyond the meso-level may be conditioned by such interaction.

Distribution

The final criterion is that of distribution. This has been discussed in Chapter VI where Mondragon's performance has been evaluated on the basis of the work of Horvat and Vanek, and where we gave particular attention to inequalities of earnings and of income from capital accounts.

If the Mondragon group should expand further, problems of distribution will become more difficult rather than more easy to solve, depending as they do on the degree to which solidarity is practised by the cooperators, whether within the enterprise, among cooperatives, or between cooperatives and other enterprises. The larger the group, the more difficult it will be for individuals to identify with distant structures that transcend the horizon of the own work organisation. Incomes policies will need to be coordinated at a more remote level; as that distance increases it may well become more difficult to adhere strictly to the guiding principles. Relationships with trade unions and with municipal and provincial authorities, and the policies adopted at the state level, may well endanger the internal policy of maintaining equality, and thus prevent the cooperatives from having greater influence over the surrounding community.

The relationship between trade unions and cooperators may be one of particular sensitivity. In general, trade unions have developed in a market economy in which labour's interests were opposed to those of 'capital'. As an institution the union typically belongs to the capitalist market economy; its main instrument of participation in industry is that of collective bargaining with which to obtain higher earnings. Problems of investment, of job creation, of research and development, of personnel policies, rarely belong to the union's range of activities.

Trade union activities under a market economy clearly do not fit into a self-managed socio-economic system, but a representative organisation of cooperators on an industrial or national scale could undertake a very constructive role: to engage in education, to raise political issues, to guard against erosion of the system of self-management, are a few of its possible functions. In Yugoslavia, for instance, trade unions have not been abolished but form a significant part of the socio-economic system.

Whether or not trade unions could play a dual role with flexibility   the traditional one with respect to capitalist enterprises and an innovative one with respect to self-managed enterprises – remains to be seen. The traditional role implies aiming at higher wages and having to accept the employment situation; the innovative role implies cooperation with a self-managed domain whose objective is to keep earnings constant while aiming at expansion of employment.

We have evaluated the Mondragon case on the basis of criteria that also apply to a national economy; nevertheless, it should be remembered that Mondragon is as yet only of modest significance, even to the province in which it is situated. It behoves us therefore to pay more attention to problems of transition than is usual in works on the theory of self-management, in order to discover whether there is any likelihood of transforming a larger part of the national economy.

With respect to each of the five criteria we have emphasised problems and aspects which may be connected with a new stage of Mondragon's development. In our opinion, the potential for further change is as important a characteristic as the record of equity and efficiency.

By 1980 almost all cooperatives in the province of Guipúzcoa had become associated with the Mondragon group; many small private enterprises had also joined. In quantitative terms these events are of little note; in qualitative terms they signify that the transformation towards a new system of social relations in production is taking place, smoothly and efficiently. If this were to happen on a large scale in Spain, it would be possible to see how the Mondragon model compares with new trends of worker take-overs in other countries, such as France, where Batstone has found 'a tendency for new co-ops to be established as other companies fail' (Batstone 1979: 25).

Opinions held by the Cooperators

This economic analysis of Mondragon should preferably be complemented by in-depth sociological analysis of the cooperators themselves, particularly as regards the processes of transition. Has there been resistance to change? To what is the excellent leadership due? Are the cooperators aware of what they have achieved in cooperative history? Will 'cooperativism' as an ideology withstand the greater 'individualism' which may result from a higher standard of living? These are only some of the questions that could form the subject of sociological analysis.

Whether or not the Mondragon system will keep 'on track' during each new stage of development, may be determined largely by the cooperators themselves. Their average age is no higher than 35 to 37 years; in other words, few of them are personally familiar with the events that shaped the system during its initial years. Opinions and perspectives must have changed with the times, particularly during the 1970s when great changes occurred in Spain's political system and the impact of a structural economic crisis had to be faced. Any student of the Mondragon scene must inevitably form some idea of the people involved, and our intention here is merely to flesh out that idea to the best of our ability.

In the years since the Mondragon movement started one or two surveys of these aspects have been undertaken, and their findings will now be briefly discussed in order that the reader may gain some familiarity with data that are not easily accessible. The facts are presented without the required disciplinary background. It will be obvious that further study and monitoring by sociologists, lawyers, political scientists, will be needed before comprehensive evaluation can be completed.

The first survey was undertaken by Ballasteros in Ulgor in 1965 when, given the political situation, any expression of opinion was a hazardous affair (Ballesteros 1968). Very little is known about workers' opinions in general during the Franco regime.

The majority of the 100 cooperators interviewed reported that they had never spoken in their factory's Assembly, some apparently for reasons of 'shyness', others because they agreed with the proposals made by the chair. There was no active participation by cooperators, as evidenced by their few contacts with superiors, and relatively little familiarity with information that had been made officially available. Nevertheless, Ballasteros found a high degree of satisfaction. Almost all the cooperators said that 'life is better than five years ago'; that 'they would wish that their children would also get employment in their cooperative'; and that 'their family is pleased they got work in a cooperative'. Ballasteros concludes by saying

... we have found a cooperative group in which, on the positive side, there is a high degree of solidarity, a good programme of professional training, and economic efficiency in production. It seems that there exists in Mondragon a cooperativism *sui generis*; an adequate 'climate', together with good economic development, and high morale. This is reinforced by the fact that many cooperators have been educated in the cooperative educational institutions. On the negative side, however, there is a low degree of participation in decision making which undoubtedly relates to the large size of the enterprise, although it is possible that the survey did not capture certain aspects of real participation. Another negative point is that little knowledge about cooperatives elsewhere in Spain is available in Mondragon. Concrete problems get more attention than the more abstract and theoretical aspects. Perhaps the success that has been achieved has induced a certain degree of indifference.

Finally, ... it seems that it would be difficult to transfer the Mondragon experience elsewhere if the conditions there are not similar to those in Mondragon (Ballasteros 1968: 244-45).

In the Ularco factories, a survey was undertaken in 1977 among 394 cooperators, to examine the extent to which negative attitudes with respect to work and to the own enterprise would lead to increased absenteeism (Ularco 1977). The analysis concentrated on aspects of organisation and of personality. The hypothesis was that the general atmosphere in a factory does not contribute to job satisfaction, but that the absence of favourable conditions leads to dissatisfaction. Seven organisational factors — variation of work, interesting job content, possibility to learn, participation in decision making, the group, the boss, the social relevance of work, were applied in order to construct an index of 'satisfaction'. The conclusion was that the level of satisfaction was fairly low; indifference with respect to the own work proved to be high. For instance, it was said that absenteeism creates 'free conditions of life', indicating that the work climate was not very attractive. The attitude towards the enterprise was positive, however, and appeared to be the principal reason for a low degree of absenteeism. The attitudes of men and women towards work and to the enterprise in general showed significant differences. Women were less satisfied than men in both respects. The Ularco research argued for a widespread discussion of the findings, which would lay the base for changes in the organisation of work as well as in the functioning of the enterprise at large: this could lead to greater commitment towards the own cooperative.

A survey which the present authors undertook in the Autumn of 1977 served as a tentative exploration of workers' opinions regarding a number of issues related to employment creation, distributional aspects, education and 'participation'.[22]

A favourable circumstance was that by then political conditions had changed dramatically and people had become accustomed to express their opinions somewhat more freely. Given the situation over the preceding 40 years, however, a continued bias against open discussion was only to be expected.

Of the 80 cooperators interviewed, 77 answered affirmatively when asked whether their decision to join a cooperative had been correct; many spontaneously gave reasons for their positive response. A generally positive reply was also given to a question regarding 'satisfaction'. Among the positive aspects of the cooperative movement, 'job creation' was mentioned most frequently — all those questioned already had a secure job. The great majority of the positive replies referred to aspects of job creation, to access to work for relatives and children, to the 'quality' of the own job, and to possibilities for further training and education.

The excellent design of the Mondragon cooperatives was frequently commented on, and also the fact that the cooperators themselves, of any rank, often spoil the climate due to favouritism, jealousy, carelessness, and abuse of power.

As for issues of participation, our conversations focussed on the role of the Social Council and on attitudes towards the General Assembly. It is not possible to summarise the views of these people with any precision, but the lower ranks seemed to see the Social Council as a 'downward channel' through which to spread information throughout the enterprise, while considering it an advantage that the Council provided them with a means of self-expression. The higher ranks of cooperators saw the Social Council primarily as an instrument for the expression of opinions and, a further advantage, as one which enabled the receipt of more information.

Many complaints were expressed regarding those elected; it is striking, however, that 'superiors', 'human treatment', and 'comradeship' scored highly. Issues of distribution, whether of earnings differentials or of individual capital accounts, did not play a role in these conversations.

The tentative findings of our own survey match well with those of Ballasteros and Ularco. The cooperators were of the opinion that the cooperative structure was ably designed. There was respect for competent management, and great appreciation for comradeship. Participation in the sense of personal involvement and a high degree of commitment, however, proved to be still in its initial stages; frustration was expressed regarding conditions of work and the manner in which participatory organs function. Nowadays, cooperators appear to have greater knowledge of the own situation, as well as of the social importance of the Mondragon movement in terms of job creation, than had their colleagues in the mid-1960s.

As far as the main aspects of this study are concerned: employment, education, distribution, economic efficiency, and expansion of a self-managed sector, it seems that, even after some 25 years, there is still strong support for the Mondragon model as this was designed a few decades ago, in terms of its guiding principles and operational design.

In fact, it is quite remarkable that such creative solutions were then found to complex problems and are still accepted by a new generation. Whether or not a system such as that of Mondragon will be able to develop further and to flourish elsewhere will depend on whether or not people are available who are prepared to show similar competence, commitment and persistence as that shown by Father Arizmendi and the first cooperators of Mondragon.

NOTES

1. There is an extensive literature on developments in Peru over the past decade; a comprehensive survey is given in the paper 'Workers' Self-Management in Peru' (tentative title; forthcoming) by H. Bejar, V.D. de Ferrero and S. Roca.

2. Horvat (1976b) and Schrenk *et al* (1979) give in-depth analyses of Yugoslav socio-economic developments; Vanek (1977: 48-91) evaluates the Yugoslav experience on the basis of self-management economics. See Sapir (1980) and Ardalan (1980) for further analyses of economic aspects.

3. We shall concentrate on those cooperatives that create pure surplus; education cooperatives, for example, contribute to GVA but do not accumulate additional surplus.

4. During the boom years of the late-1960s it was feared that the narrow differentials might deter highly-skilled people from joining a cooperative. Given the present employment situation, this problem may not again be acute for many years to come; if boom conditions had continued, however, it is not inconceivable that earnings differences might have had to be widened.

5. See in particular Vanek (1977: 48-91) on problems associated with unequal access to capital resources.

6. This does not mean that such large amounts could be paid out to individual persons working at CLP; CLP's General Assembly, namely, also includes representatives of associated cooperatives. If about one-third of the aggregate amount were allocated to CLP cooperators, the individual financial stakes at CLP would still be greater than those of other cooperators.

7. The fact that associated cooperatives have a direct link with the bank may be of great value. In Yugoslavia, for instance, closer links between factories and banks at a decentralised level are very recent (Schrenk *et al* 1979).

8. In 1980 Ularco's General Assembly came to a negative vote in this respect; in 1981 the matter was again put on the agenda of the Assemblies of the member cooperatives and approved by an approximate two-thirds majority on aggregate (*T.U. Lankide* 1980: 227; 1981: 239). Problems related to self-financing and to the obtaining of credit may be somewhat influenced by additional government finances. Some public funds have become available, but not to the extent – 20 per cent of the total costs of a work place – that was hoped for by CLP.

9. Given the paucity of data on Guipuzcoan industry regarding capital stock and the under-utilisation of capacity, it is not possible to calculate similar values for the provincial industry.

10. In an audio-visual (movie and sound) and accompanying monograph by Gutierrez Johnson (1980), details are given of the women's cooperative, Auzo Lagun.

11. The time available did not permit further exploration of the linkage between meso-economics and regional economics, a matter which deserves empirical and theoretical analysis.

12. The 'supporting structure' is the meso-equivalent of the National Labour Managed agency envisaged by Vanek for a self-managed economy (Vanek 1970).

13. For the requirements of a participatory internal organisation see Bernstein (1976) and Horvat (1976c). The evidence presented in Chapters II and III above on organisational aspects shows that Mondragon still faces many difficulties in this respect.

14. Oakeshott and Macrae some years ago presented their views on major future changes in industrial management (*The Economist* 25/12/1976, 8/1/1977). Oakeshott characterised the decentralised groupings of Mondragon very aptly as 'archipelagos of democratically organised enterprises'.

15. The role of the law is illustrated by the possibility of re-valuation of individual capital accounts. This is permitted under Spanish cooperative law, but under Italian law, for instance, this method of strengthening the financial base is debarred. The Spanish tax system, as that of some other countries, is fairly favourably inclined towards the cooperatives; we have been informed by several sources, however, that this is not necessarily propitious since government control over the accuracy of cooperative accounts is far stricter than in other parts of the economy.

16. For different perspectives on the Mondragon model, see Jay (1977) and Eaton (1979).

17. For a thorough theoretical analysis of different views on the firm see Nutzinger (1976).

18. The 'participation' literature can be referred to only in passing, e.g. the work by Blumberg (1973), and Bernstein (1976); Walker (1974), Poole (1979), Strauss (1979) and Loveridge (1980) give extensive bibliographies in this field.

19. The act forbidding the association of free trade unions was repealed on 1 April 1977; and the right to strike was acknowledged again for the first time in 40 years. It is quite possible that the cooperative Social Councils will in future assume a stronger position than has been the case in the past, perhaps becoming the cooperative representative partner in discussions with trade unions. These developments can go in several directions. For instance, the monthly periodical *T.U. Lankide*, which is available in all buildings of the Mondragon cooperatives, could either fall more under control of the Social Council and present voices 'from below', or become more of an information channel for the executive and managerial segments.

20. A point argued at a working conference held in London in 1978; see also Meade (1964) for an analysis of the connection between property and democracy.

21. Pateman (1970) and Stephens (1980) have provided pioneering contributions on the politics of self-management; a forthcoming study by Horvat will give particular attention to the political theory of self-governing socialism.

22. 80 cooperators in various plants of Ulgor were interviewed in a first round, each being asked 15 open questions. All of them had a job index of less than 2, the reason being that our research mostly involved contacts with cooperators in the 'higher' ranks. A second round of discussions, with another 19 questions, was held with 30 cooperators who had articulated views and opinions during the first round. In 1980, Eduardo Kotliroff and Irene Benavente held 31 interviews with cooperators of all ranks in order to prepare material for an audio-visual; these interviews were recorded verbatim (Kotliroff & Benavente 1980) and provided a great deal of insight into the concern of cooperators as regards future developments.

VIII

POLICY PERSPECTIVES

Experiences are not translated, they are reinvented
(Paolo Freire)

INTRODUCTION

In a political and philosophical analysis of Yugoslav developments with which he had been closely associated for many years, Marković argues for the need to pay close attention to the 'natural, social and cultural limits' of a particular situation and to the various options that are available at different moments in time. 'The problem, therefore, arises: Which is the OPTIMAL historical possibility in the given historical conditions?' (Marković 1970: 35).

If specific conditions are of such importance what can we learn from an historical case? In particular, could the Mondragon experience be repeated elsewhere?

It would be fallacious to ignore Mondragon's historical context. Indeed, to understand it properly such phenomena as the degree of industrialisation, the history of Basque Nationalism, and the general support that was given to cooperative ideology during the early years, have to be taken into account. The political oppression which the people then had to endure, the lack of freely-elected trade union leadership, and later the process of rapid and nation-wide modernisation, are factors which have formed the background to the Mondragon experience.

In the history and development of cooperatives and of self-management, in which each case has its own peculiar setting, 'Mondragon' is outstanding: a pioneering case in which modern and dynamic developments of industrial production are linked closely to a policy of equitable income distribution.

In our analysis we have given a great deal of attention to the economic theory of self-management and have made comparisons with other cases in the effort to reach a balanced evaluation of specific and general characteristics. The conclusion has been that there are no *a priori* economic arguments why this model could not be experimented with in other countries.

Notes to this chapter may be found on pp. 200-201.

In these last pages we shall elaborate on this point. Mondragon's development has spanned a process of change from a situation of poverty and underdevelopment in the 1940s to one of economic strength and advanced industry in the seventies: its record seems to be of relevance for developing countries which are in the process of building new industries. Mondragon's economic activities are primarily in the secondary and tertiary sectors, and no attempt will therefore be made to draw general policy conclusions for other than these two economic sectors. This theme will be dealt with briefly in the following section, after which we turn to industrialised countries which are searching for new patterns of labour- and industrial relations. Is it realistic to expect such countries to gain new insight from the Mondragon case?

Lastly, we discuss the problem of the functioning of socio-economic systems in a very wide sense, asking whether it is worthwhile to examine 'Mondragon' from the perspective of a 'third' system next to capitalism and socialism.

DEVELOPMENT AND WORKERS' PARTICIPATION

When studying different schemes of workers' involvement in the secondary and tertiary sectors of developing countries it is important to distinguish between state-controlled industry in the public sector and private industry.[1] In the former labour relations will be characterised by involvement of the state bureaucracy; in the latter by a strong position held by private entrepreneurs.[2]

If a government is determined to strengthen the position of the workers, the public sector provides it with greater scope to do so than does the private sector. Such a strategy is illustrated by the series of measures taken by the Bandaranaike government (1971-1977) in the Sri Lankan public sector.[3] The history of Tanzanian schemes of workers' participation, on the other hand, exemplifies the problems that may be posed by bureaucratic dominance in the public sector (Bavu et al 1981).

Many developing countries have introduced legislation by which to establish some form of workers' participation in both sectors of industry. Various participatory models such as works' councils, shop stewards, worker directors, characterise this development. Nevertheless, even in countries where conditions have been relatively favourable for the introduction of such schemes, e.g. India and Zambia, the results have been only modest, and it is unlikely that this trend will lead to effective workers' involvement in industry in the foreseeable future.[4]

For our analysis it is important that in some industrialising countries there are separate — though usually very small — segments of industry, apart from the public and private sector, which aim at adopting conditions of self-management. Particularly interesting in this respect is the situation in China where some 20 per cent of the work force work in collectively-owned rather than in state-owned factories (Lockettt 1981). Further developments towards self-management are expected in this sector, developments that differ considerably from the trends apparent in the USSR or in most East European countries.[5]

Some Latin American countries also show new interest in this cooperative development. In Costa Rica, Nicaragua, Colombia and the island of Dominica, for example, institutions are being designed on which the viability of a cooperative sector will be contingent.[6]

Unless new structures are found, the long tradition of failure in this sector is unlikely to come to an end.[7] Given its weak position in most countries, it is unlikely that the present cooperative movement in the form of workers' cooperatives will make any progress unless it is given political support. In our view the Mondragon case is a relevant example from which to draw lessons for those situations in which there is a political basis on which to develop a segment of industry in which the workers will be directly involved in running the enterprises and in management. If factories are linked with lines of credit, and managerial assistance is provided, some of the most serious bottlenecks in the development of self-managing enterprises could be overcome.

Any development of self-managed enterprises will most likely take place in the small-scale sector of industry, and it is here in particular that international aid could play an important role. In recent years, World Bank policies have included the stimulating of small-scale industries as an important element of its development strategies, mainly because of the potential for the creation of employment given the relatively low capital intensity required.[8] If the World Bank intends to strengthen such activities, it will confront the option of whether to emphasise owner-controlled or labour-managed development. The latter may well hold greater promise for the achievement of the Bank's stated objectives such as the provision of basic needs for as many people as possible.

The promotion of a self-managed segment of economic activity needs to be evaluated in the perspective of the position of workers in society at large. In developing countries, the first aim of the workers' movement, whether in industry, agriculture or the services sector, is naturally the formation of strong trade unions in order to improve their own working conditions. Further steps towards greater worker involvement in work organisation will need to be designed in accordance with the 'domain' of economic activity: the public, private or self-managed sector. The latter may prove fertile ground for new experiments. It has been argued by Nitish De, for instance, that the Mondragon model holds promise for the situation in India:

we find that even within the framework of totalitarian regime, it was possible to generate a local community scenario with the total involvement of the people where a parallel system could function effectively side by side with the capitalist ethos provided the people at the grassroots level could get an opportunity to work towards not only their immediate objectives of subsistence, but for the long range objective of creating a better human community (De 1978: 32).

It seems worth exploring whether such a strategy of workers' involvement, particularly in the secondary and tertiary sectors, really has any potential along-side public and private sector schemes.

INDUSTRIALISED COUNTRIES

In the industrialised countries schemes of workers' participation for private or public sector enterprises are often identical. The West German co-determination model and the English shop steward model are perhaps the best known, both being part of a wide range of possible forms of workers' participation in industry. One end of the spectrum is the situation in which trade unions concentrate almost exclusively on wages and other conditions of work through collective bargaining. At the other end are such countries as Sweden and the Netherlands where, with the aid of various policy making and advisory bodies, the national labour organisations are involved in macro-economic issues concerning employment creation, merger policies, investment programmes, and all questions related to wages and earnings, in the context of national incomes distribution.[9]

The level of worker involvement may sometimes differ between the two main sectors of the economy. An interesting case in this respect is the situation on the island of Malta.[10] In 1971 the Malta Labour Party formed a government which was closely associated with the labour movement. Supported by the General Workers Union (GWU), a process of involving workers in the own enterprise was initiated in the Malta Drydocks, the principal employer in the public sector. The developments that have subsequently taken place in these Drydocks can be seen as the 'thermometer of industrial relations in the country' (Zammit *et al* 1981: 28). Changes have been gradual and well-designed, and the issue of ownership has slowly become one of the crucial elements to be reflected upon. In 1980, for instance, the government decided to lease a new dock to the workers rather than to leave the ownership structure unchanged in the public sector. The Malta case also shows that the presence of a trade union which supports such policies is a necessary precondition for transition towards self-management (Kester 1980). It is particularly interesting here to observe the growth of a pluriform and relatively stable pattern of labour relations in industry. The fact that the Maltese economy is greatly affected by fluctuations in the world economy adds to the lessons that can be drawn from it.

The third domain, that of cooperative self-management, plays only a marginal role in both developing and industrialised countries. In our introductory chapter we have referred to the change of attitude shown by trade unions towards workers' cooperatives in England and the Netherlands. Quantitatively of slightly greater significance is the situation in France, Italy and Poland, but unfortunately these have not been sufficiently researched to allow conclusions to be drawn.

The Mondragon experience could provide important lessons to all countries which show a positive attitude towards cooperatives. As a first step, it would seem advantageous to explore whether it is feasible to develop closer links between existing producer cooperatives and those banks that have a cooperative history. Secondly, the raising of funds with which to strengthen regional and national associations may be an important step towards improving the cooperative structure, while planning at the meso-level could do much to improve the economic performance of this sector. Thirdly, the Mondragon experience has proven that it is possible to develop cooperative enterprises in the face of heavy odds; but it should not be forgotten that more than a quarter-of-a-century passed before the Mondragon system was fully developed. Experiments with other forms of support might be worthwhile in order to discover whether the process could be speeded-up, allowing similar results to be attained in far less time, perhaps within a decade. Fourthly, the manner in which bankrupt private enterprises have been associated with the cooperative group in Mondragon may be of particular relevance to various industrialised countries. In the United States, for instance, a process of worker-takeovers has given new impulse to self-management (Woodworth 1981).

In industrialised countries, too, such an evolution should be seen as part of the national labour movement. In other words, the attitude of the trade unions may be the principal factor to determine whether any breakthrough in this direction is feasible or not.[11]

SOCIO-ECONOMIC SYSTEMS

The structural economic crisis which so many countries are undergoing in these early 1980s has prompted new debate on the ability of capitalism to cope with such exigencies. One early outcome of that debate is an emphasis on what is called 'supply-side economics' as opposed to Keynesian 'demand economics'. This discussion usually focusses on the role of government, which supposedly needs to be reduced if a collapse of the existing system is to be avoided.

Another result is a renewed interest in the work of Schumpeter who analysed what would happen to the capitalist system if it would be confronted with ever-larger concentrations of power, and explored the possibility of a gradual and smooth transition from capitalism to socialism: transition to a centralised command-type of socio-economic system.

In the analysis of socio-economic systems, the world is usually divided into two major categories: capitalist and command-type socialist systems. It is only in recent years that a distinction has been made between centralised and decentralised socialist systems, Yugoslavia being the best example of the latter.[12]

It could be argued that a self-management strategy offers an alternative, next to a restoration of capitalism or a transition to statist socialism, with which to cope with the problems encountered by the welfare state in capitalist countries. The emphasis is then also on supply-side economics, but as a strategy by which to involve people actively in the organisation of their own work, i.e. through the democratisation of social relations of production. Such new production relationships are an integral part of what Horvat has characterised as 'self-governing socialism'.[13] At the theoretical level this system is at least as efficient as either the capitalist or command type of economy. The interest shown in such a system by economists other than of the self-management school, is illustrated by Schouten who has analysed the way in which industrialised countries could behave when simultaneously faced by stagnation and inflation.[14] The superior strategy would be to move towards 'anonymous capitalism': a system in which the yield of capital is determined at a national level of policy making, in which investments are decided upon centrally, and in which in each enterprise the workers bear all income and entrepreneurial risks.

Enormous problems would clearly have to be faced in any attempt to engage in a process of transition towards decentralised rather than centralised socialism. The first of these would be the probable large-scale flight of capital if one country were to undertake such a venture in isolation. This is not unavoidable, however. Huge capital resources are provided by institutions such as pension funds, and trade unions may well become more actively involved in the administration of the resources accumulated by their membership. The result would go far towards reducing the impact of external capital mobility. Moreover, in a self-managed situation the propensity to save need not be reduced; on the contrary, the cases discussed in this study have shown evidence of a high propensity to invest. A second and perhaps even greater problem to be faced would be the great speed at which new technologies are being introduced. In developing countries, in particular, these technologies are controlled by transnational companies which may easily undermine local industry by their superior efficiency. The need to command these technological developments may jeopardise transition towards self-management, unless and until labour-managed enterprises gain equal access to such developments.

If self-management is understood as having an identity of its own, then attention must be given to all aspects of a socio-economic system: to the production, distribution, and spending of incomes, and to the coordinating mechanisms. Sik's work, which touches partly on the same themes elaborated upon by Horvat and Vanek, tentatively explores a complete system which is neither capitalist nor command-type socialist (Sik 1980). A great deal of further work will need to be done before such fundamental questions as the role of government and the concentration of industry can be clarified in a third system.

Perhaps one of the most difficult problems will be to determine the correct dosage of democratisation. The balance will have to be determined between plan and market, between democracy and bureaucracy, in order that the system likely to be most efficient in running society may be found.

Self-management practice appears to have a preference for democratic planning from below and for market relationships rather than for centralised planning and price manipulation. Apart from the efficiency question, economic democracy is valuable also 'in its own right' (Pateman 1970: 83). Yugoslavia has been the major case from which much has been learned in this direction. We hope to have shown that Mondragon's wider relevance can be better understood if the issues of wide-ranging consequence raised in this chapter are also included in its analysis.

NOTES

1. A Policy Workshop on Transition to Workers' Self-Management in Industry as a Strategy for Change in Developing Countries, held at The Institute of Social Studies, The Hague (1981), takes the three domains – private, public and self-managed – as a point of departure in the analysis of problems encountered in implementing a process of transition towards self-management.

2. A good study of the state in the industrialisation of developing countries may be found in Choksi (1979), a working paper prepared for the World Bank; its bibliography on the topic is particularly valuable.

3. An interesting aspect of the Sri Lankan experiment with employees' councils in public sector enterprises was the attempt to mobilise the workers of different enterprises by organising a national conference attended by representatives of each (Abeyasekera *et al* 1981).

4. In India, for instance, the national constitution makes allowance for the role of workers, in line with Gandhian tradition. Yet in spite of national objectives in this respect, results have been negligible (Khanna *et al* 1981). With regard to participatory schemes in Zambia, see the country information published by the International Labour Organisation.

5. In an unpublished paper Saith elaborates on the equity and efficiency dimensions of the commune brigade type of production (Saith 1980).

6. For information on Costa Rica see Fletcher (1978) and Aguayo (1981); a proposal to amend Law 5185 on cooperative association in order to strengthen aspects of self-management is on the agenda of the Legislative Assembly for 1981. Williams writes on the basis of his own experience about agricultural cooperatives in Dominica (Williams 1980). On the situation in Colombia see Parra (1977), and for an interesting case of newly-established small-scale cooperative enterprises see a series by Servicio Nacional de Aprendizaje. These give detailed descriptions of all stages of the promotion of such enterprises (SENA 1981).

The Consejo Latino Americano y del Caribe para la Autogestion has become an important channel of communication; its periodical *Autogestion y Participación* provides updated information on Latin American developments.

7. Records of worker cooperatives in Turkey (Uca 1980) and of the recently-established cooperatives in Mexico (Galjart 1980) provide two examples of persistently poor economic performance.

8. Page (1979) and World Bank (1978) provide updated surveys of the various theoretical and empirical issues concerning small-scale enterprises. It is recognised that these have a potential for job creation in 'small but relatively modern manufacturing industry; organised non-manufacturing activity, such as construction, transportation, and trading; and traditional or "informal" activity' (World Bank 178: 5), but that 'special efforts are needed to help small firms overcome weaknesses and exploit their natural advantages' (Ibidem: 5).

9. An important trend in industrialised countries is the re-designing of work organisation now being experimented with in Scandinavian countries (Asplund 1981; Gustavsen 1981).

10. The Malta case which, from 1971 on, has been studied very thoroughly, shows the importance of meticulous monitoring during each stage. In a case of failure, namely, it is almost impossible to trace the historical facts; and in cases of survival it is rare that business records and other events can be reconstructed over any long period of time.

11. The International Cooperative Alliance should be in a position to exercise greater influence in this respect if its ideology were more sharply focussed and its analysis of societal structures were more critical. *Cooperatives in the Year 2000*, a policy study by the ICA, reveals these shortcomings. It also contains a different perspective on the phenomenon of cooperativism, i.e. that held by East European countries (ICA 1980: 77-99).

12. Dobb, for example, in discussing the failures of syndicalism, states that 'this does not mean that anything approaching the Yugoslav system of "working collectives" with elected councils is to be dismissed out of hand for all circumstances and for all time.' His chapter on Decentralisation and Democratisation ends: 'One may well see some rapidly changing alignments and landmarks in the socialist world in the decade that lies ahead' (Dobb 1970: 69). Ellman (1979:259), in dicussing the results of planning in socialist countries, distinguishes self-management from capitalism and 'statist socialism'.

13. In his recent work in particular, Horvat investigates the various dimensions of the process of transition towards self-management (Horvat 1978, 1979, 1980).

14. Schouten presents a macro-economic analysis of five theoretical systems: monopoly capitalism, monopoly labourism, ideal private capitalism, the centrally-guided economy and anonymous capitalism.

BIBLIOGRAPHY

C. Abeyasekera *et al* (1981): 'Employees' councils in public sector enterprises: the Sri Lankan experience' (The Hague, Institute of Social Studies)

S.F. Aguayo (1981): 'Empresas asociativas de autogestion en Costa Rica. Analisis de un projecto de legislación', *Suplemento Boletin*, May, 5-10

F. Aldabaldetrecu & J. Gray (1967): 'De l'artisanat industriel au complexe coopératif l'expérience de Mondragon' (Paris, Bureau d'Etudes Coopératives et Communautaires)

A.A. Alchian & H. Demsetz (1972): 'Production, information costs, and economic organization', *American Economic Review*, 62, 5, 27-52

J.B. Allcock (n.d.): 'The collectivisation of Yugoslav agriculture and the myth of peasant resistance' (draft paper)

G. Ansola (1971): *Euskal Herriko Ekonomiaz, 1955-67* (Bilbao, Etor Argigaratzaldea)

Anuario Económico y Social de España 1977 (Barcelona, Iberplan)

D. Aranzadi (1976): *Cooperativismo Industrial Como Sistema, Empresa y Experiencia* (Bilbao, Universidad de Deusto)

C. Ardalan (1980): 'Workers' self-management and planning: the Yugoslav case', *World Development*, 8, 623-638

J.M. Arizmendi(Arrieta) (1966): 'Experiencias sobre una forma cooperativa: Mondragon', *Estudios Cooperativos*, II, 11-12; and in Ballesteros *et al* (1968)

C. Asplund (1981): 'Summary of "Redesigning jobs: Western European experiences – trade union approaches to new forms of work organisation" ' (Geneva, ILO)

J.M.R. Ballesteros *et al* (1968): *Cooperativas de Producción: Experiencias y Futuro* (2nd ed.; Bilbao, Ed. Deusto)

Banco de Bilbao (1977): *Tablas Input-Output y Cuentas Regionales de Alava, Guipúzcoa, Navarra y Vizcaya* (Bilbao)

H. Barkai (1977): *Growth Patterns of the Kibbutz Economy* (Amsterdam, North Holland)

—— (1978): 'Incentives, efficiency, and social control: the case of the Kibbutz' (Jerusalem, Maurice Falk Institute for Economic Research, Discussion Paper 7815)

E. Batstone (1979): 'Some aspects of the economic performance of French producer cooperatives' (Paper for the Walton Symposium, Glasgow)

I. Bavu *et al* (1981): 'Policy study on the transition to self-management in industry as a strategy for change: the case of Tanzania' (The Hague, Institute of Social Studies)

H. Bejar, V.D. de Ferrero & S. Roca (1981): 'Workers' self-management in Peru' (The Hague, Institute of Social Studies; provisional title)

P. Bernstein (1976): *Workplace Democratization. Its Internal Dynamics* (Kent, Ohio, Kent State University Press)

J. Bilderbeek (1977): *Financiële Ratio-Analyse* (Leiden, Stenfert Kroese)

P. Blumberg (1973): *Industrial Democracy. The Sociology of Participation* (New York, Schocken Books)

H.H.J. Bol (1979): *Het Coöperatief Georganiseerde Bankwezen in Nederland* (Deventer, Kluwer)

K. Bradley & A. Gelb (1980): 'Worker cooperatives as industrial policy: the case of the "Scottish Daily News" ', *Review of Economic Studies*, XLVII, 665-678

—— (1981a): 'Industrial alternatives: internal organization and efficiency in the Mondragon cooperatives' (London School of Economics, an Industrial Relations Discussion Paper)

—— (1981b): 'Obstacles to a cooperative economy: lessons from Mondragon' (London School of Economics, an Industrial Relations Discussion Paper)

W. Brus (1980): 'Political system and economic efficiency: the East European Context', *Journal of Comparative Economics* 4, 40-55

J.R. Cable & F.R. Fitzroy (1980a): 'Productive efficiency, incentives and employee participation: some preliminary results for West Germany', *Kyklos*, 1, 100-121

—— (1980b): 'Cooperation and productivity: some evidence from West German experience', *Economic Analysis and Workers' Management*, XIV, 2, 163-180

Caja Laboral Popular (CLP) (1967): *Una Experiencia Cooperativa* (Mondragon)

—— (1968-1979): *Annual Reports*

—— (1968-1979): *Work Norms*

—— (1976a): *Situación y Perspectivas de la Economía Vasca* (Mondragon)

—— (1976b): *Aproximación a la Estructura Industrial del País Vasco* (Durango, Leopoldo Zugaza)

—— (1976c): *Contrato de Asociación para Cooperativas Industriales* (Mondragon)

—— (1977): *Economía Vasca Informe 1977* (Mondragon)

—— (1979): *Estatutos Sociales* (Mondragon)

—— Internal Planning documents (various years, unpublished)

Cámaras de Comercio del País Vasco (1973): *Aspectos de la Estructura Económica de Alava, Guipúzcoa, Navarra, Vizcaya*, Vol. I (San Sebastian)

—— (1978): *La Balanza de Pagos des País Vasco* (Mondragon)

A. Campbell *et al* (1977): *Worker-Owners: The Mondragon Achievement* (London, Anglo-German Foundation for the Study of Industrial Society)

Censo Industrial de España 1978: Establecimientos Industriales, Serie Provincial Guipúzcoa (Madrid)

A. Chilosi (1980): 'Income distribution under Soviet-type socialism: an interpretative framework', *Journal of Comparative Economics*, 4, 1-18

A.M. Choksi (1979): *State Intervention in the Industrialization of Developing Countries: Selected Issues* (Washington, World Bank Staff Working Paper 341)

K. Coates & F. Singleton (eds) (1977): *The Just Society* (Nottingham, Russell Press Ltd)

K. Coates & T. Topham (1980): 'Workers' control and self-management in Great Britain', *Human Futures*, 3, 2, 127-141

Cooperativas. Ley y Reglamento (1978) (Madrid, Boletin Oficial del Estado)

Cooperative Development Agency Bill (1978) (London, HMSO)

N. Daures & A. Dumas (1977): *Théorie économique de l'autogestion dans l'entreprise* (Montpellier, Editions du Faubourg)

N.R. De (1978): 'Action research as a learning strategy', *Human Futures* (Spring), 25-34

P. Derrick (1978): 'Cooperative development in Britain' (a paper presented at a conference of the International Cooperative Alliance, Rome)

H. Desroche (1970): *Epargne et Entreprises* (Paris, Collège Coopératif)

M. Dobb (1970): *Socialist Planning: Some Problems* (London, Lawrence & Wishart)

J. van den Doel (1978): *Demokratie en welvaartstheorie* (2nd ed; Alphen a/d Rijn, Samson)

—— (1980): (English translation) *Democracy and Welfare Economics* (Cambridge, Cambridge University Press)

E.D. Domar (1966): 'The Soviet collective farm as a producer cooperative', *American Economic Review*, 56, 734-757

P.J. van Dooren (1978): *Cooperaties voor ontwikkelingslanden* (Muiderberg; Coutinho)

W.A. Douglass (1970): *Death in Murelaga* (University of Washington Press)

H.F. Drèze (1976): 'Some theory of labour management', *Econometrica*, 6, 1125-1139

J.H. Dunning & F.J.B. Stilwell (1978): 'Theories of business behaviour and the distribution of surplus profits', *Kyklos*, 31, Fasc. 4, 601-623

J. Eaton (1979): 'The Basque workers' cooperatives', *Industrial Relations Journal*, 10, 3, 32-40

Económia Guipuzcoana (1971-77) (Camara Oficial de Comercio Industria y Navegación de Guipúzcoa, San Sebastian)

EFMA (1977): 'Le rôle de la Banque dans le développement: l'action du Banco de Bilbao vers les petites et moyennes entreprises' (Marrakesh)

M. Ellman (1979): *Socialist Planning* (Cambridge, Cambridge University Press)

J. Erdocia (1980): 'La Pesca', *T.U. Lankide*, 223-224, 50

J.G. Espinosa & A.S. Zimbalist (1978): *Economic Democracy; Workers' Participation in Chilean Industry 1970-1973* (New York, Academic Press)

S. Estrin (1979): 'Income dispersion in a self-managed economy' (University of Southampton, Discussion Paper 7906)

S. Fletcher (1978): 'The model and implementation strategy of labor enterprises in Costa Rica', *Annals of Public and Cooperative Economy*, 48, 2, 203-218

G. Foley (1978): in *Intercontinental Press combined with Inprecor* (New York)

Fomento de la Producción (1973): *Las 1000 mayores empresas españolas en 1972* (Barcelona)

—— (1975): *Las 1500 mayores empresas españolas en 1974* (Barcelona)

—— (1977): *Las 1500 mayores empresas españolas en 1976* (Barcelona)

A. Fox (1974): *Beyond Contract: Work, Power and Trust Relations* (London, Faber & Faber)

R.S. Frantz (1980): 'On the existence of X-efficiency', *Journal of Post-Keynesian Economics*, II, 4, 508-527

P. Freire (1978): *Pedagogy in Process: The Letters to Guinea-Bissau* (New York, Seabury Press)

B. Galjart (1980): 'People's industries: a sociological case study of a Mexican experiment in participation and self-management' (Leiden, unpublished)

Q. Garcia (1970): *Les coopératives industrielles de Mondragon* (Paris, Éditions Ouvrières)

J.J. Giele (1975): *Arbeiderszelfbestuur in Spanje* (Amsterdam, Anarchistiese Uitgaven)

C.A. Glassman & S.A. Rhoades (1980): 'Owner vs. manager control effects on bank performance', *Review of Economics and Statistics*, LXII, 2, 263-270

I. Gorroño (1975): *Experiencia Cooperativa en el Pais Vasco* (Durango, Leopoldo Zugaza)

A. Gorroñogoitia (1980): 'Lan Kide Aurrezkia Caja Laboral Popular', *T.U. Lankide* 223-224, 15-19

Z. Griliches & V. Ringstad (1971): *Economies of Scale and the Form of the Production Functions* (Amsterdam, North-Holland)

B. Gustavsen (1981): 'Workers' participation in decisions within undertakings – an overview of the situation in Norway' (Geneva, ILO)

A. Gutierrez-Johnson (1978): 'Compensation, equity and industrial democracy in the Mondragon cooperatives', *Economic Analysis and Workers' Management*, XII, 267-289

—— (1980): 'Women and self-management. A study of a women's service firm of the Mondragon cooperatives, Spain' (Cornell University, unpublished)

A. Gutierrez-Johnson & W. Foote Whyte (1977): 'The Mondragon system of worker production cooperatives', *Industrial and Labor Relations Review*, 31, 1 (October), 18-30

J. Harrod (1979): 'Social relations of production and systems of labour control' (a paper presented at a labour studies seminar; The Hague, Institute of Social Studies)

D.F. Heathfield (ed) (1977): *The Economics of Co-Determination* (London, The Macmillan Press)

D.M. Holland & S.C. Myers (1980): 'Profitability and capital costs for manufacturing corporations and all non-financial corporations', *American Economic Review* (May), 320-339

B. Horvat (1967): 'Prilog zasnisavanju teorije jugoslovenskik poduceza' ('A contribution to the theory of the Yugoslav firm), *Ekonomska Analiza*, 1, 7-28

―― (1972): 'An institutional model of a self-managed socialist economy', *Eastern European Economics*, X, 4, 369-392
―― (1976a): 'Fundamentals of a theory of distribution in self-governing socialism', *Economic Analysis and Workers' Management*, X, 1-2, 24-42
―― (1976b): *The Yugoslav Economic System* (New York, International Arts & Sciences Press)
―― (1976c): 'Workers' management', *Economic Analysis and Workers' Management*, X, 3-4, 197-214
―― (1977): 'Social property', *Economic Analysis and Workers' Management*, XI, 1-2, 95-98
―― (1978): 'Establishing self-governing socialism in a less developed country', *Economic Analysis and Workers' Management*, XII, 1-2, 135-153
―― (1979): 'Paths of transition to workers' self-management in the developed capitalist countries', in T.R. Burns (ed): *Work and Power* (London & Beverly Hills, Sage)
―― (1980): 'Searching for a strategy of transition', *Economic Analysis and Workers' Management*, XIV, 3, 311-323
B. Horvat *et al* (eds) (1975): *Self-Governing Socialism: A Reader*. Vol. I: *Historical Development, Social and Political Philosophy*; Vol. II: *Sociology and Politics: Economics* (New York, International Arts and Sciences Press)
G. Hunnius, G. David Garson & J. Case (eds) (1973): *Workers' Control* (New York, Vintage Books)

Indices de Precios de Consumo 1980 (Madrid, Instituto Nacional de Estadistica)
Inerketarako Euskal Institutoa (IKEI) (1979): *Restructuring the Basque Economy* (Final Report, Stage 1; Oslo, Norconsult AS)
Informe Económico 1976 (Bilbao, Banco de Bilbao)
International Cooperative Alliance (1980): *Cooperatives in the Year 2000* (London, ICA)

A.P. Jacquemin & H.W. de Jong (1977): *European Industrial Organization* (London, Macmillan)
―. Jakin (1973): *Koperatibak* (EFA, Arantzazu)
J. Jané Solá (1969): *El Problema de los Salarios en España* (Barcelona, Ed. Oikos-tau/S.A.)
P. Jay (1977): 'The workers' cooperative economy' (a paper presented to the Manchester Statistical Society; March)
M.C. Jensen & W.H. Meckling (1979): 'Rights and production functions: an application to labor-managed firms and codetermination', *Journal of Business*, 52, 4, 409-506
Job Ownership (1978) (London, Job Ownership Ltd., November)
L. Johansen (1972): *Production Functions* (Amsterdam, North-Holland)
D.C. Jones (1977a): 'Worker participation in management in Britain: evaluation, current developments and prospects', in G.D. Garson (ed): *Worker Self-Management in Industry: The West European Experience* (New York, Praeger)
―― (1977b): 'The economics and industrial relations of producers cooperatives in the United States, 1791-1939', *Economic Analysis and Workers' Management*, XI, 3-4, 295-316
―― (1980a): 'Producer cooperatives in industrialised western economies', *British Journal of Industrial Relations*, XVIII (July), 141-154
―― (1980b): 'Productivity and British producer cooperatives' (Symposium on Economic Performance of Participatory Firms, Hamilton College, May 3-4)
E. Jonsson (1978): 'Labour as risk-bearer', *Cambridge Journal of Economics*, 2, 373-380

E. Kardelj (1980): *Self-Management Planning* (2nd ed., Belgrade: Socialist Thought and Practice)
W. Kendall (1975): *The Labour Movement in Europe* (London, Allen Lane)
G. Kester (1980): *Transition to Workers' Self-Management. Its Dynamics in the Decolonizing Economy of Malta* (The Hague, Institute of Social Studies)
S. Khanna *et al* (1981): 'Workers' participation and development: the Indian experience' (The Hague, Institute of Social Studies)

E. Kotliroff & I. Benavente (1980): 'La alternativa Mondragon. Una serie de entrevistas con su gente' (The Hague, Institute of Social Studies)
I.B. Kravis (1976): 'A survey of international comparisons of productivity', *The Economic Journal*, 86, 1-44

Lagun-Aro: *Memoria Ejercicio* (Mondragon, CLP; various years)
J. Larrañaga (1980): 'Ulgor, S. Coop.: en la nueva frontera', *T.U. Lankide*, 223-224, 10-13
P. de Larrañaga (1977): *Contribución a la Historia Obrera de Euskalherria*, Vol. 2 (San Sebastian, Ed. Auñamendi Argitaldaria)
H. Leibenstein (1978): 'X-efficiency Xists – reply to an Xorcist', *American Economic Review*, 68, 1, 203-211
—— (1979): 'X-efficiency: from concept to theory', *Challenge*, 13-22
Liga de Educación y Cultura (1975): *Previsiones de Evolución de la Ensenanza Bilingue en el Valle de Leniz Plan Quinquenal 1975-1979* (Mondragon)
—— (1976a): *Estadisticas del Alto Deva Curso 1976, 1977* (Mondragon)
—— (1976b): *Bases para una Cooperación Educativa entre la Comarca del Alto Deva-Guipúzcoa y el Ministerio de Educacion y Sciencia* (Mondragon)
M. Lockett (1981): 'Self-management in China?', *Economic Analysis and Workers' Management*, XV, 1, 85-113
R. Loveridge (1980): 'What is participation? A review of the literature and some methodological problems', *British Journal of Industrial Relations*, XVIII, 3, 297-317
R. Loveridge & A.L. Mok (1979): *Theories of Labour Market Segmentation* (The Hague, Boston, London, Martinus Nijhoff)
Lucas Aerospace Confederation Trade Union Committee (1979): *Turning Industrial Decline into Expansion – A Trade Union Initiative* (Lucas Aerospace Trade Union Committee of the Confederation of Shipbuilding and Engineering Unions)
H. Lydall (1968): *The Structure of Earnings* (Oxford, Clarendon Press)
—— (1979): *A Theory of Income Distribution* (Oxford, Clarendon Press)
B. Lyons (1980): 'A new measure of minimum efficient plant size in UK manufacturing industry', *Economica*, 47, 185, 19-34

N. Macrae (1976): 'The coming entrepreneurial revolution: a survey', *The Economist*, 25 December, 41-65
M. Marković (1970): *From Affluence to Praxis* (University of Michigan Press)
J. de D.G. Martinez & J.I.G. Ramos (1976): *Desarrollo, Crecimiento y Diversificación en el Pais Vasco* (Camera de Comercio, Industria y Navegación de Guipúzcoa, San Sebastian)
J.E. Meade (1964): *Efficiency, Equality and the Ownership of Property* (London: George Allen & Unwin)
—— (1979): 'The adjustment processes of labour cooperatives with constant returns to scale and perfect competition', *The Economic Journal*, 89 (December), 781-788
Medio-Banca (n.d.): *Dati Cumulativi di 795 Società Italiane (1968-1976)* (Milan)
R. Meidner (1978): *Employee Investment Funds* (London: George Allen & Unwin)
J.M. Mendizabal (ed) (1978): 'Preface' to *Escritos de Don José María Arizmendi-Arrieta* (Mondragon, CLP)
D.D. Milenkovitch (1971): *Plan and Market in Yugoslav Economic Thought* (New Haven & London, Yale University Press)
F. Mintz (1977): *La Autogestion en la España Revolucionaria* (Madrid, Las Ediciones de La Piqueta)
P. Miović (1975): *Determinants of Income Differentials in Yugoslav Self-Managed Enterprises* (Ph.D. thesis, University of Pennsylvania, not published)

A Nove (1978): 'Efficiency criteria for nationalised industries: some observations based upon British experience', *Acta Oeconomica*, 20 (1-2), 83-105
L.C-Nuñez (1977): *Clases Sociales en Euskadi* (San Sebastian, Ed. Txertoa)
H.G. Nutzinger (1976): 'The firm as a social institution: the failure of the contractarian viewpoint', *Economic Analysis and Workers' Management*, X, 3-4, 217-237

—— (1980): 'Codetermination and the humanization of working life: recent trends in the
   Federal Republic of Germany', *Economic Analysis and Workers' Management*, XIV, 1,
   137-147

R. Oakeshott (1973): 'Spain's oasis of democracy', *Observer Supplement* (21 January), reprinted in Vanek (1975: 290-96)
—— (1977): 'Towards the industrial archipelago', *The Economist*, 8 January, 31-35
—— (1978): *The Case for Workers' Coops* (London, Routledge and Kegan Paul)
Organisation for Economic Cooperation and Development (1978): *Spain. OECD Economic
   Surveys* (Paris, OECD)
J.M. Ormachea (1980): 'Por la década de los 80', *T.U. Lankide* 223-224, 60-64

J.M. Page Jr (1979): *Small Enterprises in African Development: A Survey* (Washington,
   World Bank Staff Working Paper 363)
—— (1980): 'Technical efficiency and economic performance: some evidence from Ghana',
   Oxford Economic Papers, 32, 2, 319-339
J. Paroush & N. Kahana (1980): 'Price uncertainty and the cooperative firm', *American Eco-
   nomic Review* (March), 212-216
E. Parra *et al* (1977): *Empresas Comunitarias Urbanas* (Bogotá, CINEP)
C. Pateman (1970): *Participation and Democratic Theory* (Cambridge, Cambridge Univer-
   sity Press)
E.T. Penrose (1980): *The Theory of the Growth of the Firm* (Oxford, Basil Blackwell)
A. Perez de Calleja Basterrechea (1975): 'The group of cooperatives at Mondragon in the
   Spanish Basque Country' (Mondragon, CLP)
T. Petrin (1978): 'The potential of small-scale industry for employment in Yugoslavia' (The
   Hague, Institute of Social Studies)
H. Phelps Brown (1977): *The Inequality of Pay* (Oxford, Oxford University Press)
P.J. Pinillos (1967): 'España: sus caracteristicas estructurales más importantes' (Santander,
   Banco de Santander)
M. Poole (1979): 'Industrial democracy: a comparative analysis', *Industrial Relations*, 18, 3,
   262-272

Report of the Working Group on a Cooperative Development Agency (1977) (London,
   HMSO)
Review of International Cooperation, The (various issues; London, International Cooper-
   ative Alliance)
Royal Arsenal Cooperative Society Ltd (1979): *Mondragon: the Basque Cooperatives*
   (London)
Rumasa (1977): *Informe Económico y Financiero 1976 y Perspectivas 1977* (Madrid,
   Graficas Reunidas)

S.R. Sacks (1980): 'Giant corporations in Yugoslavia' (a paper presented at Hamilton Col-
   lege conference on The Economic Performance of Participatory and Self-Managed
   Firms; Clinton, N.Y.)
A. Saith (1980): 'Commune and brigade industries in rural China' (Oxford, unpublished)
A. Sapir (1980): 'Economic growth and factor substitution: what happened to the Yugoslav
   miracle?', *The Economic Journal*, 90, 294-313
D.B.J. Schouten (1980): *Macht en wanorde: Een vergelijking van economische stelsels* (Lei-
   den, Stenfert Kroese)
M. Schrenk *et al* (1979): *Yugoslavia: Self-Management Socialism and the Challenges of De-
   velopment* (Baltimore, Johns Hopkins University Press)
J.A. Schumpeter (1943; 8th ed, 1959): *Capitalism, Socialism and Democracy* (London,
   George Allen & Unwin)
A. Sen (1973): *On Economic Inequality* (Oxford, Clarendon Press)
Servicio de Estudios de la Camera de Comercio, Industria y Navegación de Bilbao (1976):
   Empleo y Formación Profesional en Vizcaya, 1975-1980, Tomo I and II (Bilbao, La
   Editorial Vizcaina)

—— (1977): *Estructura Socioeconómica del Pais Vasco* (Bilbao, La Editorial Vizcaina)
—— (1978): *Dinamica de la Población del Empleo en el Pais Vasco* (Bilbao, La Editorial Vizcaina)
Servicio Nacional de Aprendizaje (SENA) (1981): *Guia Metodológica; Material Didáctico; Lecturas de Referencia; Estudios* (Bogotá, La Empresa Asociativa – Colección PMUR)
O. Sik (1980): 'Towards an humane economic democracy', *Economic and Industrial Democracy* (London & Beverly Hills, Sage)
R. Slot & J.M. Vecht (1975): *Zicht op cijfers* (Amsterdam, Agon Elsevier)
E. Staley & R.M. Morse (1965): *Modern Small Industry for Developing Countries* (New York, McGraw Hill)
A. Steinherr (1978): 'The labor-managed economy: a survey of the economics literature', *Annals of Public and Cooperative Economy*, 49, 2, 129-148
E.H. Stephens (1980): *The Politics of Workers' Participation: The Peruvian Approach in Comparative Perspective* (New York, Academic Press)
W. Stewart Howe (1978): *Industrial Economics: An Applied Approach* (London, Macmillan)
Stichting Wetenschappelijk Onderzoek Vakcentrales (SWOV) (1979): *Werken in Kooperaties* (Amsterdam/Utrecht)
G. Strauss (1979): 'Workers' participation: symposium introduction', *Industrial Relations*, 18, 3, 247-261
J.W. Sutherland (1980): 'Corporate autonomy and X-inefficiency', *Journal of Post-Keynesian Economics*, II, 4, 549-565
J. Svejnar & S.C. Smith (1980): 'The economics of joint ventures in centrally planned and labor-managed economies' (Cornell University, Dept. of Economics, Working Paper 247)
—— (1981): 'The economics of joint ventures in less developed countries' (Cornell University, Dept. of Economics, Working Paper 254).
Swedish Institute, The (1978): 'Consumer cooperatives in Sweden', *Fact Sheets on Sweden*

R. Tamames (1965): *Estructura Económica de España* (3e Edición, Madrid, Sociedad de Estudios y Publicaciónes)
—— (1976): *Introducción a la Economía Española* (10th ed., Madrid, Alianza Ed.)
H. Thomas (1973): *Personal Income Distribution in Yugoslavia* (Cornell University, Ph.D. thesis)
—— (1980): 'The distribution of earnings and capital in the Mondragon cooperatives', *Economic Analysis and Workers' Management*, XIV, 3, 363-391
P.J. Thonet & O.H. Poensgen (1979): 'Managerial control and economic performance in Western Germany', *The Journal of Industrial Economics*, XXVIII (September), 23-37
L.C. Thurow (1975): 'Education and economic equality' in D.M. Levine & M.J. Bane (eds): *The 'Inequality' Controversy, Schooling and Distributive Justice* (New York, Basic Books)
—— (1976): *Generating Inequality* (London, Macmillan Press)
C. Timmer (1970): 'On measuring technical efficiency', in W.O. Jones & C.W. Reynolds (eds): *Food Research Studies in Agricultural Economics, Trade, and Development*, IX, 2, 99-171
Trabajo y Union (TU) *Lankide* (various issues)
P. Trivelli (1975): 'Algunas consideraciónes sobre las cooperativas industriales de Mondragon', *Revista Eure*, 97-126

M. Uca (1980): 'Workers' participation and self-management in Turkey: evaluating the past and considering the future' (Ph.D. thesis, Cornell University)
Ularco (1977): *El Absentismo Laboral en ULARCO* (Mondragon, Ularco Servicios Centrales)
Ulgor (1973a): *Estatutos Sociales* (Mondragon)
—— (1973b): *Reglamento de Regimen Interior* (Mondragon)

Jan Vanek (1972): *The Economics of Workers' Management: A Yugoslav Case Study* (London, George Allen & Unwin)

Jaroslav Vanek (1970): *The General Theory of Labor-Managed Market Economies* (Ithaca, N.Y., Cornell University Press)

—— (1977): *The Labor-Managed Economy* (Ithaca, N.Y., Cornell University Press)

Jaroslav Vanek (ed) (1975): *Self-Management, Economic Liberation of Man* (Harmondsworth, Penguin Books)

Jaroslav Vanek & P. Miović (1977): 'Explorations into the "realistic" behavior of a Yugoslav firm', in Jaroslav Vanek (1977), Chapter 5, 104-134

R. Velasco (1977): *Financiación y Desarrollo. Aproximación al País Vasco* (Durango, Leopoldo Zugaza)

S. Vines (1981): 'A Mondragon for Wales?', *The Observer* (8 February)

K.F. Walker (1974): 'Workers' participation in management — problems, practice and prospects', *Bulletin of the International Institute for Labour Studies* (Geneva)

B. Ward (1958): 'The firm in Illyria: market syndicalism', *American Economic Review*, 48, 566-589

J. Wemelsfelder (1978): 'De afbraak van de Nederlandse industrie en de internationale handel', *Economisch-Statistische Berichten*, 63 (11 October), 1024-27

A.N. Williams (1980): 'Self management, social transformation and development: the experiences of the Castle Bruce workers, West Indies', *Economic Analysis and Workers' Management*, XIV, 1, 149-161

S. Windass (ed) (1981): *Local Initiatives in Great Britain* (Oxford, Foundation for Alternatives)

A. Wood (1978): *A Theory of Pay* (Cambridge, Cambridge University Press)

W.P. Woodworth (1981): 'Towards a labour-owned economy in the United States', *Labour and Society*, 6, 1, 41-56

World Bank (1978): *Employment and Development of Small Enterprises* (Washington, Sector Policy Paper)

A. Wright (1977): *The Spanish Economy 1959-1976* (London, Macmillan Press)

P. A. Yotopoulos (1975): 'Rationality, efficiency and organizational behavior through the production function, darkly', *Food Research Institute Studies*, 14, 1, 263-274

E. Zammit *et al* (1981): 'Transition to workers' self-management' (The Hague, Institute of Social Studies)

Zeggenschap (Amsterdam, various issues)

A. Zellner & N.W. Revankar (1969): 'Generalized production functions', *Review of Economic Studies*, 36, 241-250

INDEX

absenteeism, 9, 42, 49-51 (G.1), 52, 58, 71-72, 143, 190
accident prevention, 28
accountability, 28, 77
age of cooperatives
 cost curve and, 123 (G.4)
 productivity by, 121 (T.13), 122
 profitability by, 121 (T.13), 122-23
 see also economic performance
agricultural cooperatives, 31-32, 34, 48, 92, 175
Alava, 79, 177 (T.3)
Alecoop, 32, 52, 54, 56-59, 72, 184
 see also education cooperatives
Alfa cooperative factory, 16-17
alpha-coefficient, 11, 150-51, 154, 162n.
Amat, 56
Arizmendi-Arrieta, Don José María, 14, 17-20, 22, 38, 39-40n., 52, 54, 57, 62, 94
Arkitle Club, 36
Arrasate factory, 21, 30
associated cooperatives, 22, 26, 30-31, 34, 49, 73n., 79, 82, 89, 94, 95n., 170, 172-73
 sales of, 1965-79, 85 (T.6), 86, 88
auditing, 23
Auzo-Lagun, 36, 176

Banco Urquijo, 19
banking, 5-6, 19, 39-40n., 79
banks, 19
 commercial, 75, 79-80, 93
 savings, 79-80, 93-94, 95n.
 see also Caja Laboral Popular
Basque General Council, 36
Basque Nationalist Party, 16, 40n.
Basque Provinces,
 autonomy demand, 33, 194
 banks, 19, 93
 Caja Laboral Popular objectives in, 90-91

cooperatives, 40-41n.
culture, promotion of, 63-64, 78
economic structure, 129n., 175 (T.2)
education in, 74n.
investment in and from, 93-94, 95n.
language, 36, 63-64, 74n.
primary sector, 31-32, 175
private sector, 2
recession in, 33, 48
savings in, 185
structural changes, 14-17
trade unions, 15-16
unemployment, 48
Benn, A. Wedgwood, 3-4
Biharko group, 37
Bilbao Federation of First International, 15
Bilbao University, 73n.
bilingualism, 36
Bulex Contigea, Brussels, 30
bureaucratisation, 179, 181
business cycle, 10, 104, 112, 170

Caja Laboral Popular (CLP), 6, 9-10, 12n., 22, 31-32, 34-35, 40n., 59, 125, 128
 account-holders, 84 (T.5), 86, 88, 93, 178
 assets, 83-88 (T.4-7), 92-93, 170-71
 branch offices, 79 (T.2), 94
 Contract of Association with, 22-26, 76-77, 79-80, 119, 179, 185
 decentralisation by, 181
 employment expansion, 169, 170, 186
 entry fees, 86, 91
 expansion of, 30, 37, 49, 79, 85, 91, 93-94, 168, 170
 functions of, 37, 49, 76-78, 80, 85, 89, 178
 importance of, 92-94, 95n.
 income and expenditure, 79-80, 81 (T.3), 82, 86

References to tables and figures are given in brackets after the relevant page number, T. indicating a table, D. a diagram and G. a graph.